STILL

LIFE

WITH

RICE

A Young

American Woman

Discovers the

Life and Legacy

of Her Korean

Grandmother

HELIE LEE

SCRIBNER

NEW YORK   LONDON   TORONTO   SYDNEY   TOKYO   SINGAPORE

SCRIBNER
1230 Avenue of the Americas
New York, NY 10020

Copyright © 1996 by Helie Lee

SCRIBNER and colophon are registered trademarks of
Simon & Schuster Inc.

Text set in Adobe ITC New Baskerville
Designed by SONGHEE KIM

Manufactured in the United States of America

10 9 8 7 6 5 4 3 2 1

Library of Congress Cataloging-in-Publication Data
Lee, Helie.
Still life with rice: a young American woman discovers the life
and legacy of her Korean grandmother/Helie Lee.
p. cm.
1. Korean Americans—Biography. 2. Lee, Helie.
3. Baek, Hongyong, 1912– . I. Title.
E184.K6L44   1996
973'.04957'00922—dc20
[B]   95–41921
CIP
ISBN 0-684-80270-8

To

family,

love,

and

home

CONTENTS

ACKNOWLEDGMENTS

Thank you Mom for filling in the blanks when Grandmother's memory failed, though you would have preferred to keep some family stories a secret, but didn't . . . and for feeding me.

Thank you Dad for your many hours of translation services and unlimited knowledge of Korean history and culture whenever I needed your help . . . and for feeding me.

Thank you Aunt Dukhae, Tracey, and Jessica for giving me a place to sneak away to and write . . . and for feeding me.

Thank you my brother David for turning our parents' attention from my unmarried status to your long "rocker" hair, body piercings, and tattoos, so I could write in peace . . . and for feeding me.

Thank you Jill Dove, Elizabeth (Nelson) Suhr, Melanie O'Connell, Stephanie Covington, Mrs. Kim, Lily Siao, and my sister Julie

ACKNOWLEDGMENTS

for correcting my grammatical errors and run-on sentences with gentleness . . . and for feeding me.

Thank you Barbara Lowenstein for selling my grandmother's story with lightning bolt speed . . . and for feeding me.

Thank you Scribner and Hamilton Cain for your overwhelming enthusiasm and friendship . . . and for feeding me.

And thank you to all those who encourage me, provide me with an outlet to plug my computer into, love me even on my bad writing days, comfort me with spiritual pep talks, sing me songs . . . and for feeding me.

You're all welcome to my home for Korean food. I'm cooking!

ROTTEN FRUIT

"I don't need a husband to have babies, Mother."

"*Yah*, you killing me." Mother clutches her heart.

"Soon you be too old, fall off tree. No man want rotten fruit for wife." Grandmother clucks her tongue in disappointment.

"But I'm only twenty-five," I say defiantly.

"When I twenty-five, I already marry. Next year maybe too late for you. Young girl should listen to parents. Parents very smart, we know." Grandmother glances around the restaurant's dining room, searching for prospects; none are to be found among the group of Big Noses and hairy chests.

"We find you nice Korean boy. Maybe lawyer, but I like doctor, more stable. Must be Christian and have good family background." Mother beams as she makes mental notes for my mail-order husband.

"Great," I moan. "You want me to marry someone who's boring."

"What boring?! That not important. *Ii-ee-goo*." Grandmother clucks her tongue again.

"These are different times, Grandmother. No one gets married anymore. I want to enjoy my life. It's hard enough supporting myself, much less some kids."

"That big problem. Your generation think too much only about yourself." Disappointment rings clearly in Mother's voice.

I, too, scan the restaurant to make sure I am not lost in some Far Eastern *Twilight Zone* episode. It's America all right; the "all-you-can-eat salad bar" is a definite giveaway.

How unrealistic and backward they are being. Grandmother was the one who devised a plan for us to flee Korea. And it was Mother's idea to raise us like the other American kids in the San Fernando Valley. She filled my head with dreams, telling me I could become anything I wanted. I believed her so much I thought I could be white. My light-eyed friends were my role models, people I emulated. I copied their dress, manners, and Valley girl speech in order to lose myself and fit in. Like all the other "normal" teenage girls, I cheered in thigh-high miniskirts, ditched classes, and bleached my black hair and tanned my yellow skin to conceal the last traces of my Koreanness. In college, I lived in a rowdy coed dormitory and pledged little sister to a fraternity. And I had even bigger nontraditional dreams for the future that included none of my past, my mother's past, my grandmother's past, and hundreds of other generations of purebred Koreans before them. The bright lights of Hollyweird—its psychedelic energy and rebel men—were more enticing. To me, my parents and grandmother were from Mars—out of sight and out of touch—too Korean for my good.

"Your makeup too heavy. Try soft color. Dark lipstick make your face look sick." Mother's voice steers my mind back to the moment.

"You sick? Stick out tongue." Grandmother sticks out hers to demonstrate.

"Grandmother, not here," I whine, embarrassed.

"Grandmother right. You not eat enough," Mother remarks as she brushes the bangs out of my face, ruining a perfectly styled hairdo.

"It's too late," I protest. "I am who I am. I'm not like you."

"What?! You think you better than your mother? You shame because we Korean?"

"No, I didn't say that." I'm totally flustered. I regress back to a little whimpering girl whenever I'm with these two women who intimidate me so much.

"You Korean, you always be Korean. Our people so good." Grandmother rubs her moist eyes.

"Then why did you bring us to America if you didn't want us to be American?"

After a long pause, Mother speaks in a tone that is strong and yet solemn, too solemn. "Your father and me give up everything, our home, our life, to bring you kids to America, not to be American people, but so you can be Korean. Here, there is no Cold War, no hunger, no losses. I know you tired me tell you eat more, do nice hairstyle, change lipstick color, wear nice dress, but I do because when others see your Oriental face I want them to say, '*Ah,* she Korean lady, they so proud people.' "

The hairs on my arms are standing straight up and there is a lump in my throat the size of a foot. I had always thought we had immigrated here to pursue the capitalistic dream. I remember that day we left Korea so well. The year was 1968. My little brother, David, wasn't born yet and my father had flown out four months earlier to find a job and a place for us to live, so Mother, older sister Julie, and I had moved into Grandmother's house.

Tears trickled down Mother's cheeks, leaving black rivulets under each eye. She had to keep reapplying her liner and regluing her false eyelashes for the seemingly endless snapshots. Neither Grandmother nor Mother smiled in any of the pictures; that was the Korean way of posing for the camera.

I remember standing in the doorway of the plane and looking down at the people below. Grandmother stood apart from the others, her arms reaching out toward us.

"*Uhmoni!*" Mother shouted, but the engines roared over her last cry, denying Grandmother her daughter's final farewell.

With one whoosh of the latch, the door was clamped shut, locking us in and Grandmother out. Now, as I look back at those crinkled photos, I realize that Grandmother and Mother shared a deeper grief. They were separated many times before, but this time an ocean would stretch between them. Would they ever see each other again?

Days, weeks, months have passed since the conversation with my mother and grandmother, but what I heard hasn't left me. It never occurred to me that it was a sacrifice to move to America: no wonder, then, that their hearts still cling to Korea's anthem and traditions, even so far removed by years and miles.

I, on the other hand, view Korea as a bleak place. The country's divided, the men are selfish lovers (so I've been told), and the women marry too young and have too many babies, too soon. That's not the life I've chosen for myself. I desire independence, I desire a jet-set career exclusive of kids and a nine-to-five husband, especially a Korean one. But as hard as I try, I can't stop thinking about my mother and grandmother, and the tragedies they must have suffered before and after the Korean War. Once someone said to me I am my mother's daughter. I never believed it to be true and now I believe it even less. I've always hated being Oriental/Asian. I hide my face and camouflage my eyes, but not my mother or grandmother. They are both the same, so proud and certain of their identity. They annoyingly intimidate me, yet at the same time, their stubborn loyal spirit draws me toward them. The more I attempt to figure out these two women, the more confused I become as to who I am and where I belong.

So I do something risky: I return to my birthplace. With no preset itinerary or companion for moral support, I fly into Seoul's Kimpo airport on a one-way ticket. I'm not exactly sure what I'm searching for in this homogeneous country where everyone calls each other Brother and Sister. The moment I deplane into the terminal, a flock of cousins and extended, extended cousins greet me with warm embraces. Their yellow faces light up with huge smiles—such uncensored affection is overwhelming.

We all cram into a green taxi, me squeezed in the middle. The driver weaves madly in and out of chaotic traffic. Here no one obeys traffic lines or signals. Through the window, the city of Seoul whizzes by. Although I envisioned thatched rooftops, rice paddies, and war refugees eating dogs like on the TV show

M*A*S*H, to my surprise this place is like any congested metropolis in America: subways, skyscrapers, rush-hour traffic, McDonald's.

Our taxi lurches to a halt in front of a large iron gate. Instinctively, I take off my combat boots inside the entranceway like the others. I guess I'm not so far removed from customs after all. The women, old and young, work busily in the kitchen to prepare a welcoming banquet of rice, *mandu kuk*, "ravioli" soup; *twikim wanja*, deep-fried appetizers; and *kimchee*, cabbage fermented in tons of garlic and red pepper. I gorge until I am full, then they insist I eat another serving. What was my mother talking about? There's no hunger problem in Korea.

Although jet-lagged, I venture alone through the neighboring streets of Apkujongdong. I'm eager to begin my journey even at the early hour of eight. I initially thought I would just blend in now that my hair is dyed back to its original black and my skin is three shades lighter, but there is no mistaking I'm a *jaemikyopo*, a Korean living in America. Small children and their grown parents point fingers at me, remarking on my gray sweatpants. I hear one woman tell her friend I am wearing pajamas. I feel a little self-conscious, but it doesn't inhibit me from taking in all the unusual sights. The cobblestone alleys are humming with early risers and shopkeepers. All the colors and smells seem so strange and yet familiar. Suddenly I don't feel so alien.

Back at the house, I slip off my boots, and then I'm escorted into the men's quarters, where all the men lounge together in a circle on the floor. A place is reserved for me next to the eldest man, *Samchoon*, uncle. Actually he's my mother's cousin, but because he's a generation older than me, I must address him by his respected title. Immediately a young pregnant woman, the wife of my twenty-one-year-old second cousin, serves me a large tray of peeled apples, melons, and persimmons.

Samchoon clears his throat; the excited chatter dies down. The women stop their work and crouch in the back of the room behind their husbands. I feel awkward thrust in the inner circle with the men when the other women remain in the outer. "I am so honored to have the granddaughter of Big Grandmother here in our home," he begins in his low authoritative voice. "As long as you are here consider me your uncle, father, brother, mother, guardian. It is the least I can do for Big Grandmother."

I had no idea my grandmother was so appreciated. I strain my brain to understand every word, for my Korean is very rusty from lack of practice.

"She is a woman of unshakable conviction and great heart. Many, many years ago when she was a young wife and her husband wished to take his family to China to escape our Japanese intruders, she followed him dutifully. Her clever mind built up a large empire of opium, allowing her family to return to their home in North Korea and purchase land as far as the eye could see. She bought this rich and fertile land for her sons' sons, but the Reds came in and stole everything. This loss did not break Big Grandmother, though, it only made her stronger and she bought yet another plot of land, almost as great. Then the greedy Reds came again for her property, and when she had no more land to give they wanted her husband and eldest son, for her family was branded as religious traitors. She refused, so they unjustly threw her in prison. Her faith, however, never flickered out even after the war claimed her husband's life and tore her first son away from her. Since then, she has endured many more tragedies and losses; nevertheless, she continues to be an inspiration to all her family and those lives she has saved with her *chiryo*."

I am numb; goose bumps sprout everywhere. When I was a young girl, I had heard Grandmother ramble on about being born in North Korea and she told a few censored war stories, but she never mentioned living in China or selling opium or being imprisoned by Communists or losing a son. It's mind-boggling that this woman *Samchoon* is praising is my grandmother, because when she first came to live with us in California she seemed so helpless and ancient in her backcountry dress. She didn't know how to operate a toaster, much less drive a car. Sometimes I'd come home from school and find Grandmother squatting on a pile of newspapers on the kitchen floor, chopping weeds she had picked from the backyard, planning to serve them for dinner. Other times I'd find her wearing only her Korean slip and slapping herself black-and-blue. She called it *chiryo*, which means "healing treatment." I called it self-mutilation.

"We expect great things from the granddaughter of Big Grandmother and the daughter of Dukwah." *Samchoon*'s tone is very serious. I'm filled with anxiety: the most drama I've ever had to deal with in my comfortable life is my mother trying to find me a boring husband.

Here in Korea, I feel as though I straddle the modern present and prehistoric times. The women's liberation movement and tampons haven't reached this part of the world. My worth is still measured by marital status (or should I say diminished by the lack of it?). Every relative is on a crusade to marry off the foreign girl.

I live at *Samchoon*'s place with all seven of them—*Samchoon*, his mother, his wife, his two sons, and their pregnant wives—in their three-bedroom home. "We always have room for family," proclaims *Samchoon* as he happily grins at his daughter-in-laws' protruding bellies. For me, the cramped adjustment is a hardship. I moved out of my parents' house at age seventeen, and have fought hard to maintain my independence and my right to be on my own even at the "rotten" age of twenty-five. If my parents had it their way, my siblings and I would be living under their roof even after we got married, as they do here.

During the day, while the other women busy themselves with house chores, I take Korean-language classes and teach English at the *Korea Herald*. In the beginning, my classes were filled with mostly young professional men, but when they discovered my disinterest in marriage they quickly transferred out . Now I teach only college women with promising careers in education and medicine. But to my disappointment, each one of these intelligent women is willing to trade it all for a husband and dirty diapers.

"Our first responsibility must be to the family and not to the individual. It is our duty as women to raise future generations," a medical intern states proudly as her classmates nod in support.

"You can do both. Many women in America are working mothers," I argue.

"Korean women consider our positions as mothers and nurturers to be the most important job. Asserting our rights outside the household is not worth sacrificing the family's well-being," another student adds.

I'm surrounded, ambushed, by mirror images of my mother and grandmother. What makes them this way? Is it the rice and *kimchee* they all eat religiously? I feel disconnected. A total outcast. A black sheep. Complete strangers—taxi drivers, street sweepers, doormen—lecture me constantly on my snobbish Western attitude. I'm emotionally fed up. The only thing that's changed about me during my grueling year-long sojourn is my bulging waistline. Disheartened, I decide to leave the country and abort the search to find myself before I'm tossed out of a taxi or beaten by a broom or I outgrow my entire wardrobe. Spreading a borrowed map of the world on the floor, I turn my back and toss my lucky U.S. penny to see where destiny will propel me. It lands in China. Groovy. I was hoping for European civilization, like Paris.

Within a few hours, I purchase a plane ticket to Hong Kong and say good-bye to my relatives before I chicken out and cheat destiny. Carefully I stuff a backpack with only lightweight essentials—camera, passport, toothbrush, a pair of 501 jeans, a few T-shirts, two wool sweaters, a warm winter coat, sweats, plenty of clean underwear, and a journal.

Loaded down with a twenty-pound pack strapped to my back, I'm ready to embark on a mysterious journey to an unknown country. Fear is forgotten, and a sense of relief flushes through my body as the plane lifts off, away from Seoul.

Hong Kong is a neon-lighted cultural extravaganza where the West mixes nicely with the East. English pubs and rave dance clubs are a welcome reminder of home, sweet home before I cross over the freedom border into Red China on the rusty old train. The scenery changes dramatically: the modern skyscrapers and colorful double-decker buses of Hong Kong are replaced with boxy gray cement buildings and thousands of bikes. Suddenly I'm curious about the lives my grandmother and mother had led here in China. I wonder where they lived and how they survived without knowing the language. In China for less than an hour, I attempt to order a simple meal consisting of broiled chicken and fresh vegetables; instead, I get duck stir-fried in a tub of grease.

With much difficulty, I make my way to Zhongshan University in Guangzhou to see about a room. I'm greeted by an art professor named Chi Ke, who speaks enough conversational English.

"A Korea-America. Well, that different," he exclaims, delighted.

"My grandparents once lived in China."

"Yes, many Korea people did. In fact, I know older Korea couple who still alive in Shanghai."

My ears perk up: Koreans still living in Communist China. "Can you help me find them?" I can't believe I'm asking to find more Koreans when I've just escaped a whole country full of them. He copies down an address on a scrap of paper, and then on the back side he scribbles a letter of introduction, informing the couple who I am. I thank him with a deep bow.

Next stop: Shanghai. I fly into the city a few days later, after many delays due to the travel agent and red tape. Nothing moves quickly in China. There's no incentive to. I check into the hostel recommended in my travel book. Seven men and three women are my roommates. All of us have sought out this place simply because it's the cheapest joint in town. Also, it gives us lonely travelers a chance to meet the other youths of the world who have come to expand their experiences. But most importantly, we gather to exchange valuable information. Here, word of mouth is the most reliable and trustworthy form of news. The country's too vast for even the People's government to know which territories are unsafe due to local "unrest."

A tour of Shanghai is like walking through several countries. One section looks distinctively French, another like Denmark, another like Philadelphia. And so many people, people, people: thousands racing down the streets on rickety old bikes. It reminds me of Disneyland during the height of tourist madness. No wonder the government only allows one child per couple.

I decide it's time to search out the Korean couple Chi Ke spoke about before I'm squashed by an uninsured bicyclist. Somehow fate again guides me to my destination. As I approach an abandoned neighborhood, an elderly man is tending to his scanty garden. He's wearing the classic blue Communist garb with the Mandarin collar. His round, aged face looks Chinese to me. I hope he speaks English.

"Hello, sir." I bow as his weary eyes peer at me. I can tell he understood nothing; then remembering we are both Korean, I make a second attempt, this time in *Hangookmal.*

"Excuse me, are you a *Hangooksahlam,* Korean person?" I enunciate each word.

His eyes open wide and he responds in an excited voice, "*Uh-moh-nah,* where did you come from?"

"From America," I reply. "I have a letter of introduction from Chi Ke."

"Come in, come in. You must sit for a while and rest yourself after such a long journey. My wife will prepare you something to eat." I accept humbly and follow him to the shack he calls his home. We walk through the doorway, which is just wide enough for me and my backpack to pass. They live very simply, only one room. No carpet, just a dirt floor, a twin-sized cot with a thin mattress, a small table covered with plastic, a broken wall clock, a portable stove with two burners, and a stained poster of North Korea's beautiful mountain scenery tacked to the wall above the entrance.

"Food for our visitor from America, *Yobo,*" he announces to his wife, who is bent over, cleaning a black iron pot.

"From where?" She looks perplexed, then with her pinkie she digs out wax from each ear.

"From America," I echo a little louder.

"*Ii-ee-goo,* it has been so long since we have heard another speak our beloved *Hangookmal.* We should have gone with the others when we still had the strength," she says with a sigh.

"Now we are the last ones," the old man mutters in the same sorrowful tone, then wipes his nose and adds, "We can talk later after your belly is filled."

I watch in silence as the elderly couple slowly shuffles around preparing my meal. In my honor, a dusty can of American Spam is opened and placed at the center of the table surrounded by small bowls of rice, roasted peanuts, egg soup, lukewarm beer, and mild *kimchee.* I eat sparingly, copying my host and hostess. The conversation is enough. It fills me completely. Every now and then they forget a Korean word and replace it with *Songhai,* the dialect of the people from Shanghai, unaware of what they've done.

"A long time ago our family fled here to escape Japanese oppression. We hid in the French Embassy when the Japanese police tore up the town, hunting for Korean freedom fighters. Our courageous compatriots were being [wiped out] all over Manju (Manchuria) and even as far down as in Chungking. They knew exactly how to [distinguish] us from the Chinese by the way we ate and the foods we cooked. My wife and I had to retrain our [mannerisms] and eating habits. After the war, we stayed behind, not knowing the fate of our country. Now we can never go back home on the south side of the 38th Parallel. So those of us who are trapped behind the lines have formed a community near the North Korea and China [border]."

It's nearly nine by the time I leave their company. The city is pitch-dark, but not my mood. My head is buzzing from their incredible story. I am eager to journey farther northeast to see for myself this minority community of Koreans.

My urgency is delayed again an extra day before I secure a seat on a small charter plane to the remote industrial city of Shenyang. From there, I'll travel from city to city by train. The plane is like something out of an old Soviet war movie. The faded red hammer-and-sickle emblem of the U.S.S.R. is still noticeable on the fuselage. The Chinese have converted this relic into a commercial airliner. Inside, the aisle is quite narrow, and with difficulty I maneuver my oversized backpack to a tiny seat at the plane's rear. Moments later, a six-foot-four-inch Russian-looking woman with brown curls spreading everywhere plows through the aisle and plops down next to me. She stands out more than I ever could.

I hold my breath, mumbling a prayer, as the rattling plane taxis off down the runway and soars into the air, bouncing between clouds. The engine sounds as though it's about to stall. A few perilous minutes into the flight, the flight attendant balances her way over and says something in Mandarin. I don't understand, but the woman next to me does.

"God, we're going to crash." I verbalize my fears outloud.

"Oh, you speak English." She sounds surprised, not half as surprised or thrilled as I was to hear her speak. "They want us big people to move to the front. The back is too heavy."

We share a nervous laugh, then quickly follow instructions.

This traumatic experience bonds us and we become good buddies quickly. Small world—two Southern California women exchanging bizarre travel stories somewhere over mainland China. I reveal to her my search plans and she asks if she can tag along. I welcome her company, for I could use a translator as well as a friend.

Finally the plane lands safely in Shenyang. The temperature is at least ten below. It's so cold, the battery in my camera freezes. The locals are smartly draped in Russian-style fur coats and caps. Lisa and I shiver as we try to find shelter. From out of the misty fog, a big yellow bus screeches in front of us. The driver offers us a ride and we accept. He chauffeurs us to the doorstep of a university dormitory. As a token of our appreciation, Lisa hands him a hundred RMB, People's money, but he refuses. So I reach into my pack and grab the orange "I ❤ LA" T-shirt and offer it to him. He accepts and grins, revealing tobacco-tarred teeth.

We wake after noon in our warm room. Famished, we decide to chance the weather outside. Insulating ourselves as best as we can, we roam the streets, holding hands. Apparently every restaurant in Shenyang closes between two and four o'clock in the day. Running on empty and a very short fuse, we tread farther. And the farther we go, the more cabbage I see piled in yards, on the sidewalk, in carts.

"That looks like *kimchee* cabbage," I remark, light-headed with hunger. All of a sudden my nose picks up a familiar scent, which leads us around the corner into an alley. At the nearest stall, a young woman is selling *kimchee*. Her pretty, smooth cheeks are highlighted with bright red blush. Two imperfect circles. Her lips are painted as if a child had done them. Behind her, posted on the wall, is a warped calendar from 1969 with a picture of a Korean woman in traditional dress, fanning herself.

"Are you a *Hangooksahlam?*" I ask in Korean.

"Why, yes. Are you a *Hangooksahlam,* too?" she says. Her Korean is almost perfect, except for her intonations. She singsongs her words, similar to the Chinese. It's difficult to understand her at first, but my ears adapt quickly.

"Were you born here?" I inquire nosily.

"Yes, and so were my parents and grandparents."

My jaw drops in amazement. Three generations removed and yet she speaks our language better than someone who was born in Korea—me.

"Can you tell me where the other *Hangooksahlam* live?" I ask.

"We live and work all around here. This is our community."

I had arrived and I didn't even realize it. It was my nose that led the way. I give myself credit for recognizing authentic Korean food, and now I was craving a mouthful. Although, after leaving Korea, I swore off garlic and red peppers, just the thought of the delicious spices made my mouth water. I order plenty of extra-red extra-spicy *kimchee*. The young woman won't accept our money. It's too cold to argue with her.

So with the bundle of food wrapped in plastic, Lisa and I venture into a quaint family restaurant and order rice to go with the *kimchee*. The place isn't open for business yet, but the head cook takes each of us by the arm and seats us at a table nearest to the furnace. She brings us plates and chopsticks, then two bowls of rice and a basket of steamed bread. I clutch the tin bowl, and instantly the heat thaws my fingers.

As we feast, the other cooks join in on our conversation, slurping their own bowls of rice. I notice they eat like the old Korean couple in Shanghai. They bring the bowls up to their mouths and shovel the food in with chopsticks. This is the way the Chinese eat. I think it's because China has had such a history of famine that once they receive food they waste no time getting it into their mouths. Also the closer it is to their lips, the more unlikely someone can come between them and the food. It makes sense.

Between Lisa's Mandarin and my Korean we manage to carry on quite an extensive conversation. These people may have lived here a long time and they may have acquired Chinese table manners, but inside they're all Korean. When they speak of Korea, it's as if they're talking about a heaven on earth.

I'm revived and ready to battle the chill outside. I count out some money, but the head cook pushes it back into my pocket, winning a friendly struggle. "Nonsense. We wouldn't want you to go back home and tell your family we treated you poorly." She brushes the hair out of my eyes, and her wrinkled lips curve into an affectionate smile.

"Home." It feels as though I've been away for such a long time. Suddenly this loving woman reminds me of my own mother and grandmother, who are waiting for my return, probably worrying about my safety. All at once, the hardship of my extended journey weighs heavily on me, and tears streak down my cheeks.

"I'm sorry." I am weeping, overcome with emotion. "I guess I'm getting a little homesick."

"Dry up your tears, you are among family. We are all your brothers and sisters, because we share the same history, the same blood."

"Thank you," I reply, rubbing away the tears, feeling comforted by her kind words. She speaks from the heart, just as *Samchoon* did when he told me he was my father, brother, mother, guardian.

Lisa and I depart, hand in hand. We say very little. She senses something inside me has softened, and leaves me to my thoughts. The bitterness and resentment I had felt for all Koreans has left me. As I glance around and absorb the scenery, I can't believe I'm here, walking down the same roads and experiencing the same wondrous feeling of discovering a new land, half a century later than my grandmother and mother.

"A church?" I hear Lisa's stunned voice.

I turn my head in the direction she's pointing. A newly carved church steeple rises above the other houses. We approach in shock: this is a Communist country where religion isn't tolerated. A Christian hymn wafts from the church. The melody's calming. Lisa and I exchange glances, and she nudges me forward. Inside it resembles my parents' church in Koreatown, even down to the large velvet painting of the Last Supper. Just then a nice plain-faced woman introduces herself as the reverend.

"A woman reverend?"

"Why not?"

"Why not?" I repeat.

"We *Hangook* women can do anything once we put our minds to it. Look, it has brought you here."

I realize for the first time that I am my mother's daughter and my grandmother's granddaughter.

"We've worked equally beside our husbands and children to build this church and our schools and shopping mall."

"Schools and a mall? How's that possible in a Communist country?"

"I told you, we Koreans can do anything and will do anything to preserve our culture and language. Not even the revolution destroyed our community."

I'm astonished. This reverend, the cook, the girl with the red cheeks, my students, my mother, my grandmother are all such remarkable women, but they are not unique or rare. They are all around me, here, in America, everywhere in the world, creating and nurturing Korean communities because of their deep love for our culture and customs. I belong simply because I'm one of them.

Driven by a unquenchable thirst to learn more, I fly back to California and begin to ask all those long-ignored questions I never bothered with while I was busy exploiting my privileges as an American teenager. Hungrily, I dig deep into my grandmother's and my mother's memories. Looking at myself through the prism of their lives, I've finally come to peace with who I am. The emptiness and chaos I once felt is now filled with the past I rejected and the future I will passionately embrace.

I no longer desire to be a "rotten fruit."

YEAR

OF

THE

RAT

In 1912, the year of the rat, in the summer month of May, Hogin, surname Baek, and his wife, Hwaksi, were expecting another baby, their fifth child. Hwaksi, who just passed her thirtieth birthday, had delivered her last son nearly five years before.

During the long labor, she clamped down on a piece of cloth to muffle her pain. As she lay on the floor bedding helplessly, her contracting abdomen took on a life of its own. She could not remember the others being quite as agonizing. Unfortunately, though, only her first son was strong enough to fight for his life. Her daughter and second son died shortly before their *paikil*, one-hundredth-day birthdays. Her third son died tragically when Hwaksi was just beginning to discover his potential. So much unhappiness and bad fortune, yet she would bring another child into this world. It was her burden to birth sons—a woman's supreme duty. Sons would ensure her husband's ancestral rites, thus guarantee his own spiritual eternity. Hwaksi prayed faithfully and tirelessly to the tiny naked jade Buddha that perched on a low stand in their home. Each morning and each night she gave offerings of extravagant gifts, for her husband was a man of great wealth.

"A son. A son to lay on my bed. I shall clothe him in fine garments and give him a precious stone to play with," she prayed, rubbing her beads red-hot, till exhaustion overtook her.

After forty-eight hours of labor, she finally gave birth to her fifth child, an unusual girl, strong and willful.

Hwaksi thought to herself: If this daughter of mine had only come out a son, he would have been a very powerful man. Disappointed, Hwaksi laid the infant on the bare floor, clothed only in a diaper and nothing but her fingers to play with.

The child was given the name of Baek, Hongyong, which Hogin carefully constructed himself. Some thought him foolish for spending so much energy on such a task, for many families did not even bother to name their daughters, but not Hogin. "Baek" linked her to her father's ancestral tree. Even when married, a daughter never changed her surname. It was a way to identify all individuals to their lineage. "Hong" connected her to all the other siblings and cousins born of the same generation. Usually *yangbans*, the elite class of government officials and scholars, observed this family-tree naming system to name sons. This system was based on Confucian philosophy, incorporating five signs—gold, wood, water, fire, and earth. The third part of the name, "yong," belonged only to the owner. Hogin was pleased with the name. "Hong" represented "big" and "yong" was the sign of the dragon, the mystical beast.

Hwaksi, encouraged by the strength of her daughter, decided to try again; perhaps the next child would be an even stronger boy. A year later, her karma did change, she thought, when she birthed a son. Surely, he was a gift from the great Buddha.

Those were blissful days. Her son successfully passed his one-hundredth-day birthday, which was celebrated with festive foods and gifts of gold. Then one afternoon, as he napped nuzzled between his mother's full, warm breasts, he passed away suddenly and silently. Struck by another heartbreaking loss, Hwaksi made two more attempts. Both times screaming girls sprouted from her burning womb. She would try no more.

There was an old saying: A house with three daughters, a thief would not even enter such a place. For after three daughters married, there would be nothing left. Daughters were viewed as lovely bandits, who would take possessions out of their father's home and bring them to their husbands'. Hogin, a kind, gentle man, never paid any mind to the many gossiping whispers. He did fuss over and dote on them, for he found unusual delight in his three daughters. Carefully he selected two more names. The second girl child he called Baek, Hongeun, "big middle," and the last was named Baek, Hongsam, "big third."

He admired their will and curiosity to conquer life when even their elder brother grew pale at the challenge.

SIX

When I was six, I ruled my small kingdom, Hongyong's world. Every room in our house, including the men's quarters, was mine to explore. "Hongyong-yah, young girls must not be so curious," Mother would warn, but even she could not refuse me the tiniest or most greedy request, for I was Father's favorite.

I loved our huge one-story home. It formed double L's, with the L's fitting perfectly together to construct a stretched-out square. In the center, a courtyard was bordered by walkways and living quarters. Gently curving tiles roofed the house and mud plastered the walls. We had very little furniture: a small dining table, wooden chests to hold bedding, and a black lacquered stand for the jade Buddha. We sat, slept, and ate on the floor, thus all the furniture and ornaments were built low to harmonize with our way of living.

Every room in the house had *ondul* floors. Flues ran heat from the kitchen stove to the adjoining rooms. Layers of cement, sand, lime, clay, and rocks were pressed under the sturdy paper called *jangpan*, which was derived from mulberry wood. Then a polish made of ground soybeans and liquid cow dung was spread over the sheets and dried, turning the floor a lustrous yellow, smooth and easy to clean.

"There is no floor as great as ours in all the Orient. Koreans are a highly innovative and intelligent people," Father would boast.

Mother spent most of her time in the *anbang*, inner room, near the back of the house next to the kitchen. The men's room, *sarangbang*, love room, was separated from the women's *anbang* by sliding lattice screens covered with paper. The division of the house symbolized just how separate men's and women's lives were. Young boys and girls from an early age were properly trained to stay in their respective quarters with their own kind.

The front rooms Father converted into a shop. Large swinging doors opened to the busy street. Rice, corn, millet, nuts, dried salted fish, fruits, vegetables, sugar, rice candies, and *panchan*, side dishes, were colorfully displayed to tempt those who passed by. Other businesses along the streets sold everything from handwoven silk to utensils and rubber slippers. Each day was an exciting adventure of new faces as people from the neighboring villages and provinces came to shop for bargains in the capital of Pyongyang, located in the northern region of our boot-shaped country.

Safely insulated in my father's house, I had no worries or fears. Thoughts of rice cakes and mischievous games filled my days. I was too young and naive to comprehend the ruthless oppression of our people outside by the Japanese, who marched into our country on August 29, 1909, three years before my birth.

All day long three-year-old Second Sister and I clung to Father's side, soaking in his affection and generosity. He adored us as much as sons. He lavished sweets on us, making sure our bellies never hungered for anything. Whatever we craved, he provided. If I desired a pomegranate, he would give me a basket loaded with the finest and reddest from his store.

Whenever he could close the shop and slip away for an afternoon, he would walk me to his favorite spot down by the river. I was delighted that Second Sister and Baby Sister were too young to tag along. The stroll always seemed a wink's time, as Father filled the long roads with amazing folktales of heavenly maidens, foxes, tigers, and dragons. Just a few miles from our house, the Taedong River cut right through Pyongyang. During the warm summer months, private fishing boats and ferries hauled people back and forth while on the banks women washed their family laundry and gossiped.

Father taught me to fish there. For hours, we sat at the river's edge, side by side, waiting for a fish to nibble on our homemade lines. A clump of rice, a rock, and a hook were all we needed. They were wrapped tightly in a cloth mesh, tied with a long string, then lowered into the water. Father and I lounged in each other's company as we waited patiently for a tug. Sometimes when the fish were too clever to bite, I would watch Father float in the water, paddling his hands under his chin and squirting a jet of water from his pressed lips.

One day on our trek back from the river, I overheard a man describe a big round machine that popped corn kernels into large fluffy balls. I begged Father for the magical machine, and the next day a servant was sent to find the mysterious popper. The neighborhood children and I anxiously waited in the courtyard until the servant returned, balancing it on his back. It had a large, round metal body with a hatch where the corn was poured in, two sturdy legs, and a handle. A low fire blazed underneath it as the servant cranked the handle, and we heard the corn roll and fall, then roll again. Faster and faster he churned. Sweat dripped from his forehead. The temperature rose, the metal glowed red-hot. A cloth sack was placed over the hatch just in time to catch the fluffy white corn that shot out. *Pong!*

Dozens of small hands reached into the steaming bag. The freshly popped corn scorched our fingers, but we kept grabbing. The puffy corn was as light as winter snowflakes, only it tasted better. As the sack was being passed around for the second time, I snatched it and barricaded myself in the farthest corner of the courtyard. I dared anyone to try to wrestle it away from me. I was ready to beat them down with my fist. No one did; even the boys twice my size refused to challenge me.

The servant promptly poured in a second batch rather than

confront my greediness. I watched, plotting my strategy to swipe the next one. Minutes passed, and the temperature rose again. All watched with anticipation, pressing their hands to their ears. But there was no explosion.

"Something must be wrong. What are we going to do?" Second Sister cried as smoke spiraled between the cracks.

In a crazied panic, the servant quickly opened the hatch and a plume of black smoke filled the courtyard and seeped into the rooms. The other servants frantically ran through the large house, flapping their arms like birds, trying to chase the smoke out.

Hearing the commotion, Father rushed in, thinking it was a fire. The smoke was so thick, his presence went unnoticed. He cleared his throat loudly as he always did when he commanded our attention. It was his way of announcing, "I have arrived." Everyone immediately froze.

"What happened here?"

The servants all dropped their heads and clasped their hands in distress. Father scrutinized their many faces, staring hard and long at each one. "This machine is dangerous. I will not have it disturb the peace in my house," he said authoritatively. There was no arguing with Father when he had made up his mind. His word was law, but Second Sister, being too young to hold her tongue, dared to ask Father what he planned to do with it.

"It must be destroyed," he declared.

We watched helplessly as he flung an ax down the center, splitting it in half. Again and again he swung the ax until there was nothing left but scrap metal. For weeks, the mutilated pile cluttered our yard like an odd piece of sculpture, the kind no one wanted to buy. It was there to remind us of the hazards of modern machines, to remind me of my selfishness.

WOMAN

AT

NINE

Before I knew it, my seventh, eighth, and ninth birthdays came and went. And with them my childhood freedom. I was forced to take on a woman's responsibilities. It was my punishment for being born a girl rat. My life became as divided as the house itself and as closed in as the walls. I was no longer allowed to leave the grounds. The outside world had shrunk to the size of a gate's single peephole. Sometimes I could steal glimpses jumping up and down on the seesaw, my head stretched way out to see over the wall.

Whenever I wanted to do something, anything, I had to sincerely and in elaborate detail ask for permission. Being a daughter, though, I never asked to learn letters. Besides, the idea of reading other people's thoughts on a piece of paper sounded boring except when it came to the family's book of records. It was a magnificent book filled with pages and pages of names and birth dates going back hundreds and hundreds of years. Yellow and soft from generations of handling, these pages felt like the skin on an old person's arm. When left alone, I would creep into the waist-high teak cabinet decorated with fine brass, and shut the door, leaving it open just a crack for light. There I would steal peeks at the intricately brushed ink characters until I heard Mother call me for my lessons.

Daily, she drilled me on the virtues of being a woman, which involved everything from the tone of one's voice to making tea properly. All this was in preparation for my wifely duties someday.

"If followed diligently, the peace, purity, and happiness of a home may be maintained," Mother proclaimed.

These lessons were difficult. It was impossible to memorize them all. "You must try harder," Mother stressed, with patience for my confusion and blunders. The lessons always centered on obedience and chastity, the two most important virtues according to Mother. Obedience denoted "blind obedience." I was instructed always to say "yes" to my parents, and my future husband and in-laws.

"Say 'yes' in a quiet voice and do not let that voice go beyond the walls of your house or it will bring bad fortune." Mother demonstrated in her birdlike whisper. "You are merely here to serve and not be heard."

Obedience was straightforward enough to grasp. Chastity, on the other hand, was like fumbling blindly through a forbidden maze. I was warned to separate myself from boys, even Older Brother, whom I used to pretend would be my husband someday. This was before I discovered sisters could not marry their brothers. It all sounded so silly to me. I was supposed to protect something I did not know existed, something to do with my private parts. Originally, I thought Mother was hinting at my knees, for she constantly nagged me to keep them covered. Only when I began to bleed at the age of twelve did I suspect what she meant.

"Now you are a woman." Mother grinned.

"Am I dying, Mother?" I asked.

"No, it is a woman's curse. Only when you are married and a good wife and daughter-in-law will the blood give way to a baby."

"Why do I bleed there?" I dared to ask.

"You do not need to concern yourself with such curious questions. It is dangerous," she answered simply, and then she guided me to her private dresser cabinet. Down below on the lowest shelf was a hiding place for unspoken female necessities. "Here," she said discreetly as she handed me a thickly padded bundle of cloth. "You must take care of it and wash it well after each bleeding."

Later in the privacy of the women's quarters, I unraveled the cloth. It was about two arm's lengths long and a hand wide. The thought of washing it sent acids of nausea up to the back of my throat. It was humiliating to reach the threshold of womanhood only to wear diapers. Again, I thought, this was my punishment for being born a girl.

Afraid my shame would leak for all to see, I locked myself in the room. For hours, I sat with my legs sealed closed. The pressure and cramping built with each drip, and tears formed in my eyes as I wished the bleeding to stop. The thought of enduring cramps and dirty diapers for the rest of my life only brought fresh tears.

"Hongyong-yah!" Mother called.

I refused to respond. All I wanted was to be left alone, to drip in my own misery. But there was no hiding in a house full of servants. Mother glided through the door and sat gracefully by my side. Her dissatisfied eyes burned through the side of my head as they outlined my plain features.

"As long as you are untouched, you will be worth something. Protect it with your life." Her voice was uncommonly tender.

Now I was more confused than ever. I could not comprehend why the unmentionable part of my body could at the same time be so valuable. What did all this mean? Was this a cruel grown-up joke? I nodded anyway, pretending to understand the impossible.

I preferred the household lessons over the lessons in virtue and womanhood. A broom was a broom: there was no mistaking it for a washbasin. It was something I could touch, see, and use freely.

Of all the chores, I enjoyed the family wash the best. In fact,

I looked forward to it since I was permitted to walk to the river's edge, where a smooth flat stone was used to beat the clothes. The chores I detested the most required patience and skill, such as ironing. It was an onerous task if one lacked strong arms, expert timing, and firm lips. First, one pounded the fabric on a stone block, using two sticks. Next to the block, a small bowl of water lay on the ground. On the other side, a flat black metal iron heated on coals. The temperature had to be constantly monitored, as I learned by painful error. When the iron overheated, the heat would go through the protective cloth and burn my hand. Mother made it look so simple and graceful. She would take a sip of water and spray the fabric evenly from between tightly puckered lips, then glide the iron across Father's wrinkled trousers. My sprays usually dribbled out in puddles, leaving a wet trail down my chin and the front of my dress. I also had a heavy hand, which often left rows of brown marks along the length of many skirts and jackets. Time and again Mother attempted to guide me through the arts of ironing, cooking, spinning, and sewing, but without success.

"Who would want to marry such a worthless girl?" she cried hopelessly.

I knew Mother's cries would someday be mine if I could not properly press trousers or mend socks. I forced myself to do better, because I did not want to suffer under the wrath of a dissatisfied mother-in-law whose only duty was to make my existence miserable.

After many aborted disasters and a matching collection of unwanted singed clothing, Mother concluded that my talents were best suited for larger housecleaning duties. I agreed (the bigger the task, the less noticeable the mistake). It became my responsibility, then, to prepare for the "Big Cleaning Day." Once every spring and autumn, the Japanese health inspector barged into each household, checking for dirt, cobwebs, insects, and rodents. It was part of the Japanese campaign to establish an orderly and clean colony, because they saw Koreans as uncivilized and incapable of keeping their homes decent without supervision.

Father violently despised their intrusion into our country and into our home, but he knew no amount of bolts could keep them out. Thus, the entire family had to work together to prepare for the inspection.

Cotton quilts were hung on branches of trees and beaten. Their covers were boiled and wrung till the stains vanished. The furniture had to be carried out into the courtyard for a wash, then rubbed with oil so the wood shone luxuriously bright. A long homemade broom swept away the intricate cobwebs in the corners of the ceiling, disturbing the spiders that had taken permanent residence inside them.

In the kitchen alone, it took at least a dozen trips to the well and back to wipe down and patch the counters and floors of earthen bricks, which were made from our own mud and straw. It reminded me of when I used to serve mud rice balls and mud bean cakes to my sisters on Mother's old chipped dishes. Not once did I burn the rice then.

If a house passed the inspection, a round tin button of approval was nailed on the front gate for all to see. For those that failed, the inspector would make several return visits until his vigilant eyes, nose, and fingers were satisfied.

As a reward, the town's people would gather at the river and scrub their bodies clean. The men bathed first, then it was our turn. As the sun was setting, the women would call on one other as if we were going to a social function. Together we strolled the two miles through the streets, the air humming with fresh gossip. Everyone carried blankets and washcloths. Since our family was well-off, we could afford ground bean powder to scour the layers of dirt and dead skin. The less affluent households used plantings picked around the riverbanks, which left green stains on the skin. Green knees and elbows were common sights.

If the weather permitted and the summer monsoons were calm in their fury, we bathed once every two weeks in the Taedong's cool refreshing water; every week was considered excessive. Oddly enough, the restraints of modesty and humility washed away at the river. Women peeled off layers of jackets and slips. They stood pale and naked in front of one another, without any inhibitions. Only when my body began to fill out did I notice the sights. There were no two bodies exactly alike among the masses of curves, peaks, and folds. The young women were all grossly slim. Their hipbones and rib cages, as if wrapped in thin rice paper, stuck out harshly like mine. Other women were classically plump, their skin swelling with good eating. Some were simply massive, their rolls overflowing at the waist. They looked almost comical with their twiggy legs supporting all that bulge.

What shocked me the most was the mound of short black hair sprouting like a man's beard between the women's legs.

"It is improper to stare." Mother would scrub my back harder to divert my gaze. But how could I not stare? Was this what I had to look forward to?

They squatted all around me with their legs spread open as they washed themselves vigorously. Perhaps their mothers did not beat into them that that part of their bodies was to be protected and concealed at all cost, even when bathing.

As I grew into my womanhood, I began to listen carefully to the talk at the riverbanks. Information concerning childbearing and marriage was collected; however, when it came to physical acts performed between husbands and wives, the voices suddenly hushed to a secret whisper. All winter long I would puzzle over scattered bits of gossip I had overheard, wishing for summer to come. During the winters, we bathed inside, for the frozen river was good only for crossing to the other side, like a ghost skating on top of water.

WORMS

FOR

DINNER

With age, I started to become more "unruly and unmanageable," as Mother used to claim. Later in life, I learned it was due to intestinal worms. Many people, in those pre–germ awareness days, suffered from the same maddening infection. Farmers used human waste as fertilizer. No one knew about the importance of washing and cooking food well or the consequences if one did not.

During the summer months, when the fields were plentiful with vegetation, we brought heads of lettuce, radishes, green onions, and chili peppers straight from the ground to our tables, still crispy and raw. A spoonful of steaming rice wrapped in lettuce with a dab of spicy red bean paste was worth waiting for all winter long. Not once did I see or taste the tiny parasites that slid down my throat with every swallow. Soon a whole family of worms nested and bred within my belly's cramped walls, causing it to burn and swell. It grew worse always at night when Mother rolled out the bedding. The moment my head touched the grain-stuffed pillow, demons used my belly as an oven to start a roaring fire. The pressure was so unbearable, I would spring to my feet and pace around the room, stumbling over the shoulder-linked bodies.

"Hongyong-yah, stop playing around. Decent young women do not walk around at night," Mother scolded.

Nothing, not even her threatening hand, ended my midnight ritual. My family could not understand what caused such craziness. Pacing, though, was the only way I knew how to remain sane. Lying still, I felt vulnerable.

Mother became convinced that demons were besieging my innocence, and she was determined to exorcise them herself. She took wisps of fabric from my dress and tied them to a distant tree in hopes of tricking the evil spirit to stay with the clothing. It was all part of her shamanic belief that good and evil forces were allied with natural objects.

Confident that the demons were flying over a tree far from our house, I finally let my heavy eyelids slide smoothly shut. I once again dreamt I was soaring high into the sky on a seesaw. The wind blew under my dress. Higher and higher I jumped, tranquil at last, and then I saw them flying toward me, their distorted faces glowing with fury. The demons knocked me down and pinned me under their weight, and I cried aloud. Mother was furious. She ran into the kitchen and brought back a large butcher knife. I was sure she was going to plunge it deep into my stomach. Paralyzed with fear, I lay helplessly as she circled the sharp tip inches above me. In a low, droning tone, Mother chanted the same undecipherable words over and over again.

"Please, Mother, stop!" I whimpered. "I will be good, I promise!"

Then I heard her shrilling command: "Be gone!" Her arms stretched to the ceiling.

No longer did I pace the nights away after that mortifying exorcism. I learned to endure my madness internally, suffocating from the inside out. My mind became clouded, and I was incapable of thinking clearly. Mother would order me to burn the trash and wash the clothes; instead, I would burn the clothes and wash the trash.

"A virtuous woman must never defy her elders. She must be unheard, gentle, and weak," Mother preached endlessly.

Her words went inside my ears and disappeared somewhere in my head. My ability to distinguish right from wrong, appropriate from inappropriate, swam around aimlessly with all the other information I was instructed to remember.

Soon the infection grew larger than I, and my body surrendered to its control. Each morning, I would wake and find myself soaked in a pool of urine. Mother insisted that it was due to laziness. As a result, each wet morning commenced with a scolding. "What decent man would want to marry a girl who wets her bed? You are not a babe. You do this to spite your mother, I know. What have I done to deserve this?"

It was not my intention to spite anyone, but it was useless to try to defend myself—Mother was always right. So one morning I plotted a plan. While the family was still soundly asleep, I rolled Second Sister on top of my crime, pretending it was hers as I slipped onto her dry bedding. When Mother discovered the puddle underneath Second Sister, her powerful hand slashed across my cheek. The shock stung more than the slap itself. We both stood there stiff, afraid to move. I could see Mother's hand quivering. Suddenly I felt bad for her. Needless to say, I never attempted that trick again.

With mistake after mistake, trouble after trouble, I cringed under Mother's hand as it whacked me indiscriminately. The punishments came so frequently, my reaction to crouch and shield myself became automatic at her slightest movement. She was determined to break my will, as her mother broke hers years before.

A
THOUSAND
PRICKS

After Second Sister's fourth year, the playful laughter that rang through our home halted. Friends were no longer allowed to visit, and Father stopped taking me to the river. The household was so gloomy. I could not understand why Second Sister had to stay inside the women's quarters all day long. In fact, she lay in the same spot, unable to move. Her arms and legs grew weak and lifeless. Her tiny right foot curled tightly under itself and her stomach muscles contracted into a hard knot, making it impossible for her to eat regular amounts of food. It was an effort to merely turn her neck.

Several weeks earlier, she fell ill with a fever and vomited up all Mother's remedies as fast as Mother poured them down Second Sister's parched throat. No amount of Cornish hens stuffed with ginseng or meat reversed the fever's paralyzing effects. Frightfully, she withered away to half her normal weight. Her starved flesh dangled from slender bones. She was completely helpless, unable to feed or relieve herself.

Father sent for the best physicians and herbalists. I began to resent Second Sister for all the attention she received from Mother, Father, and their important guests.

A famed herbalist, educated in potions and needles, was called in. The brittle old man lugged in a wooden case filled with hair-thin needles and bitter herbs, the kind of weeds you ripped out of your garden if they sprouted. All day long he pricked Second Sister's loose skin with the needles, rolling the ends between his bony thumb and crooked index finger. He tried to generate feeling back into her frail legs. After many unsuccessful attempts, he began setting coin-sized balls of herbs on fire all over her body. The potent combination of stale herbs and sweet human flesh left an eerie perfume that settled into all the blankets and clothes. My resentment vanished. I was grateful it was not me on fire.

A thousand pricks and burns later, she looked worse than before the treatments. As a final attempt, Mother persuaded Father to send for a shaman to drive away the evil spirits that had invaded Second Sister's body. The shaman woman made offerings of food and wine as she flirted and sang and danced for them. When that too failed, she sacrificed our prized chicken, slicing its head right off. Obviously the spirits were neither hungry nor in the mood to be seduced, for Second Sister's condition only worsened, which tormented Mother.

"I cannot bare to watch another one of my children die."

Having surrendered all hope, Mother carried Second Sister to the top of the large stone wheat grinder in the middle of the courtyard.

"It hurts, Mommy. I am cold, Daddy," she cried.

Father and the servants did try to rescue her from the stone grinder, but Mother held them back. "Let her die now. What value is a crippled girl? Who will care for her once her parents are in the ground? Surely not a husband."

Father ached terribly, because he knew the wisdom of his wife's words. Second Sister would be a burden on Older Brother's family someday or end up on the streets as an outcast. Death was more merciful and practical. I peeked through downturned eyes as Second Sister attempted to drag her coiled body off the grinder. But her struggling efforts were useless; the treatments left her too bruised.

Early the next day, I awoke with the morning sun, but I lay there pressed in between Baby Sister and the wall, waiting for Mother to rise and rescue Second Sister. Finally she did stir, her body heavy with grief. Each move required great effort—getting up, changing clothes, folding blankets, breast-feeding Baby Sister, chanting, and overseeing the preparation of the morning rice. She did a whole day's work that morning to avoid going out to the grinder. And at the same time, it took all her will to keep herself away.

"Now we must bury your sister," Mother announced, her face empty of any expression. She picked up a burlap sack and headed for the courtyard. She looked like she was going out to pick some vegetables, rather than the remains of my younger sister. When she reached for the body, Second Sister lifted her lids. Her face was dirty with dust and gravel, and tears still trickled out of her bloodshot eyes.

"Mommy," she pleaded weakly. With a slight hesitation, Mother retreated back into the house. Just like that! I was never so frightened in my entire life.

She ordered me to remain inside for the rest of the day. I felt unfairly sentenced. Why was I being punished? I could still walk and use my arms. To pass the time, I poked a tiny peephole through the small wooden lattice window. I stole glances of Second Sister whenever Mother was not around to catch me. Second Sister moved very little. I kept willing her to jump off the grinder and call out, "Here I am. Come and catch me!"

Gathering for supper was unbearable, knowing Second Sister had not eaten since noon the day before. Looking over the low table, I stared at Father, sitting cross-legged, back straight, at another table across from me. He appeared poised and calm, though I could tell he felt the guilt of each grain of rice that touched his lips.

"Eat, eat! I will not have this food go to waste," Mother urged unconvincingly.

My thoughts locked on to the image of Second Sister shivering on the cold stone grinder. It must have been deathly chilly last night, and yet another was quickly approaching. Father stood up, his rice bowl still half full. Mother held her tongue; instead, she vented all her anxieties on me. "You will not leave this table until your bowl is clean," she warned.

I sat there studying the food for a long time. An army of tiny soldiers attacked my legs. Without thinking about the repercussions, I emptied the rice into the hem of my skirt, hoping neither Mother nor the servants would notice the bulge between my legs as they removed the table with all the uneaten meats and spicy vegetables. Once all was clear, I carefully peeled each flake of rice from my skirt and squeezed them into a tight ball, the size of a fist. As I was about to take the ball of rice outside, Mother caught me concealing my crime. She dragged me by the braid of my hair and flung me against the wall. I had never been lashed before, but I knew I was going to pay dearly for my disobedience.

"Turn around and hold up your skirt," she ordered, squatting behind me. I bent down and pulled up the hem just below my knees, revealing two pale calves. "Higher!" she commanded as she reached for a long, thin bamboo rod. The blows came quickly and precisely, each lash stinging more than the last.

"Do you think you know better than your parents?!" She whipped again.

"I am sorry. I will not disobey you again," I whimpered. "Sorry, I am sorry."

No amount of apologies, though, would have stopped the beating. Mother was taking out her agony on my legs. I stood defiantly as long as I could, but my virgin legs betrayed me and I slithered to the ground, cradling my knees to my chest.

"Why must you always go against me?!" Mother dropped to her knees, whipping, slashing the floor next to her. The cries were so deep and loud, I was not sure if they were mine or hers. Then from out of nowhere I heard Father's gentle voice.

"That will be enough," he announced plainly.

Mother and I both stopped crying, stunned at his unexpected emergence. The women's quarters were considered sacred and no men were allowed to trespass.

His strong protective arms scooped me up and carried me to bed. His eyes were moist as he drew the covers over me. I fell asleep right away, knowing Father, at least, still cared for me. The following morning, I awoke very late because I did not want to face what I was expecting to see—Second Sister in Mother's vegetable sack, lying at the bottom of a concave grave.

A small meal tray was put aside for me. On it was a bowl of

rice and my favorite *kimchee chigae*, spicy cabbage broth. Hungrily I sat up, ignoring the ache throbbing down the back of my legs. Unable to cross them, I stretched them out underneath the table, something Mother would never have approved of. Like a peasant, I buried my face in the bowl of rice, forgetting to chew in my rush. I was so consumed with satisfying the emptiness inside, I did not hear Mother come in. When I gazed up, I was startled to see Mother carrying in her arms the twenty-five-pound girl. Second Sister was still alive! Mother's heart must have melted for this sorrowful creature and brought her back into the house.

Things were never the same again. Second Sister became Crippled Sister, and her handicap crippled my life. My legs were her legs. Hauling her on my back, I carried her from room to room. If that was not enough, her handicap robbed the one thing that mattered most to me in the whole world—Father's affection. He began to favor Crippled Sister more. I watched jealously as she soaked in all of Father's attention. The only thing I was soaking in was a basin full of dirty dishes and soiled clothes. Together Crippled Sister and Father made many trips to the river, trips that were once mine. He even bought her a small boat.

Many hours I sat on the steps outside the women's quarters waiting for their return. Sure enough, she would arrive, bouncing on Father's back, her skin brown and shiny from too much happiness.

"Shield your face. Do you want to look like a rice picker's daughter?" Mother tried to scare me into obedience.

"Why not Hongeun?" I questioned, pointing to my tanned-faced sister.

"She is crippled. What harm can it do?"

It seemed everyone was under her spell of helplessness. Older Brother also treated her as if she were someone very important. He encouraged her to learn a special woman skill. So on his advice, Father built her a tiny play store next to his. There in her own shop, she learned to weigh grains and roll cigarettes.

She became very demanding with her new privileges. She ordered me around as if I were her subordinate and she were my elder. If I refused, she would squeeze her eyes, forcing fake tears to swell, a skill she mastered after much practice.

"Hongyong-yah, take your sister for a stroll around the courtyard," Mother ordered.

"She is too heavy," I protested. Why they did not trade me in for a mule was a wonder to me—a trade that was possible for daughters in those days.

Then I figured out a way to use Crippled Sister to venture outside our gate. One year when a traveling troupe of actors were performing in town I asked Mother's permission to take Crippled Sister to see the exorcism. She agreed. So Baby Sister and I played a game of rock-paper-scissors. The loser had to carry Crippled Sister. I lost.

A long cloth strap was wrapped securely around our adjoining waists several strangling times. The rope cut deeply into my sensitive belly. It was not an easy task balancing a spineless snake with only a thin layer of skin to grasp on to. Her dragging feet flopped on the ground, kicking up dust, choking me. Her two arms clung tightly around my neck, ready to finish off the job. No matter how hard I struggled to keep her from slipping, she would slide down lower. I would bump her back up and she would scream out in pain as her bony chest banged against my ribbed spine.

"*Ay-ya!*" Crippled Sister squawked.

"Be quiet," I growled.

"You are hurting me." Her fingers clawed into my neck.

"Stop it!" I huffed like a dragon.

Up ahead, the tuning of instruments was teasingly close. Too excited to wait, Baby Sister ran ahead. I chased after her as fast as I could.

"*Ay-ya!* I am going to tell Mommy you were hurting me and she is going to whip you." Crippled Sister pinched.

Having endured enough of her complaints and pinches, I dumped her in a cluster of bushes. "But first she will have to find you," I snickered as I skipped away.

"Older Sister, please do not leave me here. I was just teasing!" she yelled after me.

It felt incredible to discard my burden. I was six years old again, free to laugh, skip, and play. There were so many people gathered. Vendor carts crowded the streets, each vendor fighting to shout over the others. That was an amusing show in itself.

"Steamed silkworms!"

"Sweet potatoes!"

"The finest corn!"

The exorcism resembled nothing like the knife trick Mother performed on me. The actors wore colorful masks with exaggerated expressions. They shook, danced, and sang, and skillfully flicked their trained voices at the audience. Flirting. Enticing. Threatening. They swayed their arms as if the wind carried them to their next positions.

The men laughed with their mouths wide open, showing all their pinkness inside. The women giggled silently, with their small fanlike hands smothering their laughter. I laughed like the men, throwing my head way back, mouth stretched open.

On the way home I had forgotten where I had dumped Crippled Sister. Which bush could it be? I wondered. There were so many that lined the path to our home; none sparked a note of familiarity. Slowly Baby Sister and I inched down the road, our eyes and ears scanning opposite sides. Then I heard a muffled whimpering. I peeled back the curtain of leaves and there she was, just where I had dropped her.

"Stop your crying." I slapped her. We were late and I knew Mother would be waiting. I stooped down next to her, my forehead pressed to the ground as Baby Sister lifted her onto my back. I ran as fast as I could. Step, bump up, "*Ay-ya!*" Step, step, bump up, "*Ay-ya!*"

Suddenly I felt light again. Crippled Sister's tiny waist had slipped through and out, and she had landed headfirst on the gravel. Blood oozed from her hairline. Our faces mirrored each other's horror. Hoping to escape punishment, I smeared a handful of dirt into the cut to hide the bleeding. However, the instant we walked in, Mother's observant eyes darted in on the tiny blood-speckled pebbles that marked the spot. Once again I faced the wall, clutching my skirt high above my thighs. My calves received a double whipping for abandoning Crippled Sister behind a bush and for dropping her on her head. The next day, I carried Crippled Sister behind the outhouse and pinched her arm where I was sure she could feel the pain. My sweet revenge.

MARRIAGE

OF

STRANGERS

The union of marriage was too important a decision to let young hearts choose for themselves, so a matchmaker was called in to select a bride for Older Brother. He had no say in the arrangement, because the ceremony was more of a ritual to receive a daughter-in-law into the family. Respect, discernment, and honor came before friendliness and affection, if there ever was any.

As Older Brother was Mother's only surviving son, Father paid the old weathered matchmaker dearly. She searched villages near and far for a suitable bride from the same *yangban* breeding.

"You are a very lucky boy." The matchmaker winked. "I have found the most beautiful bride for you right here in our own province. Hips so wide, she will give you many offspring."

Several letters of marriage bearing the red family stamps were exchanged. Beyond the bride's ancestral name, her mother's surname, social status, and birth dates, we knew nothing except what trickled from the matchmaker's flapping tongue.

Mother was satisfied with the scraps of information she received. "Now we must take all this knowledge to the fortune-teller, who will tell us if my son and this girl are compatible," she said gaily.

The fortune-teller pulled out his chart of stars and planets and examined the horoscope of the groom and his bride, based on the couple's birth times, days, months, and years. "A good wedding," he announced eagerly, knowing he would receive a handsome fee. "The marriage is well matched."

He then calculated the perfect wedding date, set for the following month. No detail was left unattended to; elaborate gifts of jewelry and fabric were prepared for the bride's family; the guests invited; tasty dishes chosen; and the worn sedan chair painted and mended to fetch the bride to our home.

Three days before the bride was to arrive, Older Brother awoke early and filled a shallow basin with cold water which he drew from the well himself. He carefully set it on the floor and washed his face, neck, and hands. Then he unwound his hair, combed and oiled it. To signify his adulthood, he coiled a top-knot like Father's on his head. Once he was fully dressed in his horsehair wedding hat and a wedding belt, a banquet was held with relatives and friends, who came to help Mother and Father celebrate their son's reaching adulthood. The eldest literary man among the guests gave him a new name. The name he had as a child would not be used again. Then, together with Father, he went to the shrine of our ancestors to bow. From there Older Brother went to the house of the bride with his friends. The largest male acted as the horse and carried on his back the *hahm*, a wooden box filled with gifts for the bride's parents.

For three days, we all waited anxiously for Older Brother's return with his new bride. Finally, they appeared late in the evening on the third day, he on his mule leading the way and she in her sedan chair, rocking on the shoulders of six sweating bearers. The bride was not a "beautiful" woman as the matchmaker had bragged—that was expected. But the creature that walked into our home that evening was less than desirable, even for the most desperate man. Her features were far from soft and refined, and her lips were dark and full. She had intensely large round eyes that slightly popped out of their sockets, and she walked with a slight limp.

"At least she is not deformed," Mother commented grimly.

"At least," Father repeated with dismay.

"It is a good thing," Mother said after some thought. "It is unimportant to have a pretty daughter-in-law. A pretty daughter-in-law will be more concerned with how attractive her face is than tending to the house and bearing children."

"It is a good thing," Father echoed again.

Older Brother and his bride both looked unnerved as the white papered lattice doors sealed them alone in their wedding chamber. I was filled with curiosity; it was the first time I would ever witness a man sleeping in the same room with a woman. On occasions, I would see Mother slip into Father's quarters and return late in the night to take her place next to mine.

In the morning, Older Brother crept out when all the dishes were cleared away. Moments later his wife emerged with her head drooped low and her hands clasped tightly in front of her. They seemed more distant than ever. Father and Mother pretended not to notice, but I saw her battling for each step, strangling back her agony. Did he beat her? I wondered. I saw no bruises or welts on her hands or face, though I searched for them.

Promptly Mother assigned her to her new wifely duties, taking over most of my household responsibilities. I was ecstatic with the thought of leisure time. Mother, unfortunately, had other plans for my time: I needed to perfect my sewing and knitting skills. Older Brother's wife was also given the job of my tutor. She sat very patiently beside me as I fumbled through the lessons. Never once did she turn her head in frustration as Mother often did, causing me to skip a stitch. Her tenderness eventually won my heart and devotion. I began to resent Older Brother's coldness toward this frail woman, who was so kind and devoted to her new family.

Like a faithful daughter-in-law, she dutifully gave birth to two girls and a treasured grandson for Father and Mother to coo over endlessly. Having fulfilled his husbandly responsibilities, Older Brother began to leave his wife to tend to their children alone. In his loneliness, he sought out the pleasures of *kisaengs*. *Kisaengs* were famous for their captivating beauty and cultivated skills in pleasing a man in every way. They were poets, musicians, singers, flatterers, companions.

Father remained sternly silent as Older Brother stumbled in, reeking of rice wine, night after night. Father also said nothing when Older Brother brought home Second Wife. We called her by that title, though they were not formally married. She was not actually a *kisaeng* herself, but because her older sister entertained in a *kisaeng* house in Pyongyang, the family's reputation was blemished. So when Older Brother asked her to come live at our house and serve only him, she came willingly. It was the best proposal she would receive from a respectable man.

Everyone could see why he adored her. Stunning, she had all the exquisite qualities that First Wife lacked. From then on, she replaced First Wife in his bed. There was never any mention of her desertion. With time and some adjustment, First Wife, Second Wife, and Older Brother all lived courteously together under one roof.

Father and Mother secretly rejoiced in their son's happiness and the woman who made him so. But her sweet manners and sugary words frightened my sisters and me. We were sure she was a demon perfumed in flowered scents and expensive powders. She fell into the habit of dawdling around the house, and eventually became a kind of enormous breathing toy. She let herself forget she was only the concubine, and behaved as though she were the first wife. Every morning, she rose late and wasted the rest of the morning. Only after she was served her delicately prepared tray did she call out for her bath. "Hongyong-yah, come help me," she summoned.

To my displeasure, I had to fill the deep, round porcelain tub Older Brother had bought for her use. (She refused to bathe in the river with the rest of the women.) No one else was allowed to wash in the tub. She had me prepare the water precisely to her specifications—two brimming buckets of hot water to every three brimming buckets of cold. No more, no less. With eyelids half closed, smiling, she would sink into the water with a satisfying moan. Even with her hair uncombed, lips unpainted, skin pink and pruned, she still was exquisite. When finished she would rise with arms stretched high in the air, and bid me to dry her dripping body.

As a reward, she would let me admire her as she painted her face, a painstaking and time-consuming ordeal. First she evenly matted on a heavy mask of white powder, stopping at the base of the chin. Then the seeds from the *bongsoungang*, balsam, flower were crushed and mixed with water. No matter how careful I was, the reddish orange dye left stains all over my hands, but somehow Second Wife avoided a mess.

"Am I pretty?" she fished for a compliment.

"Yes," I admitted, hating to fuel her already monstrous ego.

"How pretty?"

"Very pretty," I answered, just to shut her up.

"Yes. I suppose I am. I could have married anyone in my younger days if it was not for my sister. Damn her." She often cursed, but only in my presence. She masked her true self from everyone else as well as she covered her facial blemishes. "I could still lure any man to do my bidding."

"I am sure Older Brother would disapprove of your luring skills," I said dryly.

"Do not think you can threaten me. Who do you think your precious brother will choose to believe? You are only his younger sister. I am the one who warms his bed. I advise you not to forget that." She gave my arm a good long pinch, then just as suddenly her face changed and her voice sweetened. "Now, come, Little Sister. Brush my hair."

The moment I had wished for so long came one explosive afternoon with a chilling shrill.

"*Uh-moh-nah! Uh-moh-nah!*"

The wails came from the women's quarters. Sisters, Older Brother, First Wife, and I rushed in to investigate.

"Why do you steal from me when my husband and I have welcomed you into our home?!" Mother's cheeks were scarlet and her eyes black fire.

"I was not stealing," Second Wife retorted, her hands still in Mother's jeweled coin box.

Older Brother picked up a shovel and swung it over her

head. Then, in the midst of his fury, he froze, the shovel still in midair. His whole body shook and twitched. Drops of sweat poured out of his high forehead as he lowered the shovel.

With a regretful sigh, Mother said solemnly, "I am lost. I cannot punish my son's wife."

I could not believe my ears: another injustice gone unpunished. I felt the anger swell inside of me until the words blurted out. "Then I will punish the thief!" All eyes whirled toward me as I gathered my courage. This was the day that Second Wife would be tossed from our home and out of my life forever.

"If Mother cannot beat her because she is Older Brother's wife and Older Brother will not because he feels too much with his heart, then I must," I stated boldly.

No one attempted to block my path as I marched to the corner and grabbed Mother's bamboo rod, the same punishing rod that left welts and bruises across my calves. I clutched it with quivering hands. Suddenly I felt powerful, holding the rod. So this was how it felt to possess it. I glanced over to where Mother sat to see if she would stop me, but she did not. Older Brother's eyes avoided mine.

Although Second Wife was five years my senior, I clutched her hair with one hand and lashed her over the backside with the rod. "Troublemaker! Troublemaker!" I yelled, mustering all my strength. Whack! The stick broke in half.

Second Wife huddled into a human ball, jerking with pain. "*Ay-ya! Ay-ya! Ay-ya!!*" I released my grip, wanting to flee as far away from this demon woman as possible, but she dug her reddish-dyed claws into my arm and held on.

"Little beast, I will kill you!" Her nails dug deeper.

Using the heels of my feet, I kicked myself free and ran straight into the men's quarters. She chased after me, scratching and barking. "Die! Die! You little bitch."

Father walked in unknowingly, startled at the disruption that swept his house. "What is going on here?! I will have silence in my house!" he demanded. Mother flew to his side and told him what had occurred in his absence. Father's face blazed with controlled anger. "You, come here!" He jabbed his finger at Second Wife, who slithered to the ground, hiding her tearful face between her knees. "What kind of woman cries so loudly?"

He glared down at Second Wife as she rocked back and forth, shielding her face. "Get out of my sight. What bad manners to cry so in my house!" Then I heard Father yell out my name. "Hongyong-yah! Where is she? Find her and bring her to me."

"I am here," I stammered from behind the screen.

"What is the meaning of this disgraceful act? You must be punished!" he said in a jesting tone I recognized. I melted with relief.

That night Father and Mother confronted Second Wife. She sat motionless, her legs folded beneath her, her head bowed down, and her hands lifeless on her lap. Tears were still pouring. She looked like she wore a painted mask left out in the rain.

"We cannot kick out our own daughter although she did a very disrespectable thing. But she is our daughter, hence you must leave our home at once so that peace may be restored," Father stated calmly. It was believed if a woman's voice rose high and loud, it would bring ill omens to the home. A loud angry voice, an excited voice, a high screaming voice: all were taboo.

"We will find our son another wife to share his bed," Father said bluntly.

And that was the end of Second Wife. She left early the following morning without her perfumed bath. Something ruptured in Older Brother's heart at that moment. The sight of his misery petrified me. It was a gentleman's duty to discard his lover if his parents so desired, no matter the personal loss. First Wife and I cooked Older Brother's favorite meal of *kwae chorin*, blue crabs in soy sauce; *kalbi*, short ribs; and *kaktugui kimchee*, turnip squares and served it to him with the hope of restoring his appetite, but he had lost all will to eat. He sat rigid, eyes fixed on the closed gate. Weeping, Mother begged Father to save their son, but Father would not listen to her cries.

"What kind of man would I be if I do not protect my household from the winds of tragedy?"

"A man with a son," Mother answered with great pain. "Is that not enough to make you change your mind, *Yobo*?"

"I have no son, only a childish boy who still needs to cling on to a woman's breast. Let him be."

Father would not give in to her pleading. For twenty more

days Older Brother barely ate, slept, or spoke a word. That was all Father could endure.

"Get up!" Father broke his silence at last. "If you are not man enough to live without her, get up and bring her back. It is your fate. There is nothing else I can do to save you." Father raised his arms in defeat.

Immediately Older Brother stumbled weakly to his feet and went out in search of Second Wife. He found her entertaining in a third-rate *kisaeng* house, pouring drinks and making friendly conversations. This time he did not promise her grand gifts to come serve him, only his heart. A few days later, they arrived at our gate. She was no more humble or tame than when she left, and Older Brother was more hopelessly in love.

Only later did I understand the true reason for Father's fury. It was not due to my outburst or Second Wife's thievery, but Older Brother's weakness. It was his duty to punish his wife. By failing to rise to his position, he gravely disappointed Father. In Father's eyes Older Brother was not the true man he had hoped his son would be. Secretly he wished I had been born the son. Nothing would have made me happier, but my fate was to remain ghostly pale and to wear tight rubber slippers, two sizes too small.

MATRON

BRIDE

The birthdays rolled by, and soon I found myself, at twenty-two, nearly past my prime and still unwed. Most daughters of rich families were already married and had added two or three grandchildren to their worth. Unmarried, I lived suspended between adulthood and childhood. My long braided hair uncoiled and tied with a red ribbon bore witness to the fact that I had not rightfully passed into womanhood.

Trapped.

I waited patiently, anxiously, knowing in another year or two no matchmaker in all of Korea would be able to find me a suitable husband. Although I felt doomed to be a rotten fruit, left to wither on the branch before ever being plucked by a man's hand, never once did I question my parents' tardiness in securing my future. It was none of my business. Instead, I busied myself practicing table settings and other procedures in preparation for marriage just in case. My thoughts, though, churned endlessly. I sketched in my mind the image of my groom. Would he be handsome? Would he be tolerant? Would he offer me lasting affection? Would I like him? I chanted to the Buddha, who sat there, inscrutable, with his eyes closed, as I laid down my prayers before his fat, naked belly.

More precious months passed and still no husband. Convinced I was ugly, I cursed my childhood illness for leaving its nights of torment etched in my face. I hated the shape of my lips, full and dark like First Wife's. My nose, unattractively flat and wide, dripped constantly from the demons burning a fire in my belly. Finally I gave up the foolish notion of marriage altogether. I am a lucky girl, I told myself, hoping the more I repeated these words, the better I would feel. He might have turned out to be an old widower with foul breath and warts or cruel and abusive. I am a lucky girl. A very lucky girl!

I was certain Older Brother would permit me to stay on and care for our parents in their old age. The security of remaining in the comfort of my father's home brought great relief and joy. To live forever in my childhood home was more than a daughter could ever wish for. Then one day as I was mending socks in the privacy of the women's quarters, I was formally summoned to appear before Father. Not since I was a young girl did Father request my company. The request was so startling I drove the needle deep into my thumb. Only when the blood oozed out did I realize what I had done.

Quickly I raised myself and cut across the bright sunny courtyard, then lightly tapped at his door.

"I am here, Father," I announced.

"Enter," his strong voice commanded as his hand motioned me to come in. He and Mother sat side by side on matching cushions. Obediently I slipped off my rubber slippers at the doorway and stepped before them in Father's inner office. He sat grimly, without his usual smile. In spite of being prepared all my life for this moment, I shivered with panic.

"Hongyong-yah, come closer so your Father and I can take a good look at you." Mother sighed impatiently.

I was hoping they would ask me to sit, for I was about to lose my footing and topple like a tree whose roots were suddenly uprooted by a storm.

"Your mother and I have arranged your *napchae*," Father said briskly. He wasted no time on small talk, for this was a business arrangement. "He is from the family of Lee. His given name is Lee, Dukpil. His age is nineteen and he is the first and only son, like his father and grandfather before him," Father recited from memory.

The son of three generations of only sons. A prestigious ranking for any man. No doubt the matchmaker had been well compensated. What snagged my attention, though, was that he was nineteen years old. I was his senior by three disturbing years. A man-child I was to wed and carry on my back to manhood. This kind of marriage was actually quite common: elderly parents desired experienced daughters-in-law who were capable of managing all the household responsibilities immediately and not a fourteen-year-old bride who still needed her mother's grooming.

Suddenly it all seemed so unfair. My parents never once asked me what I desired. "Does this please you, Hongyong-yah?" would have been sufficient. I was unsure if I should drop to my knees and bow deeply in gratitude or barricade myself in a room or threaten to throw myself into a well. Frozen, I just stood there, mute.

My future in-laws requested the *munmyoung*, the giving of Mother's surname, as a way of ensuring that families with the same bloodlines did not intermarry. This exchange of information, however, was one-sided. The bride's side, my side, had to be approved by the groom's side. When all was satisfactory, a fortune-teller set the wedding date and Mother and the servants had to work diligently to prepare a trousseau worthy of a daughter from a well-to-do *yangban* household.

"Only the finest fabrics and jewels," Mother insisted snobbishly.

Father only shook his head and poured more coins into her palm. I was grateful for my parents' generosity, for I had heard that the richer the dowry, the kinder the in-laws.

Days before the wedding ceremony, my in-laws sent over the *hahm*, carried on the backs of two male servants. Inside there were a pair of carved wooden wild geese and bundles of blue, red, and green silk.

"The green signifies that you two young ones will grow together," Mother remarked as she unpacked the gifts.

"The red represents passion. Every marriage must have passion for happiness," Second Wife added.

Mother shot her a disapproving glare. "Keep that knowledge to yourself. Hongyong should not concern herself with such things. She has more important duties to fulfill."

For once I agreed with Mother. I did not care to hear any more. Just the thought prickled my face with heat. I preferred the wooden ducks: the symbol of eternal love and devotion, partners for life. When a duck died, its mate would starve itself to death. Then I realized the benefit of being promised to a man three years younger. He would have a long life unless a flood, famine, or disease took him before his time. This was good news, for I was not ready to die.

Surprisingly, I slept well those last precious nights in my father's home. No nightmares of a mother-in-law with horns and fangs haunted my dreams. In fact, I hardly dreamt at all, but during the days I fantasized about my groom's face. Sometimes I envisioned him as being plain; other times I was quite indulgent, carefully molding his nose to slightly pinch in or outlining the corners of his mouth so they sloped upward. All these tiny details made a plain man exquisite.

The day of my wedding, I rose as usual. "Hongyong-yah! Hongyong-yah!" I heard the servant woman call just outside the screen door. "This is your wedding day. You must bathe your whole body." She giggled in delight.

A hot chill rushed through me, even my toes tingled. On this day a man would look upon my body. "My husband"—how hollow the words sounded. "My husband," I repeated, letting the title roll around in my head.

It was annoying being so ignorant about the relationship between a man and his wife. All I knew from stolen bits of conversations was that a husband would touch his wife in disgraceful places like her belly button and . . . breasts. Why must he touch mine when he had his own? Suddenly a strange urge possessed me to touch myself. The curiosity was overwhelming. It stirred my hand to action. I slipped it under my blouse and lightly moved it over the fullness of my breast, pretending it was his hand. It felt warm, smooth, and round. Very round. Enough for more than one handful. Slowly my fingertips inched toward the rising peak. Magically, the soft nipple hardened. I squeezed it, imagining it was his mouth sucking on it like a baby hungry for milk, but no milk trickled out, only a strange building of tension down below, between my legs. My hand became more daring and aggressive, sliding down between the valley of my cleavage, following the trail of surging energy. It continued along the length of my smooth belly, admiring the plush layer of skin. Down, down, my hand ventured lower to the sparse bush of black hair. Like a protective blanket it covered my private woman part, a place even unknown to me. Never explored, never penetrated. My breath became short and rapid as I peeled back the folds of skin. It was warm and moist with my own juices. It was unlike anything I had ever felt before, more tender than an infant's bottom and warmer than any touch. Then a memory flashed, spilling its horror all over me. Were the gossiping whispers true about the man's thing? The women at the river told tales about it hanging like a wilted pepper between a man's legs, and when it was time to go to bed it grew to an unnatural size. Then he would stick it between his wife's legs and relieve himself inside her. I jerked my hand away, refusing to pretend any longer.

My fingers were sticky and smelled of a distinct fishy scent I was afraid would be detected. Petrified, I concealed the hand behind my back as the bathwater was brought in. On this special occasion, Second Wife's porcelain tub was mine to use. For once Second Wife served me. I sat there, Buddha style, savoring every drop of hot water she poured over my back as the servant scrubbed vigorously. Although I ached, I felt incredibly refreshed, and stepped out of the tub. My skin glowed a new vibrant color of pink. I stood naked in the middle of the room as the two women wiped me dry and massaged perfumed oils deep into my pores, and wrapped me in a dry cloth. The whole room filled with exotic flowers.

They sat me down, still wrapped only in the cloth. They combed a straight furrow across the center of my hair, then coiled the single braid at the base of my head, securing it with a long pin worn only by married women. My hair was slicked back so tightly it felt as though each strand was pulling out of its root, making my eyes appear more slanted than they already were. My scalp throbbed with pain, but I had long learned to endure discomfort.

For the first time ever I wore makeup, just like Second Wife. She rubbed cream over my face, and then applied white powder, stopping abruptly at the jawline. "Do not move your face too much and be a good bride," Second Wife warned.

I took her advice very seriously; I had seen her face crack under all that powder before. Then came the dye, stirred from a crushed *bongsoungang* flower mixed with water. With the dye, she painted my lips and fingernails, then dotted both my cheeks and the center of my forehead. The small red dots were believed to ward off harmful spirits.

I picked up the hand mirror and was amazed to see a strange pretty woman staring back at me. "Could she be me?" I stammered.

"Silly girl, no woman should look like herself on her wedding day. If she did there would be no wedding." Second Wife chuckled. The other woman muffled her giggles behind a hand.

"What happens on the second morning when the makeup is all rubbed away?" I questioned, bewildered.

"That I cannot help you with. Let us hope the groom will be still under the effects of the wine."

The women hurried me into my wedding dress, for the guests and my groom would soon be arriving. The *hanbok* was pressed and laid out, a beautiful dress with hand-painted floral trimmings. Originally Mother had decided on the ceremonial *wonsam* gown with its brightly striped sleeves and elaborate gold crown. Alas, though, the gown, once worn only by the upper class, was now popular among commoners.

"Let the commoners wear the *wonsam* if they please, but as your father's daughter, you will wear an elegant blue silk *hanbok*." Mother raised her nose and went to work promptly.

With expert skill, she perfectly blended and cut the dress. The *chogori*, a short jacket that fell just below the breasts, was sewn from a fine sky blue and yellow silk, as she promised. It tied at the bottom of the starched white V-neck collar with a pair of long, wide ribbons. The sleeves were straight on top and curved slightly below. The *chima*, a full-length puffy skirt, was made of a magnificent red silk. Underneath the skirt I wore a five-layer knee-length slip to give it fullness. Under the slip I wore a white unlined see-through jacket and pantaloons. So securely were they wrapped, I barely had room to breathe. One sneeze and the entire dress would have unraveled at the seams. Like everything else in our lives, the *hanbok* harmonized with nature and the prudish Korean code of ethics. Nothing was seen. No feminine curve could be detected under all the silk. It was either hidden or flattened.

On my feet I wore padded socks with upturned toes and colorful rubber *komusin* slippers. The slippers were two sizes too small, but Mother insisted they made my feet more attractive. Upon my head a bridal crown was placed, a short veil that graced the tops of my shoulders and had wildflowers arranged in my hair. I had no idea Mother was so stylish.

When all was complete, Mother came in with scrutinizing eyes. "Fine," she said, after a long inspection. "You may leave us now." She waved everyone out.

Suddenly the room was unbearably silent. The walls seemed to close in, forcing the two of us to press against each other's guarded space. She stood up abruptly, breaking the trance, and untied her coin pouch, hanging from her breast ribbons. Carefully she dumped out its contents, and there on her palm was a single brass key. She carried it to her private cabinet and unlocked the latch; it clicked open. I waited anxiously to see what was hidden behind those sealed drawers. From the top drawer she lifted a narrow rectangular box. To my surprise Mother presented me with the red tassel ornament that had lain undisturbed for many years. Her small delicate fingers fastened it to my jacket strings, where my heart beat heavily with emotion.

"With this tassel you carry the hope of ten generations of women." Her voice cracked.

I was chocked with sorrow. I wanted to embrace her, to be close to her, to tell her I held no hatred for her for all those times she whipped me. If only I could have known this proud yet fragile woman I called Mother. Now I belonged to another man's family. And another woman I would call Mother.

A tear escaped from her eye as if she had read my thoughts. She took one more longing gaze before saying, "Remember, Hongyong-yah, a woman can always learn to love her husband."

There was another saying: "A bride who could not control her laughter on her wedding day would give birth only to girls." Such a woman was no better than a servant, I was warned. This was a heavy burden, because the wedding ceremony lasted several days, and it was filled with ruthless teasing from relatives and neighbors.

My groom arrived on his mule just before noon. During the earlier part of the day the soles of his feet received a beating from his friends, who tied his two legs together and hung him from the beam of the house to make him promise them another feast. As the mule carried him, I could hear the cheerful cries of children flocking around him. Guests and relatives crowded into the middle room, where he was brought in. After closely inspecting him, they awaited my entrance.

I walked in with my elbows out and my palms raised to meet my bowed forehead, completely dependent on First Wife and an elderly female servant to guide me, for my sight was obstructed. I saw only my rubber slippers scooting, one tiny step at a time, careful not to trip over the hem. Laughter tinkled throughout the room. In spite of all the teasing, I easily kept my face tight against any hint of a grin or smile.

A light hand pressed gently on my shoulder, directing me to sit. My groom sat across from me at the low lacquered table, only a whisper away. How I wanted to raise my eyes, to gaze at this newcomer full in the face, but tradition forbade it. All I could manage to see was his long, slender hands. Striking hands they were, as beautifully manicured as a woman's. Obviously they had been spared from raising a hoe or working the land. A pampered man's hands.

Everyone watched as a single ceramic cup of *makkoli*, a

creamy wine made from fermented rice, was poured for the groom. Father offered the first toast, welcoming my new husband. He referred to me only as the wife of Lee, Dukpil, who now lived in the house of Lee. My position as the first daughter of Baek, Hogin was over. My memory would forever be erased in the book of records, as was done for all the other generations of Baek daughters, who were sent out of their fathers' homes. From this day forward I would never be called by my childhood name. "Lee, Dukpil's wife" was my new title.

While all the guests settled around two large banquet tables for the elaborate feast, I felt the same light hand touch my shoulder. This time it told me to rise. The dreaded moment had arrived. First Wife supported one arm and Mother slid her hand in the crook of the other. Together they steered me through a path of snickering onlookers and into the inner room. The teasing and laughter that rang all through the wedding feast halted abruptly. I was wrong, the dead silence was more paralyzing. The vision of First Wife's face the morning she limped out of Older Brother's chamber came haunting back. I wanted to run away as fast as my rubber slippers could take me. But where? Perhaps to a monk temple. I could pledge myself to their gong-ringing, incense-burning lifestyle.

"A woman's place is not with religious nonsense, it is to follow her husband," I could just hear Father mutter.

A single candle flickered in the corner, throwing shadows on the surrounding walls and on the ancient silk screen embroidered with waterfalls and forest scenery. In front of the screen and on the floor, the bedding was spread out and the heavy cotton comforter pulled back to receive us. I was positioned on the bedding's edge, facing the empty wall, my profile to the door. Mother worked meticulously, dabbing the sweat from my brow, straightening my headdress, fluffing my skirt.

"That will have to do." Mother sighed heavily, lifting herself off the bedding. "Do not dishonor us. He is now your husband," she added coolly. I watched feebly as she moved toward the door, wanting to cry out to her and beg her to stay. Then she turned her head slightly, her back to me, unwilling to meet my pleading eyes. "Keep your eyes closed," she forewarned.

A whirlwind of images crashed through my head. I pinched my fingers, trying to think what the coming night might actually bring. Girl I would go in and woman I would emerge. If only it were that simple and painless.

I waited nervously, propped up and posed. Outside, the festive chatter of men, women, and children celebrating my wedding without me resonated. Toast after toast, husky voices urged my groom to drink yet another cup of wine. As I waited, my head began to feel heavy with the day's exhaustion, and I nodded off.

I was uncertain just how long I sat there asleep until the screen door slid open, startling me awake. All my doubts and fears thundered back. I could not see him, but I heard the sound of his feet lightly pacing back and forth about the room. Instantly my breath left as I sensed him kneel behind me. He was near, so very near: the smell of his drunkenness sizzled my nose hairs. I felt his eyes move up and down the back of my neck, my body, examining each detail. "Just do what you must," I wanted to blurt out, but once more tradition commanded me to remain submisssive.

Finally he placed his thin fingers on my shoulders and pivoted me toward him, scrutinizing my face. Mustering my courage, I lifted my eyes a few inches so they rested on his mouth. It was flawless in shape and red, the skin around it freshly shaven and smooth. Lost in my own exploration, I forgot myself and I raised my eyes to meet his. This was my groom?! For once the matchmaker had not lied. His features were well defined—a strong prominent nose, large round eyes with double lids, high cheekbones, arched ink-brushed eyebrows, and not a single missing tooth in front.

We sat face-to-face, rigid in our shyness. It was the groom's duty to do the undressing. He was expected to remove the headdress, undo the breast string, and take off only one sock. The bride must sit motionless. Clumsy with fright, he painfully plucked several long strands of black hair along with the headdress. When he reached for my breast strings, he must have caught the horror in my eyes, because he stopped and coiled back his hand, a retreat. At that moment, I felt his terror, and I was no longer afraid.

I could not let this happen. I had to quickly restore his confidence so he could perform his duty, for it was a great sport for wedding guests to peep through holes they punched in the paper door. They must not see him reject me. I let out a little whimper, then another. My simple plan worked. By letting him believe I, too, was frightened, it emboldened him.

No one could have prepared me for what happened next. Completely disrobed except for a single sheer slip, I lay still on my back with the covers drawn tightly under my chin as he peeled off his clothing, one item at a time. First he removed his padded socks, then he pulled off the navy-blue-and-crimson jacket. Lastly he untied the silk baggy trousers at the ankles and when he unfastened the waistband they dropped to the floor. My eyes focused on the male part dangling between his legs. I blinked hard, hoping the darkness was playing tricks on me. I blinked again and it was still there. So all the hushed gossip about the male thing was true. How strange, though, he had the same black mat of hair down below. As he stepped toward me it swung from side to side, limply. I wondered if it was broken or dead, like Crippled Sister's legs.

Committed to memory and not to reason or to passion, he lowered himself on top of me, his body clammy. My own body stiffened, arms and legs were straight and locked at the joints. Without further delay, he slipped his hands between my legs and strained before prying them open. I felt his thing rub against my upper thigh, growing harder and longer with each movement, searching for something. When he shoved it inside of me, I forgot to breathe, stunned beyond belief.

"Close your eyes," I heard Mother's voice echo within the walls of my head. I shut them tightly as he continued to move in and out, in and out. Faster and faster he pumped, ripping me open, wider and wider.

"Muffle your screams. Be brave." I told myself.

I bit my lips hard, and the taste of my own blood made me want to retch. Then unexpectedly, he stopped pushing. Every muscle in his body tensed up as he groaned and shuddered several times. He rolled off onto his back and lay there lifeless beside me. He seemed near death.

"I killed him! I killed him!" I cupped my face with my hands, wanting to hide.

I remained motionless for a long time, waiting for him to say something, anything. Then I could not lie there any longer. I needed to separate myself, but my numb leg was crushed beneath his. Unable to free it, I struggled to hold back sobs.

"Mmmmm . . ." he moaned faintly, followed by deep snoring.

I pressed my ear close to his mouth and felt his breath on my cheek. He was sleeping! A mad chuckle of relief escaped me. I was saved.

The encounter was wretched. Not even Mother, if she had tried, could have prepared me. It was the furthest thing from my wildest imaginations. How grotesquely uncivilized it was. We were no better than the livestock we butchered.

That entire night was an unnerving blur of pain. Bloody, swollen, consumed with shame, I rose early and left my groom's side before he awoke. I did not want to have to speak politely to him as though nothing had happened between us, because something had that changed me forever, and the stained sheet was my evidence.

I avoided the questioning stares of my younger sisters, who looked to me for answers, secret answers which I wanted to spare them. With no one to share my troubled heart, I stayed mostly to myself, though I kept up the pleasant facade everyone expected of me until it was time to leave. Three days had passed, and my in-laws had sent the wedding sedan chair to fetch me to my new home.

Again I was scrubbed, dressed, and painted. As I stood in the women's quarters one last time, a deep sadness grew inside me. When I would be allowed to visit these familiar rooms depended on the mercy of my mother-in-law, whose temper I would learn soon enough. I was determined to bargain for her affection through hard work and obedience. I knew, however, some mothers-in-law could never be won over, no matter how low the faithful daughter-in-law bowed or how small her sewing stitches. Bitterness and cruelty were handed down from the older generation of women to the next.

"It is time," Mother delivered the message herself.

I gathered my dress around me and stood to attention. "Yes, I am ready."

"Good," Mother replied, but there was a hesitation on her lips as if she wanted to say one final thing. I waited, yearning to hear comforting words.

"You have entered womanhood. There are things you must remember to keep peace and harmony in your husband's household."

A flood of knowledge gushed from Mother's mouth. I had never heard her speak so much before. Wasting little time to think out her words, she steadily presented a detailed verbal list. I realized then that she had planned this moment earlier, all on her own.

"Marriage is the relation between heaven and earth, between solid and soft, and between sovereign and subject. And it begins from the distinction of the two. The distinction should be kept between man and woman, as it is proper and will lead to the stability of the world." She went on by telling me my supreme duty as a married woman was to inherit the ancestors' spirits by performing sacrificial rites and to give birth to male heirs for the continuation of the Lee line.

She advised me that short words were best. "Talk in a soft, thin voice only after you have made your mind undisturbed and have thought deeply first. Avoid attracting attention to yourself. Try not to cough or sneeze or make any indecent noises. Avoid saying evil words people dislike. Instead of saying 'thief' say 'night guest.' Eyes must be low, head straight, hands polite, posture virtuous, expression sublime, and appearance clean. Clean also means chaste. Do not be adulterous. Refrain from jealousy and pretend not to notice his indulgence. Otherwise, you will be considered narrow-minded. Do not steal. And do not disobey your in-laws. Treat them as . . . your first parents." Mother heaved a sigh which wrenched my heart. She was ordering me to toss aside my devotion to her and Father. Only years later when I had given my own daughter away for marriage did I understand her sacrifice and camouflaged agony that day.

All of Mother's words cluttered my head, dizzying me as I

was lifted away on the shoulders of six men. The bearers marched to their own separate internal counts; thus with each miscalculated step my head banged against the ceiling of the tiny box. Each careless sway propelled me from side to side on the satin cushion. The sun's rays warmed the red silk that hung over the window, enticing me to tug back the curtain. And in my solitude, I boldly stole several quick glances. The hills appeared larger and more abundant. The trunks of the trees were as thick as a cow's belly.

By the time we arrived, people were already happily stuffed with rich foods and rice wine. They shouted teasing remarks through the window as the bearers lowered the sedan chair. Like a prized gift, I was presented to the crowd. As I rose to climb out, all the blood shot straight down to my feet, making my rubber slippers tighter than ever. I was pale with discomfort—this would have pleased Mother. Weeks before the wedding she kept me shut away inside the house and out of the tanning sun; the mark of a peasant who labored in the rice field.

Up ahead, I heard the sound of hooves. I restrained myself from raising my head in order to see my groom's face in brilliant sunlight. Then once again bold curiosity overwhelmed strict social etiquette, and I glanced up through lowered eyes just in time to observe my groom lose his footing as he dismounted and land on his behind. To my astonishment, he appeared much younger than his nineteen years in the direct light. The guests cackled joyously. My baby-faced groom laughed along with them as he sprang back onto his feet and dusted his rear.

Inside, everything was festively arranged. The wedding gifts from my overstuffed dowry were displayed prominently on a low table. The clothes Mother had sewed for each member of my new family were neatly laid out. Quilts and bundles of fine silk Father had imported from China glistened with wealth. But the most valued gift was the jewel-covered box filled with gold and jade earrings, bracelets, rings, necklaces, and pendants. There, on that table, was my security. I hoped Father's generosity would be appreciated by my in-laws so they would treat this new servant well.

Immediately I was summoned to appear before the family. Perched at the head of the receiving room, an ancient grandmother and a kindly man and his wife sat on cushions on the floor, clothed in lustrous silk. "Step forward, wife of my only grandson," the old woman beckoned. Her sharp eyes narrowed. "Closer, closer, let us get a good look at you." She flicked the small silver knife she was polishing.

One by one, they loudly scrutinized my height, weight, the shape of my face, the flatness of my nose, the size of my hands, the broadness of my hips. Now I felt like crying as I stood before them all.

"Dukpil-yah, stand by your bride so these tired eyes of mine may see you as one," she bid.

Side by side we stood before those sunken sharp eyes of hers, as she imagined the offspring we would produce. "You two have a heavy responsibility. I expect a great-grandson within a year's time." Grandmother's brows arched. Something told me she would make it her burden and mine to see to it that I fulfilled my obligations.

"Look, he is eager to make you that great-grandson you desire, Grandmother. The groom cannot seem to tear his eyes off his new bride!" a man shouted out, his voice laced with amusement.

The blood shot to my face. I was outraged at my groom's lack of decency. How could he embarrass me so in front of all his family and neighbors? Suddenly I hated him; it was all his fault I was torn away from my parents and sisters.

"This is a good sign. I will have that babe soon enough. But first thing is first, the couple must perform the *paebeck*."

At her request, we sat at the wedding table and I offered my groom a cup of rice wine, respectfully using both hands. I held it up to his lips as he drank. Then I sipped the bitter wine, turning my back to him slightly. It burned a trail down to my empty stomach. Everyone laughed in delight as I choked to keep it down. This was how we pledged our troth.

Together we rose. My legs shivered uncontrollably as I bowed slowly in front of my new in-laws. Cross-legged all the way down, down, until my rear touched the floor, then my forehead; a skill which required weeks of practice to accustom my legs to the strain. He bowed next to me. His legs were pressed together into a kneel as the back of both palms met his forehead and he then descended to the ground in the same but less strenuous fashion. Up and down we went till every last elder received their tribute. And when that was complete, we faced each other and performed our final bow. Perspiration pushed its way through the crust of face powder; beads of sweat trailed down my neck and back. Afterward, I sat before my in-laws as they tossed jujubes, red dates, and chestnuts into my skirt. The more I caught, the more children and luck I would bear. I caught only five.

Now it was time to eat. I watched, amazed, as my groom tipped his head and emptied his wine cup in one quick gulp. He was more animated and confident among his own relatives and friends, and they clearly favored him over the other young men, regardless of how foolish he acted. I, on the other hand, sipped modestly, letting the wine linger on my tongue for a moment before I released it down my throat and into my system. The attempt, however, had no diluting affects.

I had a chance to nibble on some wedding noodles before being escorted into a private chamber to fulfill my obligation to the old woman. Again I waited in a darkened room while my intoxicated groom bumbled through more drinking games. He stumbled in, stinky drunk. Every muscle in my body tensed up at the sight of his silhouette. He looked grisly, the way the yellow candlelight flickered on his reddened face. His particular bashful grin told me he was ready to force himself on me. With each approaching step he swayed. If it was not for my speed and agility he would have tumbled onto me with all his bloated weight.

"Are you hurt?" I eased up to him, careful not to touch him.

To my joyful relief, he passed out, facedown and still fully clothed. I undressed him and tucked him under the quilt. In the morning I let him believe he had conquered me once again.

How startling all this was. Only a few nights ago I shared a bed with my sisters. What crime had I committed in my previous existence to be born a female? I sulked over these questions for a while when it dawned on me that it was not my groom's fault I was here. He was as much a victim as I was in this unfair arrangement. I realized then I held no bad feelings for him. In fact, I felt nothing toward him. There was no affection, no emotion, nothing.

I was awakened by my mother-in-law and assigned to morning meal duties right away. "You must learn to cook specifically for my son's palate. He dislikes his food bland. The exact mixture of spices can make a simple meal mouthwatering. Your first lesson begins now."

With those brief words of introduction, I was swept off into the kitchen. There I spent most of my early weeks, chopping, measuring, mixing, and sampling recipes. I slaved from five o'clock in the morning till the last member of the family retired.

Each morning commenced with the refueling of the oven, to warm the chilly *ondul* floor. As the rest of the family slept peacefully, knowing a freshly steamed meal would await them when they awoke, I went to work. These meals required elaborate preparation. And no meal was complete without rice, *bahp*, the staple of our diet. It was so central our spoken word for food was also *bahp*. A woman's ability to cook it garnered her either praise or disgrace.

Early in life, my own mother had taught me to wash the rice seven to ten times, rinsing by dipping the basket into the water and scrubbing the grains with strong hands. Only when the milky water turned clear and the rice shone white as wet pearls was the water measured. The amount had to be as precise as a doctor would measure the dosage of medicine.

Once the rice was cooking, I busied myself with the rest of the meal, but always I kept one eye and one nostril on the simmering kettle. My biggest worry was nodding asleep and waking to the smell of burnt rice and having to face my mother-in-law's anger. Finally, I understood the reasons behind Mother's persistent naggings and whippings. A fluffy grain of rice, a tiny stitch, a nicely ironed jacket, obedience were my insurance that I would be able to eat, sleep, and have some peace.

Always the meal tray was loaded with the household's favorite dishes, all precut into small pieces, for only spoons and chopsticks were used. While they ate, I folded quilts and listened with relief as the family chewed and slurped loudly. No praise was expected; however, the noise assured me of their satisfaction. Dutifully, I waited in the corner for the head of the house, Father-in-Law, to place his chopsticks directly on the table, officially signifying the meal was over. Only then did I carry the tray back into the kitchen. There I sat and scraped the leftovers for myself, hidden away from the others.

After the morning meal, the dishes needed scouring, the floors needed wiping, the clothes needed washing, the furniture needed dusting, the socks needed mending, the house needed patching, and before I knew it, the day was half over and the noon rice needed rinsing. The whole tiresome process would be repeated again and again until the day's last dish was cleaned and put away. Once the sun set, I was allowed to retire because of a superstition. It was believed if the sound of ironing sticks were heard after dark it would bring death to an elderly person in the house.

Soon even my nights were interrupted with the change of seasons. It became my job throughout the chilly winter nights to monitor the warmth of the *ondul* floor. Regardless of how cold it got, I sweated constantly. The garments clung to my shoulders. Several bean-sized calluses had grown on both palms right below the joint of each finger where I gripped the handle of the pail when I hauled water from the well to the house. I was weary with exhaustion, but I kept working. Quickly I forgot my homesickness. There was simply no time or energy to think of anything but the many chores at hand. Gradually the sharp memory of my parents' and sisters' faces dimmed; it seemed as though I had been here serving these people all my life.

As the months sped by, my early-morning rising became the most treasured time of the day. No mother-in-law or grandmother scrutinized my every move. It was a moment of absolute solitude, a moment to lose myself in thought. Thoughts that increasingly gravitated toward Husband.

Perhaps because I was not looking for love or friendship in

my marriage, I was dumbfounded when love stroked my heart. It began with a simple, abrupt compliment on the fluffiness of my rice, then progressed to the silkiness of my hair.

"It is improper to stuff a woman with such praise. She will see your weakness, and use it to seek power over you." His mother frowned at him. "Repress your emotions, or else people will think you are uncultured. Women are not meant to be the companions of men."

"Yes, Mother, as you say," he would agree.

But every once in a while, he let another escape whenever his mother's alert ear was out of hearing distance.

"You have spoiled me with your cooking. I fear I shall outgrow my clothes," he said in a plain voice, looking past me.

Concealing my excitement, I humbly pretended to be unworthy of his sweet words so that I might hear him speak again. "I am undeserving of your compliment. I am a poor cook. And if you do outgrow your clothes, I shall be honored to sew you new ones," I answered him in the same dull voice.

"Then I shall try my best to fill out my flesh if this is what you desire. I wish for you to be happy," he added discreetly.

It was all so splendidly bizarre. I was not accustomed to receiving such praise from a man. It seemed almost immoral to declare our affections, but I savored every exchange. The only way I knew how to return his sweetness was to wait diligently on him. I folded his clothes just the way he liked it, and stored them with fragrant flowers and leaves. I learned to cook all his favorite spicy dishes, dropping in an extra chunk of meat or fish. All these things I did just to please him.

For the first time in my life, I obsessed over my appearance. I studied my naked reflection whenever I washed, exploring my flesh to see if I could arouse the same heat, but it was futile. Husband's touch was magical. The mere thought of spending the coming night wrapped in his arms sustained me through the day's hardship. A primitive, uncontrollable giggle welled up through my body until it filled me completely with desire. Cautiously, I bottled up these feelings, concealing them from him. I feared he might think he had married a foolish woman.

By late afternoon, I was giddy with anxiousness. I watched out of the corner of my eyes as he retired to bed earlier and earlier each night. Unfortunately, the three old ones failed to follow his lead. I had to wait until they tucked themselves in before I was free to creep into our room.

A single candle on the nightstand near where he lay was always lit for me. I would watch his face as he watched me disrobe. His roaming eyes made me extremely uncomfortable. He, however, seemed to find it endearing the way I quickly untied my jacket and wiggled out of my skirt.

"Why do you hurry so? I enjoy watching my wife undress in the candlelight. It is a beautiful sight."

"That is the one thing I will not allow you to indulge in," I answered uneasily as I stood above him in only my thin white slip.

"We shall see." His gaze narrowed to focus on my bare shoulders.

"We shall," I agreed as I hastily crawled in next to him on the smooth cotton bedding. He was already completely naked below. I never had to wait for him to take me; his hardness told me that he was ready. It warmed me all over, knowing how urgently he desired, needed me. He drew me in closer to suck in the perfumed scent of my hair. I knew how much he fancied such things as a woman's smell, so I made sure I was well oiled.

I playfully struggled as he rolled on top of me. The weight of his lower body settled completely on mine, while lifting his upper body with his arms. Every inch of him was smooth and firm. He began to kiss my face, hot smothering kisses. I held back, though I wanted to swallow him up and possess him. He withdrew his kisses teasingly, allowing me only a maddening taste. I was enraged. He saw my pouting lips and grinned, gratified, knowing I, too, was eager to make love to him. He pinned my arms slightly above my head with one arm and with his free hand he skillfully moved down the front of my slip and untied the strings, exposing my heaving chest. The pent up tension built throughout my body. His mere touch aroused so much heat it was overpowering. I dropped my head back on the pillow, no longer wanting to resist. My back arched with uncontrollable ecstasy. Every gesture and sound was amplified. His long, slender fingers reached way down and lifted my slip high above my hips, then I felt him enter, leaving me breathless, just like the first time. At once it grew, past the boundaries of my walls. There was no pain now, only the lasting pleasure of his controlled thrusts. Spasms surged through my body. I did not understand their meaning and tried desperately to hold on to the building sensation, but it was impossible. Mind and body were separate. My body had discovered his rhythm and would only respond to his bidding. I felt fire. My skin burned. I wanted to moan. We clung to each other closer, tighter, in a desperate lock to fuse together. He groaned! I groaned! I felt him pouring into me, drenching me with his warmth.

He collapsed on my chest, his heart pounding against my rib cage. As we lay there in the darkness, I heard his angelic voice.

"I am too happy to sleep."

His breath, so close in the blackness, soothed us both. I sank into his comforting arms and listened late into the night as he recited to me one of his favorite folktales, wondrous stories I had never heard before. I became small again. A child who loved to be cuddled, spoiled.

"Now let us talk together. What runs through that secret head of yours?" he pressed delicately. Always he encouraged me to share my thoughts with him.

"You speak so well and your stories are so much more entertaining," I answered shyly, wishing him to conjure another tale.

"It would please me to know your mind."

"There is nothing of worth for me to say."

"You must not be embarrassed to share your thoughts. Everything you feel, think is of great value to me. I wish to know my wife's gentle mind as well as I am getting to know her flesh."

"My mind is all a-clutter. It has been since I was a child."

"That is untrue. I know your heart, and it is expansive; so must your mind be."

"It is problematic when a woman's mind is too large."

"And why is that?"

"Because . . . then the household will be disturbed. There can only be one voice. One master," I recited Mother's words.

"This is true; however, do you not agree that two thoughts bring better solutions, more wisdom."

"Perhaps . . ." I stammered, pausing for a moment to ponder

his question. "Perhaps if the two thoughts have the same vision at heart."

How wise he was. I had never met such a person who pried my mind open with his questions. It was perplexing to believe I belonged to such a man. With that thought, I closed my eyes and was ready to receive my dreams, though none possibly could equal the one I had just lived.

MY

LITTLE

RED

PEPPER

Husband gave me the strength and inspiration I needed to work the hardest I had ever worked. For him, as well as for my sake, I concentrated on winning his mother's approval. If I failed her expectations, she had the right to turn me out in disgrace, and out of Husband's company. Determined to stay by his side, I woke up an hour earlier each morning, to get a head start on the day's chores. Slowly her complaints faded, for I taught myself to anticipate her every need before she realized it herself. On a rare occasion there was even a hint of affection in her voice. My intrusion into her son's heart was at last forgiven. The beast had been tamed and I had won her favor. The household was finally at peace, but not for long. She passed away unexpectedly in her sleep. A few months later, Husband's father followed her to the grave. That was the way with the old ones. When the man died first, the woman lived long after him in the leisure of her eldest son's home, but when the woman died before the man, his time usually came quickly.

Husband and I mourned in our coarse white hemp garb

which we would wear for the next three years. Though I wore white, the colorless color of death, I bore little sorrow in my heart, but custom demanded I wail loudly with forced tears. I knew it was shameful the way I was feeling deep inside, but I was caught up in the joy of rising to the position as the head woman of the house. It never occurred to me that Husband's ancestors would punish me for my wicked thoughts.

Grandmother emerged from her long hibernation and snatched the reins from my reaching fingers. Bitterness poisoned her mood, a bitterness that grew more sour each morning she awoke and realized she had outlived her only son. No matter how diligently I served her she was entirely impossible to please. She was trying to wear me down with her authority. Whenever she barked, I jumped, skipped, snapped to do her bidding.

"You are useless and lazy. See how frail my grandson looks because you neglect your duties."

True, Husband did seem undernourished, but it was due to the lack of food. Grandmother controlled our daily consumption. Once a day she took a stick into the storage room to measure the rice supply. She vigilantly kept count on the number of chickens and pigs slaughtered, paranoid that one would land in my stomach. We ate like peasants, although the storage room brimmed with rice, millet, barley, corn, and beans.

"Stupid girl! Do you think food falls freely from the sky? Cook less rice, chop less meat, pour less tea!" she squawked until my head throbbed from maintaining self-control.

Three times a day I humbled myself to ask Grandmother for the key which was tucked in a secret pocket sewn into her pantaloons. She always trailed me to the storage room, and hovered over my shoulder as I scooped rice from the sack. Carefully I leveled the ground with my free hand, making certain not to spill the grain, then I poured the rice into a basket woven of finely split bamboo.

"How careless you are. You waste my precious rice!" She waved her crooked finger at an invisible speck on the floor. On my knees I searched for the single missing grain.

I learned to scrimp and do without. For myself I took smaller portions of food and poured my share into Grandmother's bowl. It was not because I desired her to live any longer than she must; I was petrified she might accuse me of hoarding all the food. The soft plumpness of my figure waned, growing lean, accentuating every muscle and bone. This only added to my shyness. I went to great lengths to conceal the ripples in my concave stomach and my sharp hipbones from Husband. I could not endure it if he found me undesirable, so I learned to undress in record time.

Often, I would steal into the kitchen late at night when Grandmother and Husband were fast asleep. In the darkness I scavenged for leftovers like a starving animal. Many nights, as I crouched in the corner sucking on splintered chicken bones and wilted cabbage stems, I dreamt of the feasts we used to have in Father's home. Mother would cook up a huge steaming kettle of rice. Chunks of vegetables from Father's store floated in a delicious broth of spicy red-bean paste. Conversation was a rarity at our table, only the sound of clicking chopsticks, slurping mouths, and hearty belches.

I knew I could not survive on discarded chicken bones and wilted vegetables for long. I must secure power, and the only way to accomplish it was to bear children, sons. With sons came position, prestige, and authority. I wished for the day I, too, was Grandmother's age, enjoying my sons' and grandsons' fruits. Desperate, I chanted to the Buddha, for it had been nearly a year since I was married off and still I was barren. I had little faith in that fat bald-headed man, but I turned to him once more. Soon enough, someone or something heard my plea. At first, I had thought my childhood ailment was causing my belly to bloat and whirl. The mere mention of food made my stomach heave. Dark shadows formed beneath my eyes from worry. Grandmother gave me permission to visit Father's home to recuperate. The gesture arose not out of kindness; it was caution. She wanted to guard herself against contamination.

Mother greeted me at the gate. I had been gone only twelve months, but it seemed her hair was dusted with more gray and her face older. Judging by her concerned expression, I, too, must have aged prematurely. Her face also communicated some additional worry. Perhaps she thought Husband had turned me away.

"This is such an unexpected visit. How is our son-in-law?" she hinted.

"Very well, thank you. I must return to him shortly to attend to my duties," I assured her, immediately releasing the wrinkled tension from her brow.

"Come, I wish to hear about your life." She spoke in a carefree voice I had not heard since I was a young girl. Instantly I was six again, yearning for my mother to make the hurt and aches vanish. Her easy touch on my cheek broke the dam of emotions.

"Mother, I think I am dying. The demons of my past have come back to finish their wicked work." Nearly in tears, I told her how my hunger was insatiable and yet the thought of food violently sickened me.

Once we were alone in my former quarters, she eagerly probed my illness further. "When was the last time you bled?"

"Bled?" I pondered this odd question for some time before answering. "There is so much work that needs my attention, the exact number of weeks has slipped my mind . . . I suppose I am overdue."

She patted my hand affectionately. "You are with child." She beamed at the idea of being a grandparent. "Let me take a look at your belly."

Mother examined my protruded belly, hidden from all others under my full skirt. Her featherlight fingers brushed over the swell.

"It is a boy child, I am sure of it," Mother declared.

"How do you know, Mother?" I questioned, wishing it to be true.

"See here. Your child clings to your belly very low and the nipples are brown as the earth. This is how I know, and I am always correct."

Suddenly the knowledge of a tiny person growing inside of me stirred a new sense of protectiveness. I was so anxious to share my joy with Husband I returned home almost immediately. The entire way there, I rehearsed just what I was going to say. It had to be special, it had to be perfect. Then it dawned on me that Husband might not share my excitement. He himself was barely out of childhood. How would he respond to sharing the attention with another?

Once home, I waited for the night's intimacy when we were pressed together. He held me so longingly, reclaiming the nights lost during my absence. At that moment, I knew he had more than enough love for our child. The image of him coddling our babe brought forth tears of joy.

"Am I holding you too tightly?" he fretted.

"Never," I assured him, stroking his chin.

"I am afraid in my urgency to possess you again, I forgot how delicate you are."

"These are not tears of pain, but tears of absolute joy. In a few short months, you shall have another to hold in your arms, our child."

"Are you certain? A babe? Can it be true?" He sounded genuinely astounded.

From then on, every thought, every conversation revolved around our coming child. Nothing else mattered. The news, however, hardly softened Grandmother's disposition. I was still required to perform my household duties, but I was spared from doing anything unclean or killing animals. She did become less stringent on the amount of food I could take from the storage room. This failed to curb my cravings, because many items were now banned from my diet, including rabbits, squids, crabs, eggs, peaches, ducks, and chickens. Although peaches and chicken were my favorites, I observed the strict taboo, for I did not want my child to be born with fuzzy, prickly skin.

By the fifth month, miraculous changes occurred within the wall of my belly without any conscious effort or manipulation on my part. While I sewed and cooked, my body was forging a tiny hand, a perfect toe, two eyes, two ears—a whole other person. The first time I felt it kick, I was speechless.

"Uhh," I sighed.

"What is it?" Husband rushed to my side.

"It is the child, it moves," I answered, smiling.

"Does it ache?" he asked innocently.

"No. Such a miracle can never ache," I assured him, touched by his naiveté.

He looked at me, desperately wanting to feel the wonder that I felt. So I took his hand and laid it on my round, taut stomach. He waited, awed and stunned at the intimacy of the moment. With his palm conforming to the shape of my flesh, I could see him will the child to stir once more. And it awakened as if it knew its father's touch.

Husband's damp hands traveled, unchecked, from my enlarged breasts to the protruded navel. His touch was new in his discovery of what his planted seed had aroused. His exploring hands pressed gently on the soft curve of my belly. I could tell Husband wanted to take me, his eyes had that spark of desire, but the baby objected to all the crowding, and kicked harder in resistance. Husband and I shared a frustrated grin, then reluctantly put aside our urges for the sake of the demands of the child.

As my time drew nearer, my slender frame gave way to the babe that grew and grew and grew. My back hurt, my ankles became puffy, and my bladder bloated. I wobbled around with my arms crossed protectively in front of my engorged chest. One slight bump could have provoked a milky mess. I wanted nothing more than to purge myself of the pressure, but apparently the child was content, tumbling inside my womb.

The worst of my ordeals occurred at night, when I tried to settle into a bearable position on the thin blanket mattress Husband and I shared. An inch of padding provided minimal cushioning between me and the hard *ondul* floor. If I attempted to sleep on my stomach, it felt as though I were flattening the babe. If I slept on my back, it crushed me. All I could do was flip from side to side, each turn battling gravity.

Finally, when I was seriously considering fetching a butcher knife and slicing the burden out myself, I experienced my first labor pain. All the muscles in my stomach contracted into a tight fist, then released. It was time. Husband had begged me to go to Father's house weeks earlier to await the birth, but because of my stubbornness he allowed me to stay with him too long.

"I shall ride in front of you to clear the path," Husband assured me as he gently lifted me into the sedan chair.

"*Ay-ya!*" A moan escaped from my lips, then another. "*AY-YA!*" This time it was deeper and more desperate. I was annoyed at myself for not being able to conceal my pain from Husband. I wanted to spare him.

"*Iiiii!*" My hand gripped his like the jaws of a trap.

"Does it hurt badly?"

"I apologize for my weakness."

"On the contrary, you are much braver than I am. It is a noble thing you do, to bear me a child, *Yobo*, beloved." His distressed eyes stroked my face, comforting me the best way he could.

When we arrived at the house, Mother had the birthing room all prepared. First Wife and Second Wife knelt by my side, holding my hands and dabbing the sweat from my face. Crippled Sister and Baby Sister, who were still unwed, were forbidden to witness the ordeal, nor was Husband or Father allowed near at my hour.

I lay on the same wooden mat that was built with the house many decades ago. Here in the birthplace where I was born I would bring forth a new generation.

A strange rhythmic pattern formed, starting with the muscles tightening at the sides, changing the shape of my belly. A fountain of water gushed from between my legs, dousing my slip, warm and potent in smell, the smell of hot blood. I panted through my teeth so fiercely beads of perspiration funneled through my hair. At the height of the contractions, when my stomach arched, Mother placed a wooden stick in my mouth to bite down on, silencing my screams. Then as quickly as it came it ended, the muscles relaxed and settled down again. I wondered how a full-sized baby was going to squeeze through such a tight hole.

Mother's cool hand probed between my legs, massaging and measuring the opening, yet I found nothing shameful or appalling in the way she touched me, entered me. "Try to calm yourself, because you will need to summon all your strength when the next pain comes," Mother skillfully guided.

I shut my eyes and pursed my lips together tightly, anticipating the next contraction. The biggest one yet!

"Push, push!" First wife twisted my hand.

"I cannot," I whimpered.

"Push with all your might," Mother coached.

Unwillingly I pushed, but nothing came out. I was straining so hard the veins on the sides of my head pulsated feverishly.

"Again, push! Push!" Mother encouraged as she lifted her head up from between my legs.

"I cannot. It hurts too much," I gasped.

"I tell you, you must!" Her voice sounded more urgent.

Once again I bore down on the wooden stick and pushed.

"I see the head!" I heard Mother's relieved chuckle. "The child is almost here."

I felt the fullness of its round head pry open my hipbones. The pain was excruciating, as if a hot iron scorched my lower back. I bit down harder and gave one final push. The baby shot into Mother's awaiting arms. A thin fierce cry pierced through all the ache and exhaustion, and at once I focused on that single cry.

"It is a boy!" Mother proclaimed, her face wrinkled in smiles. "A grandson."

I had fulfilled my most important wifely duty. Joy rushed into me as he was placed between my breasts. As he lay there, I could feel our heartbeats continue together. I sensed he knew instantly that I was his mother. I snuggled his body a little closer to mine, wanting him to feel secure as much now as when he was unborn.

He was beautiful, even coated in thick ashy slime and blood. So calm and serene. He did not squirm as his grandmother cleaned out his mouth, nose, and ears with a cotton swab. Immediately I recognized he had his father's sleek olive body and my grave expression.

My heart lurched as Mother pulled out a knife and held it against the long cord that dangled from the center of his belly. I was so terrified for his precious life that a sudden surge of power rushed through me.

"Calm yourself. We must all cut our ties to our mothers at birth," First Wife said knowingly.

I watched with amazement as Mother tied a tight knot, then severed his lifeline. Now he was breathing on his own, but I knew he would never truly be separated from me. He was of my flesh and of my blood.

"Be still. This will sting," Mother warned.

She reached deep inside of me, her right hand fully immersed up to her wrist, and scooped out the bloody bag of afterbirth. Salt could have been poured on my wound and I would not have noticed. As my child drowsed, I examined closely each finger, each toe, comparing them to mine. I checked the size of his forehead for intelligence; the wideness of his eyes; the evenness of his ears; and the fullness of his lobes. To my exhilaration, he was perfect, and I drifted into sleep.

Evening passed calmly toward a new morning before I awoke. I glanced around, disoriented: everything appeared normal again except for the small cherished bundle beside me. The women must have scrubbed all the blood off the floor and removed any traces of afterbirth while I slept.

The infant looked so angelic, wrapped in a gold silk blanket. As I lightly ran my finger over his lips, he opened his mouth. I untied my slip straps and gently offered my nipple. Instinctively, he began suckling. Milk as white and pure as snow trickled forth for him.

First Wife was the first to discover me awake. She informed me that Husband had hurried back home to tell Grandmother the wonderful news. "But do not fear, he returned bright and early this morning. He is a good one, that husband of yours. His heart is devoted only to you—that is a rarity among even the finest men," she said soberly. Suddenly I felt guilty about all my good fortune. I could have been she if the winds of fate blew in another direction. "Treat him well and give him many sons."

I, too, used to wish for that same thing. Many nights, I had dreamt of giving Husband sons upon sons. I would imagine their bedding lined up from one wall to the other, but now I knew the reality of pushing a baby's head through a tiny passage.

"I will fetch Second Wife and she will make you presentable to receive your husband. She is more knowledgeable in the art of making a woman appealing." Her tone sank lower but there was not a hint of jealousy or malice.

Still damp from my agony, my hair had to be washed and combed. Moments later, Second Wife came in, fully equipped to do battle. After rinsing the sweat of childbirth from my body again, she persuaded me to let her dust my face with powder and add a touch of rouge.

"Of course you want to look pretty for the father of your

son," she teased me as she applied another layer of powder. I suspected she was unsatisfied with the final outcome. "Perhaps more blush?" she asked herself while unconsciously tapping the tip of her nose with her forefinger.

"I am sure it is fine. There is little that can be done with a face such as mine," I interjected.

"True, true. I did the best I could with the subject I had."

She handed me a small mirror, and I gazed at my reflection. All I saw was this flat white object with two red smudges where my cheeks were once supposed to be. "Are you presentable?" Mother sneaked her head in.

I was far from presentable, but I nodded a nervous yes so as not to keep Husband waiting any longer.

"Good." She smiled and escorted him in.

His hair was disheveled and he needed a shave, yet he still radiated beauty. My adoration for him swelled up. Though my mind was still a bit foggy, I could see his face twitched in his attempt to disguise his pride. In his arms, he carried a gift wrapped in splendid cloth.

"Are my son and my son's mother well?" He spoke in his deep public voice, but his eyes expressed the indescribable closeness we shared.

"Very well, thank you," I answered shortly, aware we were under survey.

"Grandmother had prepared these things for you and our son," he said as he handed the package to me.

I wished we could be alone, but I knew the women were eager to see what he had brought. Inside were several outfits for the child and rice cakes sprinkled with millet flour and aromatic mugwort leaves. Grandmother's generosity jolted me a bit, but this was no time to be miserly—the future patriarch of the Lee clan had been born.

Satisfied with Grandmother's token of goodwill, Mother, First Wife, and Second Wife withdrew to the other room, sliding the door closed behind them. Once we were alone, shyness overtook us both. He turned his body slightly sideways away from me as if he were mindlessly admiring the morning sun. The window frame highlighted his slightest movement. He edged cautiously toward us, aware of his own awkwardness.

"I hope you both slept comfortably." His voice sounded more normal.

"Yes, very comfortably," I answered modestly. What I really wanted to tell him was how smart and wondrous our son was. And how I hoped he would grow up to be as loving and kind as his father.

"Would you like to hold him?"

"My hands are clumsy." He stepped back at my suggestion.

"Your hands are too tender to be clumsy."

"I am indebted to you forever. Never have I been so blessed and fulfilled. Now I will have a servant bring you something to eat. You must regain your strength, mother of my son."

He went out and came back quickly, balancing a tray of *miyok kuk* (seaweed soup). He was serving me. I was speechless as he placed it carefully on my lap. *Miyok kuk* was fed to every new mother. It restored the needed nutrients and helped the mother to nurse. When I thought he could show me no more affection, he lifted the spoon, blew on it, then fed it to me. In that moment, I knew I loved him absolutely. It was a love separate from passion, a love that surpassed the flesh and would flourish long into old age.

Three days after childbirth, I rose from my bed. Every muscle still ached, but that did not stop me from picking up my son and taking him on his first tour around Grandfather's house. Prominently across the arch of the gateway, a string of dried red peppers entwined with pine branches was hung to proclaim the birth of a male child. For the first time in my life I was pleased to be a woman, a mother.

I continued to stay at my parents' house for the next one hundred days, consuming vast quantities of *miyok kuk*. During the first week, the baby and I were restricted from receiving any visitors, for it was believed at that time the newborn child was especially susceptible to bad luck and evil spirits. But I knew this son of mine was strong. He drank plentifully of my milk, and thrived. And that was how he earned his name, Yongwoon. Like the "yong" in my name, the character symbolized the powerful dragon, and "woon" stood for the clouds in the sky—clouds so high that no man or demon could harm him, so pure that no evil could soil him. I loved the name right off for its greatness, its ring, and also because it would be his first and perhaps only connection to our Korean heritage. Our Japanese colonial rulers began to force us to adopt Japanese names; thus only in the secrecy of our home would I dare utter his given name. In public, I was compelled to call him Tanaka, Takeo.

Those isolated months, my son and I were never apart. We ate together, played together, bathed together, and slept together. And as he grew and responded to my outpouring of love, I noticed in myself new qualities I lacked before: patience, gentleness, and an ease of laughter.

Then Yongwoon safely passed his one hundredth day of life, and it was time to share him with others. Family and neighbors helped us to celebrate his *paikil*, one-hundredth-day party, and then his one-year birthday, *tol*. On this very special one-year occasion, Yongwoon turned two. That was our custom: children were born already a year old.

My parents let their pride go unchecked, especially Father. I had forgotten how much he adored the laughter of children. If only I could have preserved the image of Father bouncing his grandson on his lap. The two of them looked like life-sized dolls in their fancy traditional costumes. They should have been perched on top of the festively prepared banquet table rather than behind it. The sleeves of Yongwoon's jacket were a riot of brilliant colors arranged in narrow vertical stripes. He even had on miniature black shoes and a hat. And twenty-four-karat gold rings decorated his chubby fingers, gifts from wealthy relatives.

Everyone cooed and fondled my little treasure as he was passed around. He remained still as people poked at his round belly and pinched his puffy ruby cheeks.

"What a fine boy!" someone exclaimed.

"An intelligent boy!" another said, chuckling.

I, too, chuckled inside as various foods and objects were placed in front of him. If he picked up a brush or a book he was destined to be a scholar. Money or rice meant he would be wealthy. The sword symbolized a great military commander. And if he chose the thread, he would live a long life. Yongwoon grabbed the book.

"I told you he was a scholar," the same man bellowed out.

My heart burst with a mother's pride. I loved this child unconditionally. I would give up my life for him.

LOVE'S LUCKY MATCH

At the age of nine, Crippled Sister battled death again. Her temperature rose to a dangerous high and small red dots erupted all over her skin. For days she lay soaking in a pool of sweat, scratching mercilessly. When the fever finally broke, her face was covered with a bloody crust of scabs. And the scabs eventually left deep craters that permanently disfigured her face.

"What more could happen to this miserable child?" Mother moaned. Nonetheless, Crippled Sister never grew resentful of her fate or envious of the things she could not do or the things her sisters could. When she was younger she complained and wept, but no more.

As her twenty-first birthday approached, Father and Mother pondered over her uncertain future.

"She must marry and have a son who will look after her in her old age. I cannot allow her to grow old like a ghost in her brother's home when we are no longer around to care for her," Father concluded.

"What man or family would accept a daughter-in-law who is

incapable of even going to the outhouse on her own, much less with such a marked face?" Mother clucked her tongue three times in despair.

"You forget, your husband is a man of great wealth," he bragged.

Father offered a handsome reward to any matchmaker who could locate a kind family with a son of marrying age. This was Father's only specification. It did not matter whether the groom was the first son, or the second, or the third. Father hoped this would make it easier for the matchmakers. Still, no family stepped forward. None was willing to sacrifice their son to an invalid bride, so Father further lowered his requirements. The matchmakers were told the groom should be poor with deceased parents. Father felt a man on his own would be more open-minded and thus more apt to strike a deal than a man with a meddling mother. And as an incentive he was willing to offer a handsome dowry.

Father did find such a man. He occasionally worked as a servant in our yard. His age was twenty and his surname was Park. Surprisingly, his ancestors once belonged to the *yangban* class, but now he was part of the so-called ruined *yangban—chanban*, a caste that could no longer maintain the dignity and authority that marked traditional *yangban* status.

The union first occurred to Father when he saw the man in the courtyard, stacking dried leaves for our fuel supply. Park worked steadily without taking a break. Father studied him for some time through the doorframe in his quarters before approaching the servant.

"Your surname is Park, is it not?"

"Yes . . . yes . . . yes," the man stuttered, half startled.

"I have been watching you stack the fuel and—"

"If I have displeased you, I will work harder." His words came out abruptly, cutting Father off.

"Good man, I am not here to complain. I have come to offer you something that is very dear to me because I respect a man who does his work well."

"Thank you, sir, but serving you is payment enough. Without your generosity, my great-aunt, who is my only family, and I would have gone hungry tonight." He bowed his head deeply.

Hearing that all the man had was one great-aunt, Father

knew he had found the right groom. "I will give you land, a house on that land, and food to fill the house. You will never have to work as a servant in another man's home ever again if you agree to marry my second daughter," Father said without delay, then added, "But first, I am obliged to inform you about the daughter I am speaking of, because I am an honest man. She is far from ravishing, but that you do not need. Only men of wealth can afford such a luxury. Also, at the age of four, she was struck down with a fever that took the life from her legs. Now that you know all, what is your answer?"

The man thought about the shell of a house he shared with his great-aunt. He remembered the empty room made of wood and how the wind blew dirt through the cracks in the floor. Without another moment of hesitation he promptly responded, "I am indebted to you, sir. I promise you I will be a decent husband to your daughter."

"Then it is settled," Father declared. "Take her. She is a good daughter and she will be an obedient wife."

The proposal of marriage was arranged with unusual speed. Father dealt directly with the man himself, skipping all the complicated procedures and painstaking formalities.

On the wedding day the groom showed up in his gray cotton clothes, sewn clumsily together to cover his bareness. His face was brown and common-looking. The ceremony was a simple nontraditional gathering. Only the closest uncles, aunts, and cousins were asked to witness the union. No one was more surprised than the groom at the sight of the bride. No doubt from Father's description the groom had expected to see a lame fool with the face of a hog; instead, Crippled Sister never looked more radiant in her sumptuous brocaded red silk skirt and summer yellow blouse. Even the ghastly scars across the bridge of her nose were barely noticeable that day under all the powder. For once, she was a whole woman. Everyone had forgotten about her lifeless legs hidden under the skirt.

Father cleared his throat loudly, for he wanted to make an announcement. Immediately the jovial chatter of women died down to a low buzz.

"This is a simple wedding, as my wife and I have intended; therefore, we do not expect our son-in-law and his bride to bow to us."

Just then the sunburnt groom sprang to his feet. "I humbly ask for my father-in-law's permission to allow me to show you my deepest gratitude." He spoke steadily, his head lowered.

Father nodded in approval as the groom stood tall before my parents. The great-aunt, on the other hand, bubbled with anger. Pulling him aside, she objected, "I will not have a relative of mine bow to a family of a cripple." Obviously poverty had not lessened her pride.

"I must," he replied apologetically, and took his place again. He drew the back of his palms to his forehead, bent his knees, and bowed down deeply, letting his head touch the floor for a long moment. Everyone looked on with mutual approval except for his great-aunt, who averted her head in protest.

After three days, the couple went to live in their new home. Mother sent over a servant to cook their meals and another to tend house since Crippled Sister was incapable of fulfilling any of her wifely duties. Father advised his new son-in-law to start his own business. So with Father's financial backing, Park set up a glassware store. There he sold dishes, cups, ornaments, and unusual sculptures. The business prospered, due to his commitment and diligence. He worked from early dawn to late dusk; nevertheless, he always found the time to favor his wife with gifts and adventures.

Often he surprised her with sweet candies and fabric so she could make herself a new dress. He never splurged on himself; the glow on his wife's face was his treat. But his most special gift was a bicycle, although a couple of spokes were bent and missing, the paint flaked with rust, and the seat bandaged. He added a bell to the handlebars and strapped on an extra seat made from the sturdiest plank he could find. On the plank, he tied a padded cushion for her comfort.

"Now I can take you anywhere," he said with exhilaration.

"What is it?"

"A riding machine. Today I will show you the world," he said as he lifted her onto the cushioned seat.

"What if I fall?" she asked, terrified, looking down at the graveled ground far beneath her.

"Hold on to me and you will be safe," he assured her.

She obeyed willingly, clinging tightly to his back. She felt his breathing grow labored as his legs pedaled harder and farther.

He pointed out sights she missed seeing as a cripple. She saw hills, rice beds, tree groves, and wildflowers.

From that day forward, they ventured often onto new roads. In the beginning she fell quite a bit, frightening him every time she scraped or cut her flesh, but soon she learned to sway with the bicycle's turns, and eventually she could carry a picnic sack in her arms, which they spread out in green secluded valleys they discovered together. For hours they snuggled under the ever-changing clouds and dreamt about the children they hoped to conceive. Whether that was possible, no one knew until it actually happened. Miraculously, Crippled Sister carried a babe in her flattened belly. There were many disbelievers, but as the weeks progressed into months, her stomach swelled to twice its normal size. When she became completely immobile, her indulgent husband carried her from one room to another on his back.

A month before the birth, he rode her to Father's home on his bicycle, for the babe was anxious to stretch its arms and legs early. The space in her womb was too cramped.

"Her time is here," Mother announced, and sent the men away.

As soon as Crippled Sister cried out her first wail, the child slipped out in one effortless push.

"Thank Buddha," Mother said as she clasped her wet fingers together.

"It is a girl!" The cheers rang through the house. Everyone was so overwhelmed that Crippled Sister bore a child, no one seemed to notice that the infant was a girl.

Crippled Sister's husband, who hardly spoke except for the brief necessities, overflowed with laughter and chatter. "A baby! A baby! A baby!" he muttered over and over again, allowing the news to soak into his bones.

Immediately he pedaled back to their home, and the proud father hung over the gateway a twisted rope of charcoal and pine to announce his daughter's arrival.

A ROUND-FACED STRANGER

Baby Sister, who was spoiled the most simply because she was the youngest, suffered misfortune after being given away in marriage. The stranger just appeared one day at Father's store. He had a round face, a flat, broad nose, a gash for a mouth, and slitted eyes. Seeing Baby Sister near the opened gate, the stranger approached her boldly. "I have come to take care of some business with the man of the house," he stated, squinting his eyes at the young girl before him. "Is he home?"

"My father and Older Brother have gone to the river, and my mother is napping in her quarters."

"Then I will wait for their return," he declared, and sat himself down in the store.

When Father and Older Brother arrived, they were startled to find the round-faced man sprawled on his back, hands behind his head, snoring loudly among the fruit barrels.

"What is the meaning of this!" Father's voice quaked.

This odd fellow slowly rose to his feet. "I am here to deliver a proposal," he replied, handing Father his own letter of marriage. "I am a friend of a neighbor of your eldest daughter. I hear you have a third one, who has yet to be promised. That is the one I wish to have as my wife if her honorable father will permit it."

That was how I found out about the round-faced stranger. Father had dispatched a messenger to my husband's home asking for my approval of the man's good character and family name. I searched my memory for such a person, but I failed to recall who he was. Nevertheless, I sent a message back.

"Father, if you have not yet found a proper suitor for Hongsam, perhaps you should consider this gentlemen for her marriage. I feel she is well ready."

Still, Father was uncertain of this man who so arrogantly proposed his own marriage. Father decided to send another messenger to the stranger's house with a letter of introduction. A few weeks later a second letter of marriage arrived, bearing the stranger's red family stamp and wedding gifts.

"What can I do?" Father reluctantly confessed. "The deal is almost done."

Baby Sister, remembering their first meeting, shuddered at the thought of belonging to someone whose nature she mistrusted. The image of his dull black eyes and broad face haunted her.

"How can I serve a man whose face is round as a plate?" Baby Sister objected.

"Then he will never have wrinkles, because the flesh on his face is so stretched." Mother tried to sound optimistic, adding, "Your father says he is taller than the average man," as if that qualified him as good husband stock.

"I will not." Baby Sister shamelessly protested, but all her efforts were futile. The gifts were already sent and Father's honor was at stake. Up to the very day of her wedding, she cried herself into a fit. The pitiful sight reminded me of my wedding day. So many terrifying thoughts tore through my head, though my face did not display her bride's mask of pink and swollen eyes. I wished I had the chance to share with her stories of my happy union so she would have something to hope for.

When it was time for her to depart to her new home, a large procession of men and horses escorted her sedan chair. Father had hired extra menservants to carry all her dowry gifts, things he knew would lift her spirits and bring her comfort and joy.

The instant she entered her husband's home, Baby Sister quickly understood he had made false claims about his wealth. Long ago he had begun to drink away his moderate inheritance. The potent wine helped him to escape that crusty mother of his, whose hot temper was easily stirred. Now Baby Sister knew why her husband's eyes were so glassy and dull; years of abuse and rejection had tarnished their human quality. All notions of love and peace in her new household were smothered.

As the months dragged on, she rarely saw her husband, for he disappeared for long periods of time. Baby Sister rejoiced in his desertion; she preferred him with other women rather than on top of her. Intimacy with him repelled her. Somehow he sensed this and called her to his bedding whenever he reappeared to replenish his money pouch. It brought him tremendous satisfaction knowing she loathed him. The only thought that comforted her through those dark moments was the prospect of his early death. And after he was finished with her body, she would obsessively sterilize herself. Then off he went again with more of her dowry money.

Even with him out of the house, life was no less miserable. Baby Sister soon learned the depth of her mother-in-law's evil nature. For her, Baby Sister was only worth the dwindling value of her dowry. The greedy woman relentlessly accused her daughter-in-law of hoarding jewelry, but in fact she had already stolen everything Baby Sister brought with her, even her wedding hairpin. The accusations and naggings viciously escalated once the dowry was all wasted.

"You are useless to me. You are no better than a pig who eats my food and rolls around in her own shit. At least I can slice a pig's throat and cook it for dinner when it gets too fat." She jabbed her sharp index finger into Baby Sister's cheek. "All you are good for is your father's wealth. Go fetch me an expensive jeweled box. Do as I desire or die for all I care."

Emotionally drained, Baby Sister was finally permitted to return home to carry out the woman's bidding. Seeing her grief, Father went out immediately and purchased an exquisite box made from precious stones, but still her mother-in-law was enraged.

"You insult me! Do you think I am a fool? I want a box made of solid gold, not painted wood from a moth-eaten tree. Get out!"

So once again Baby Sister, filled with shame, made the trip back. She fell to her knees and begged Father for the golden box. This time Mother freely sacrificed her own jewelry box encrusted with cut amethyst, citrine, and jade. When the old woman held the sparkling gift in her paws she grumbled with dissatisfaction, then slithered away and hid it. For a while afterward, she bothered less with Baby Sister and turned her cruelty onto her widowed daughter and grandson, who had come to live with them. Whatever the daughter did displeased her mother, triggering a violent rage. The daughter crouched, shielding her head with her arms, as her mother senselessly whipped her.

One morning, Baby Sister woke to find her sister-in-law missing. She had taken only her three dresses and a broken hair comb, leaving behind her son, who still slept on his bedding. Outraged, the old woman poured her wrath on the innocent boy, beating him so ruthlessly he retreated to the farthest corner of the room, where he cowered. When Baby Sister tried to feed the sorrowful boy, her mother-in-law's rod slashed hard across her back.

"That little nuisance will eat only what the rodents leave behind," she hissed. "Why should I care for the retard when his own mother has discarded him?"

Baby Sister reeled away. Instead she boiled a large pot of barley tea and served it to the woman. As quickly as she emptied her cup, Baby Sister filled it. She watched and waited as the woman gorged herself with tea. An hour later, the old woman lifted herself off the cushion and wobbled to the outhouse. It was exactly what Baby Sister had planned. She seized the opportunity to offer the boy a handful of rice she had stored in the fold of her skirt. When she held it up to his blistered lips, he looked at her blankly. He had heard what his grandmother had said, and would not accept her kindness. She tried on several more occasions to persuade him, but he refused to eat.

Then word came from his mother; she wanted her son sent

to her. In the envelope she had wrapped money for his safe passage. The old woman spat on the paper before tossing it into the pigpen. She glowed with pleasure as she watched the pigs devour it. Witnessing his mother's letter destroyed, the boy deteriorated rapidly. His vision began to fade. Soon he was trapped in his own dark, lonely hell, and responded to nothing. It was only a matter of time before his broken heart stopped beating. And on that day, the old woman smirked.

Hearing about her son's death, the daughter returned to the house. She stayed outside, kneeling on the dirt road, scratching the ground with her fingers. Curse after curse she hurled into the house. Tears rolled down her dirtied face like oil, and her sobs sounded like the howls of a wounded animal.

"Die! Die! You wicked old bitch!" she screamed.

The old woman sat idly on her satin cushion, twisting a long strand of hair that grew from an unsightly mole below her left nostril. Baby Sister swore to herself she would never bring forth a child from such evil blood, but then tragedy befell her. On her husband's fifth stay at home, he walked in, sliding his feet, his face red with wine and some hidden pain. While crawling from bed to bed, he caught an infectious sore on his private part—his badge of infidelity. He returned to the only woman who was obligated to care for him.

He lingered at the house long enough to heal and plant his foul seed. Baby Sister tried to barricade him from their chamber, but she could not keep him out. He tore the door off its warped wooden frame in his crazed rush to be satisfied. She fought to fend off his body, crossing her arms and legs tightly, but still he ripped into her.

When she realized she was carrying his offspring, Baby Sister attempted to purge herself of it. She threw herself on the ground, punched her stomach, ate moldy food, and even tried to push it out before its time. Nothing worked; it grew stronger and bigger.

A few weeks before the child was to arrive, the old woman consented to allow Baby Sister to return to Father's home. It had been over two years since she last visited them. Not until the moment she stepped through those familiar gates did she truly comprehend her sorrow and bad fortune. She kept the tears bottled inside, wanting to spare Mother her grief, but Mother was already weeping inside for her youngest daughter.

Baby Sister's delivery was a difficult one: the child rolled around for hours in its mother's womb, unwilling to meet its doomed fate. Finally, around midnight, a chubby little girl came shrieking out. She was not a pretty baby. She had her father's round face and tightly slitted eyes.

"This one we must teach a skill." Mother tried to sound cheerful, meaning no husband would want to claim such a face.

At this Baby Sister thought: I will love her with all my being, for if her mother does not, who will?

The baby's father visited the child and her mother, bringing a package of rice cakes and clothes, then he made up a glib story about some business deal with a merchant to excuse himself.

"What business is that?" Baby Sister inquired.

"*Iiii,* such things do not concern women," he replied abruptly.

"No doubt the business of another woman," she murmured under her breath.

That was the first and last time he came to visit his wife and daughter during their entire one-hundred-day stay at Father's home.

DIVINE

DUTY

My stomach barely had a chance to flatten out to its normal size before I conceived again. The euphoric thought of another son dulled the memories of labor. I looked forward to having two or three more; then I could be selfish and wish for a daughter because every woman needed a daughter to help her around the house.

As with the first child, I worked diligently up to the final month of pregnancy. The autumn leaves were beginning to fall from the trees and there was much work that needed to be done for the coming winter before I would allow Husband to banish me to Father's house. The winter clothes needed to be sewn, the fuel stored, the roof mended, and the *kimchee* made. *Kimchee* season was my favorite time of the year. It afforded women throughout Korea the opportunity to show off their cooking expertise.

Preparing *kimchee* required great care because the spicy pickled vegetable was the most important item in every meal, next to rice. Father used to say, if at first smell the potent aroma of *kimchee* did not water one's mouth, it was not worth eating. We had to blend large quantities of crushed garlic, red pepper, salt, and other rich spices to create the distinctive fragrance. And enough had to be pickled to last through the long winter.

A six-foot-high mound of cabbages and turnips lay in the middle of the courtyard, waiting to be cut up, washed, and salted. As I strained to clean out the tall oblong earthenware crocks that would store the *kimchee* in the frigid ground, the child inside me weighed so much, I lost my balance and fell hard on my stomach. A wave of pain traveled through to the very depths of my belly. Every muscle contracted.

In a panic, Husband rushed out and brought back the only neighborhood doctor, a man with tar-blackened teeth, who examined me.

"There is nothing to fear, the child still lives," he diagnosed, blowing his bad breath into my face.

In my heart, I knew the baby was dead. There was nothing I could do but wait for seven more agonizing days. Husband insisted on taking me to Father's house for the delivery, but I hired a midwife to assist me at home. I wanted to spare Mother the sight of my stillborn babe.

Just as excruciating as my first, the actual birth gave me a cruel burst of hope. A day and a half later, the head of my first daughter popped out. The sharp stench of death rotted the air. The midwife's face showed no fear or shock as she wrapped my child in a burlap sack. Something tore at me: I needed to hold her, to see her just once.

"Please," I said weakly. "I wish to see her."

"Why torment yourself? There is nothing you can do for this one. Be happy it was only a girl."

"Please, give her to me."

She clucked her tongue disapprovingly as she placed the lifeless bundle in my arms. I unfolded the burlap. A big baby, she already had a full cap of black hair. I wanted to cuddle her between my breasts to warm her cold skin. Sad, sad little girl.

"Take her," I said finally.

And the midwife did. That night, in the same room hidden in darkness, I wept as though I had lost a son.

After three years of delay, in 1939, I finally conceived again.

Husband swelled up with excitement. Having only one older sister to play with as a small boy, he had always dreamed of filling his own home with plenty of children. At his insistence, I let him escort Yongwoon and me to Father's house two months before the baby was due. Although Husband was a bit overprotective since our last misfortune, my elderly parents welcomed our early arrival. They acted like children whenever their grandson was around.

When the time arrived, the entire household sprang into action. Having three married daughters, Mother and Father had accumulated plenty of practice over the years and groomed the servants and residents to work as a well-oiled birthing machine. The men retired to the men's quarters to await the news and the women went to theirs, for the birth of a child was our domain.

For months, I had dreamt vividly about tigers and not flowers; I was certain this meant my unborn child was a son. When the delivery time came, however, a headstrong girl emerged from between my legs. Not even my prior two deliveries prepared me for the battle I fought with this willful one. She was determined to show herself from the first contraction; I could not catch my breath for the next push. When I fell back limp, exhausted, she somehow forced herself out. And all on her own she seized the air of life with no enticement or coaxing. I knew then that this daughter of mine, Tanaka, Katsuko, whom we secretly named Lee, Dukwah, was a true survivor. The name Grand Flower suited her perfectly. She would grow and blossom even under the malevolent rule of our Japanese oppressors.

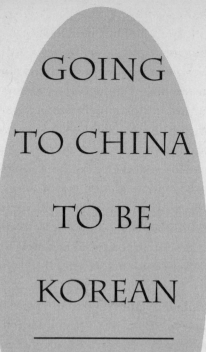

GOING
TO CHINA
TO BE
KOREAN

With my two children plump and happy, I felt content to rise at dawn, to cook meals, to clean house, and to hear Husband's praises. My family was enough, but for Husband there was only restlessness.

Husband was a proud man—proud of our pure blood, proud of our culture and traditions. By 1939, however, all aspects of our Korean society were being repressed toward complete Japanization. Japanese had superseded Korean as the official language of the country in shops and all government buildings. The next year, schoolchildren were forbidden to speak Korean even as a secondary language. They were taught to read and write only the official language of our Japanese imperial rulers.

Husband went often into the city, where the noose of our colonial pirates strangled everything. Police stations and booths held neighborhoods hostage. He witnessed the Japanese military police marching around in full regalia ready to chop up any resistance with their long swords. The clicks of the sharp metal spikes at the bottom of their boots warned us of their approach.

Then the unmentionable happened. Young unmarried women were recruited into the military under the euphemistic name of volunteers, *chungshindae*. In Japanese, they were called *daishindai*, meaning, literally, "team of offering bodies." Ordered to fill these positions, city governments notified families with eligible daughters. Husband deduced the true reason why women were being sent to the front lines. One hot, humid afternoon, he stormed into the courtyard as the children and I were resting in the cool shade. He stared at our baby daughter and his face reddened.

"Is something the matter, *Yobo*?" I asked.

"I will never allow them to take her from us." He gritted his teeth.

"Who wants to take her?" I cried out.

"If our children are ever to be safe and if we are to be free, we must escape this place."

"This place is our home."

"We have no home as long as those bastard dogs pollute our soil, pillage our mines, steal our crops, and rape our women."

"Where will we go?" My question was fraught with panic.

"China."

"China!" I gasped. "But our families are here. We will be alone. How can we survive on our own?"

"Many of our people have already settled there."

"Even there the Japanese roam. Already they have expanded their forces from Manchuria into China."

"But in China the land is too vast. We will be able to live peacefully, speak our own language openly, perhaps own our own business. Here we are little better than slaves."

"What about Grandmother? She is too old to make the journey." I grasped at any reason to change his mind.

"I will arrange for my older sister and her family to come and care for Grandmother. They will agree if I ask."

"What if—" I struggled for another excuse, but Husband interrupted me in his very serious voice.

"Please, *Yobo*, I wish to taste freedom again. I love our country as much as you do. That is why we must go and take our children. In China, they can grow up knowing their true Korean names, not the barbarian's names we were forced to give them."

What could I say after that? If it meant leaving our land to be Korean, we would go.

Husband went first to find us a place to live. Within a few months, we received a telegram, which instructed us to take a train to the city of Soju (Suchow), which was located between Shanghai and Peking. He had bought the house for very little. The previous owner had abandoned it to flee from all the fighting. And this was where Husband wanted to raise our precious children?

It felt so indecent uprooting my family and immigrating to an unknown country. The farthest I had ever traveled was from my father's home to Husband's. Now, instead of one province, hill after hill, mountain after mountain, river after river, would separate me from where I was born. I had always assumed I would grow old and then eventually die here with all my family around me. Suddenly I felt absolutely alone, but as quickly as the emotions formed in my head I pushed them aside, for there was still plenty to do. Arrangements had to be made for Sister-in-Law's family to move in and care for Grandmother.

I rushed around the house for days polishing furniture and washing and airing bedding for their comfort. I wanted to leave a good impression, because I was proud of how well I kept our home.

Her family arrived promptly, all four of them and their family cow. Grandmother seemed delighted to see her daughter return and assume my position. Her pleasure did not bother me; I was actually relishing the idea of living in my own house. The transferring of the household happened so smoothly I moved up our departure date, though Husband was expecting us much later. I did not want to delay. With deep bows, Yongwoon, Dukwah, and I said our farewells.

Once at the train station, I was frightened by what I saw. I had heard tales of this fire-breathing machine, but when I saw the monstrous iron thing huffing in the distance, I experienced serious doubts. Black smoke puffed from its snout as it twisted and slithered like a snake. Some people screamed and dashed away; others buried their faces in their hands. I held tightly to my children, waiting to see what would happen. As it thundered closer I saw long boxes locked together. There were neither oxen nor men at the head. The first one pulled the others.

Gradually it rolled to a loud, smokey stop. The braver souls boarded first; we followed their lead. Inside were narrow compartments. Rows of wooden benches with straight backs lined the side walls, and a thin aisle ran between them. At once I settled the children into seats with our bulky baggage occupying most of the space.

A sharp whistle startled the metal snake to life. The wheels began to grind. The train rocked and roared as it quickly tore into the horizon, passing swiftly through the breathtaking Korean highlands.

It was unnerving being so near other men, their hands, shoulders, and feet brushing against mine accidentally. If someone told me a week earlier I would be riding in a horse-less drawn box and touching strange men's feet, I would have blushed in disbelief. But surprisingly, it had little importance now. Being out among the vibrant and moving, I realized there were things of greater importance.

We crossed the Yalu River at Sinuiju where it connected with the Manchurian system. Many Koreans immigrated to areas just north of the Yalu to be near our own border; however, Husband thought it was safer to move farther down into China. Since the defeat of Russia in 1905 the Japanese had also penetrated into Manchuria.

After we disembarked at Soju, Yongwoon ran to the platform's edge to stare at all that passed. Along the cobbled streets, men pushed wheelbarrows laden with stacked bricks, coal, and steaming *tubu*, bean curd. On the sidewalks were people of every kind and combination, all in a hurry, jostling one another. Young girls walked arm in arm. Rich merchants, wearing light gray silk robes under black satin sleeveless coats with their hair braided back from shaven foreheads, loitered inside and outside of gambling houses. Modern women, in their well-fitted clothes and small black shoes, meandered through the shops. And in between it all, bicycles darted and weaved skillfully through the heavy traffic and chaos. It was all so bizarre: I felt like an odd extra finger on an already crowded hand.

These people were much taller than my countrymen, giants compared with the small Japanese men I had seen. I could not stop staring, and they, in turn, scrutinized me and the children in our white Korean garb. Some ventured close, but none spoke to us. I searched the streets for some form of transportation. Here and there, sweating drivers pulled rickshas. I waved my hand in the air, hoping one would stop, but they threw a haughty look and raced by. Our high pile of luggage might have been the reason. I had no Chinese money to tempt them with, only the Japanese yen stashed in a secret pouch sewn into my pantaloons. It would have been obscene to lift up my skirt and reach into my undergarment in the middle of the street. Eventually my patience evaporated and I tossed our bags into the back of one of the rickshas, claiming it. The tan-colored driver broke out in a fit of rage. Dusted with dirt and sweat, his leathery face scrunched into one large crease. Sharp musical blabber hissed out of his twisting mouth; none of it made any sense to my ears, so I stood firmly, refusing to budge. He became more animated, shaking his head furiously from side to side. This was understandable in any language. Once my stubbornness overcame his protests, he finally calmed down enough for me to show him Husband's letter with the address scribbled in bold Chinese characters.

We heaved forward along the congested streets. Here was a great city, with houses as tall as temples and shops opening right onto the streets, like Father's store. They displayed enticing merchandise in glistening glass windows. And above many doors, long silken banners of brilliant colors rippled in the breeze. Then, suddenly, I saw my first white outsider, a man with a light golden beard. How very peculiar and misplaced he appeared, standing there erect. All at once it dawned on me that I was not as foreign among these people. My dress may have been fuller and my rubber slippers curled at the toes, but my hair was black and my skin was olive.

To my astonishment, the driver halted abruptly in front of a large brick house. I should have known. Husband had high standards and taste when it came to comfort. He emerged from the front door, and paid the driver generously, the whole time holding me with his eyes. I longed for his touch, but we were trapped in a time of marital modesty; I had to restrain myself from this man I adored so much. Husband chose his words carefully, aware of the fact that we had a considerable audience.

"Mother of my children, you have done well, very well." He encircled our son in his arms, then leaned over to make funny faces at Dukwah, strapped to my back. His warm breath sent shivers surging down my neck.

"Do you approve of the house?" He asked excitedly.

"It is a fine house," I answered, and his face beamed with joy.

"Come, you must see the inside. It is more impressive."

I had never been in a two-story building. The ground floor was spacious, with several doors in the back leading to private rooms.

"There is another house at the top of these steps," he bragged. "It is thrilling sleeping in the air."

"I think I would rather sleep down here."

"But you have not seen the upstairs yet." He motioned me to follow him. "You will change your mind, I promise."

Because it meant so much to him, I scaled the creaking narrow steps. The first was the easiest and the last was the hardest, because I knew I had to walk back down them sooner or later. The second floor was as enormous as the house on the ground. And the farther back I went in, the larger and larger the space became. If I hadn't passed an opened window and look below, I might not have minded so much that my feet hovered over the earth.

Husband was indeed correct. A breeze of freedom blew here in China, unlike in our own country. Everyday life was not severely affected by the empire of Japan, perhaps because so many people buzzed about.

Following the example of earlier Korean settlers, Husband wanted to start a business. These same settlers had built a prosperous close-knit community, merely desiring to live peacefully and separately, according to Korean traditions. But as I looked around, I could already see that many had assimilated. Most of the small children spoke Mandarin as if it were their mother tongue. I knew then that Husband needed to make his fortune quickly so we might return to our own country as soon as it was possible. Also, I had other reasons for wanting to go back: I missed my parents and sisters terribly.

For weeks I kept silent as Husband futilely racked his brains for mercantile inspiration. His lack of urgency bothered me, though I knew he was not to blame. All his days, servants and women tended to his whims. Therefore, I was determined to help motivate him.

"Husband, this house is equal to two," I commented at last. "It is lonesome to spread ourselves so thinly between the house upstairs and the house downstairs. Oftentimes I cannot find Yongwoon for hours because there are too many rooms for him to hide in. Perhaps we could start a sesame-oil business in the bottom house, thus minimize my loneliness," I suggested, only after working out the details in my head. "It seems to me the sesame business is the best moneymaker, because regardless of its high price in the marketplace people seek it out. Even during times of inflation and war, people still need to cook their food."

Astonished, Husband stared at me. "I always knew there was more in that head of yours than you led me to believe. Why have you waited this long to share your mind with your husband?"

"Before, I felt it was a woman's place to restrain her thoughts concerning a man's affairs. Here, when I browse through the marketplace, I see women like myself working beside their husbands. Their sweat inspires me to support you with the same bold loyalty."

"You do, do you?" he teased.

"If you feel I am incapable, I will not be offended. A wife's duty is to maintain just the household affairs. I beg your pardon for speaking beyond my position." I replied, sincerely wounded.

"You, incapable? . . . That is the last thing I think of you." He paused for a second before finishing his thought. "All these years you have been my wife you have not once failed me. I fear I may lose face if I fail you, but I am willing to go in the sesame business if you desire it." He lowered his eyes.

When Father first announced my marriage to a man three years my junior, I viewed my future as a hardship. I thought a mother/child marriage would be more demanding and affectionless than a man/woman relationship. Now I was grateful for the age advantage, for his youth had allowed him to turn to my opinions. Rigid traditions had not hardened in his bones. He respected me though I was only his wife, only a woman.

"You will not fail, because I will never allow it," I assured him, and suddenly his spirits perked up.

The last time I had expressed myself so freely was when I was six. It felt remarkable to let various ideas percolate inside my head. Many thoughts came to me once I permitted them, undermining years of Mother's strict teachings.

Eager to purchase bags of sesame seeds, Husband and I ventured into the marketplace, a colorful area teeming with life. Any obscure craving could be appeased. Patched stalls sold fruits, vegetables, eggs, hissing snakes, clucking chickens, barking dogs, and other squealing animals. The animals banged around in their crowded cages. All around, people walked with empty tin bowls and poised chopsticks, inspecting the multitude of exotic selections. One vendor's cart sizzled with fried chicken claws on bamboo sticks, another steamed with *bao*, rolls, another bubbled with noodles. Hungry customers squatted around with their bowls pressed to their lips, using their chopsticks like shovels to push the food into opened mouths. Here, there was no ethnic division. Where food and trade were concerned, people mingled easily. Money was money and we had just enough to buy sacks of sesame seeds to fill a horse-drawn cart.

As predicted, the oil sold, and we quickly expanded our business. Soon the entire ground floor was stocked with barrels of sesame oil. I hoarded the husks of the seeds, to be sold as fertilizer. Jabbering now in the singsong way of the Chinese, Husband began to travel to larger nearby cities, such as Peking and Chunggin, to sell the oil there. Each time he went out, we packed his cart full, but still it was never enough. People acted as though we were offering gold.

Soon, sacks were bursting with coins and paper money beneath each loose plank in our floors. Just to walk over them delighted me. I was so happy I got pregnant again. The news was accepted with mixed emotions. I knew it was my prime duty, but my mind and heart were not focused on the birth as they were with the other two. I did not sew clothes or fantasize about the coming child. Instead, I obsessed about returning to work and ridding my body of the extra pounds. I was becoming a different woman. Before, I had been fulfilled by childbirth, eating, sleeping, love. Not any longer. I thirsted more.

When the first contraction came, I braced myself on the birthing bed, determined to get the ordeal over and done with. Again I had to manage without Mother's assistance. A certain sense of intimacy was lost when a midwife arrived to deliver my mother's grandchild. I felt bad, not for me, but for Mother. She deserved to be here.

The labor lasted only a few short hours and once more I was triumphant with a second son, whom Husband named Kunil, healthy one, disregarding the Confucian naming system. This son came out yawning, ready to doze again, so I let him sleep on my breast. Some time passed, and then a loud noise woke him up. I was just about to reprimand the person who was caus-ing the disturbance when a familiar aroma of *miyok kuk*, sea-weed soup, seeped into the room. I thought I was imagining things, then Husband tiptoed through the doors, carrying a food tray.

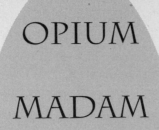

OPIUM

MADAM

After our second son's one hundredth day, I left the confines of our room and returned to work. A single day more of rest and I would have surely melted into the floor. I wanted to rise from the birthing bed that first day, but Husband forbade it. It took every bit of discipline I had to remain on the bedding.

A month back in the sesame business, I grew bored. Suddenly the money was not enough. The more I earned, the less it seemed I had. So I searched around for something new, something more popular than sesame oil. Then I overheard people talking about a white powder called opium. On the black market, a small pipeful yielded a high price, but as in Korea, the Japanese dominated the opium trade. They were the manufacturers, Koreans were the dealers, and Chinese were the users. It was risky smuggling and dealing the stuff. Those caught were tossed in jail and beaten, sometimes vanishing completely. Still, I was determined to sell it.

A Korean woman from our neighborhood, who everyone knew smuggled for a Chinese buyer, passed our brick house on her way to work one day. I seized the opportunity to introduce myself.

"I would like to help you sell your powder," I stated candidly.

She shrugged her shoulders, and without answering she continued on her way, taking long, brisk strides. I chased after her, following from a careful distance. She walked right into the middle of the open marketplace where I bought groceries daily. Here? I thought, disappointed. I suppose I was expecting something less conspicuous, with a hint of mystic.

As we weaved through the crowded aisles, a man alongside of me rhythmically clicked his chopsticks against his empty tin rice bowl. He wandered with us until we arrived at the edge of the marketplace, where there were no sidewalks. Alone, I followed the woman up a narrow path several miles outside the Korean district. Laundry hung on poles from every window. It actually enhanced the scenery, diverting one's eyes from the coal-dusted roads covered with spit and waste. A large doughy woman, balanced on a teetering stool, looked up at me blankly. She spat twice, then pressed her thumb against one nostril and shot out the slimy contents, then emptied the other nostril. As I watched, incredulous, small children in soiled shirts and blackened feet crept up around me. They pointed at my white Korean dress and started to tease me. One older boy grabbed my skirt and the others copied him. I yelled at them in Korean, more out of fear than anything else, but they laughed even harder. Then the large woman shrilled at them and they withdrew into the safety of their homes. I ran off without thanking her. I had to find the woman I was pursuing before she disappeared into an alley or doorway.

Finally, I caught up to her as she hesitated in front of her destination. Her knuckles barely tapped the gate of the home she wanted to enter. It cracked opened just enough for her to slip in. Before I had a chance to show myself, the gate shut. I gulped in a deep breath, smoothed back my hair, and softly knocked. I was not sure anyone heard inside, but then a suspicious eye peeked through.

"What do you want?" a man's voice crackled.

"Opium give." I recalled the words one at a time.

"You have come to the wrong place. My master does not have this powder you speak of."

"Me woman walk gate see. Me master see. Not go away," I said firmly, hoping I sang the correct intonations for him to understand.

The gate slammed in my face, nearly smashing my nose. A while later it opened again. "Come in quickly."

I was instructed to wait in the dim, smoke-filled room, where an old man sprawled on the floor floated between consciousness and oblivion. Beside him upon a low bench was a long-stemmed bamboo pipe, packed with opium, burning over a little lamp. Its fumes sweetened the air. A girl no older than five sat near his head, fanning away the buzzing flies with one hand. Whenever that old decaying body desired more opium, she used a silver pick to poke holes in the drop of bubbling gum as his dried, cracked lips closed upon the stem and sucked greedily. The gum vaporized into thick white smoke, which was drawn through the ceramic bowl and into his lungs. He held his breath as long as possible, but it was too much for him and he started to cough in a choking sort of way. Once he caught his breath, his yellow gnarled hand squeezed more black gum into a ball between his thumb and forefinger. I swore I would never allow myself or Husband to smoke the fumes. Not even once.

As I waited, a lanky man came in, bouncing his young son in his arms. The little boy had on pants with an open crotch. When his father lowered him, the boy skittered to his grandfather's side. Every time he took a step his tiny man part slipped through the opening. I remained standing there until the lanky man summoned me into the back room. A handful of women were already present. They had just successfully crossed the Manchurian border, past the Japanese police boxes, with stashes of opium. One by one they emerged from behind a partition, holding long rubber tubes swollen with the stuff. Several of the women had even leapt fences with these tubes hidden inside their private parts. Just the thought made me blush.

In exchange for the rubber tubes, the man handed the women pouches filled with money. Off they went, adjusting their dresses. When he had collected all the opium, he smiled broadly, and I could see that the top four front teeth were crudely chipped, instantly changing him from being semi-attractive to sinister-looking. A gasp escaped me and his eyes caught sight of my figure. For a moment he had forgotten I was there. He scratched his head, wondering if he should make use of me.

"Opium give." I spoke up before he decided against it.

"Why should I trust you?" he asked, but there was no sharpness in his tone.

"Me bring more. Lots."

"Oh, you can? And what if you get caught with twice as much?"

"No, easy," I bragged, knowing he was testing me.

And with that remark he handed me a bag full of gold and sent me out on my first smuggling adventure. Gold was the best currency when transacting business outside of China because local paper money was good for only two things: to blow one's nose and to wipe one's bottom.

A Korean woman I had never met before joined Second Son and me at the train platform. I carried him on my back. Husband stayed home with our two eldest children, shaking in his slippers. We did not part well. Against the plan, he had tried to convince me to stay. When talking got him nowhere, he stomped his foot and forbade me to leave. And for the first time, I disobeyed him. He had a devastated look on his face; I had robbed him of his manhood.

I boarded the train safely. The Japanese police, randomly searching passengers, skipped over us two women and instead hassled a young male student loitering behind us. The student was accused of being a guerrilla fighter. When he denied the charges, the police rammed the butt of a rifle into his back, sending him crashing into a seat.

I had accomplished the easy part; the journey back would be the true test of steady nerves.

It seemed like a long trip, although the distance was much shorter than when I first rode the train. Fortunately, we avoided police questioning at the many station searches. Once across the border, we hired a ricksha to drive us to the secluded factory—actually a house with crowds of people squatting around, wearing rubber gloves and cotton masks. I bought a substantial quantity of opium, white and powdery like flour. I had expected it to be black and sticky sweet, straight from the plant, but my companion informed me this was the modern processed stuff.

With a funnel made from newspaper, I packed ten long rubber tubes. I was not foolish enough to store the opium between my legs. Instead, I lined the bottom of my breasts with three tubes each and secured them with strips of fabric—a good hiding place, for my once milk-bloated breasts had dried up early and hung empty. The other four tubes I coiled inside my hat, which I pinned to my head. Once that was done, I donned my Korean dress and strapped Second Son onto my back, in the Japanese fashion. It was perfect. We Koreans carried our children on our backs using a blanket wrapped forward around the chest, pressing the breasts down, which could have ruptured the tubes. The Japanese used shoulder straps that crossed at the heart, adding double protection.

At the train stop my companion and I took an extra precaution. We separated in case one of us got caught. I boarded the train hunched over, dragging a sack of food up the steps. A Japanese policeman impatiently glared at me as I slowly made my way up. Once I reached the top of the steps he grabbed my shoulders and yanked me in. I was paralyzed with fear.

"Move on! You are holding up the line," he bellowed, as if he thought I was deaf. "All the way to the rear!"

Relieved, I staggered to the back, catching my breath. I squeezed into the last seat near the window so I could watch my companion make her way past the rude man. It was painful to stare at her face; it screamed of doom, especially her bulbous monkey eyes that could not hide her guilt. They scrunched together and up, causing her dark bushy eyebrows to do the same. Maybe she should have tried to jump the border, I thought. To the surprise of both of us, the soldier motioned her through. I saw her start in my direction, but she looked as though she was going to collapse right there and then. Her knees buckled, her arms fell heavily to the side, and her head swayed back and forth. Hastening to her, I wrapped my arm around her waist and supported her the rest of the way home.

When we returned to the lanky man's house, I handed him eight perfectly packed rubber tubes. He stared at the enormous quantity of opium in his palms, and then rewarded me with a well-earned pouch of money. I was eager to count it, but I restrained myself, for I wanted to share my victory with Husband. A gesture of peace.

Once I was home, Husband and I spoke to each other politely. Although clearly relieved, he acted differently, almost withdrawn. I pushed the feeling aside and gaily offered him the pouch of money to open. The pouch contained only the cost of my train fare and a little extra. Furious, I focused my attention on the two tubes of opium stashed under my hat.

I paid a Chinese man to act as an intermediary. He secured a buyer since I was capable of singing only a few phrases correctly in Mandarin. Neither one of us spoke the other's language well enough to carry on a lengthy conversation, but he sensed the purpose of my business right off and that was what mattered.

He brought me to a friend's home where the friend lived with his parents, grandparents, brothers, and a multitude of nieces and nephews. They bought everything I had. In that single hour, I earned as much as I would have in an entire month in the sesame business. It seemed so enticingly easy. Immediately I made arrangements to go on another run across the border. This time Husband insisted it was his turn.

"*Yobo*, are you certain you wish to do this?" I asked, concerned for his safety.

"If a woman can do it, I can do it better," he boasted in his lordly manner.

I said no more, for I knew he wanted to salvage his honor.

The children and I bowed good-bye from the gate as he marched off toward the train station. He looked twenty pounds overweight with all that gold I had sewn into the lining of his jacket and trousers.

Two weeks passed and the children and I awaited Husband's return. Worried, I blamed myself for jeopardizing his life. The desire for food or sleep left me. Scary, gruesome thoughts drove me to imagine the worst. What if he was caught and tortured? What if some bandit killed him for the opium? I felt completely helpless and alone, with no answers to soothe my fears.

Then word from the Japanese police finally arrived at our house by official foot messenger. The letter stated that Husband had been arrested and it would take a fortune to buy his freedom. At once I hurried to him, bringing along most of my savings and Dukwah, because I knew the sight of her pretty face would delight Husband. Together the three of us returned home, empty-handed and Husband twenty pounds poorer. Later, he and I decided his talents were best suited for managing the money.

Once family life was normal again, my brain churned out new and safer ways to double, triple our fortune. The perfect solution flew into my head one afternoon. Although I never received any formal education, I discovered I was clever and had a natural talent when it came to business.

"Yongwoon's father, we are going into the wholesale business," I announced.

Through an important connection, I arranged to make one big opium pickup directly from the largest Japanese manufacturer in China. I would resell it to Korean dealers, who in turn would offer me a percentage of what they peddled on the streets. It was easier this way, for I could freely communicate with my own kind. I did not have to worry that someone was cheating me in Mandarin.

Once a month I rode the train to Chungedo, hauling back enough powder to seduce a whole village. I smuggled it in tin lunch pails, lacing the bottoms with opium. On top of the opium I laid a thin sheet of paper, then covered it with rice, seasoned fish, and *bulkogi*, barbecued beef. It was a brilliant plan, I thought, as I guided my cart past many police roadblocks and checkpoints.

By the time I transported the opium home, it reeked of fish and garlic. To rid the opium of the odor, I mixed in cheap perfume, then spread it out to dry in two large iron tubs. As if performing surgery, I wore long rubber gloves and tied a wide piece of cloth over my nose and mouth. One too many sniffs of the white dust and I knew I would sink to the floor in a fog of forgetfulness. The rats, on the other hand, crept out by the dozens, licking the tiny specks of dust off the ground. They would go wild, shooting across the room several times before they would eventually tire out and doze off. As they slept, I grabbed a flat iron pan and smashed the life out of them. Their blood splattered everywhere—on the walls, on my shoes, in my hair. I swore once more that I would never allow myself or my family to smoke the sweet poison. I was terrified that we, too, might be squashed while we slept, for many envied our wealth.

After the opium dried, I mixed it with vitamins, sugar, and occasionally plain flour. Soon I had twice the amount as before, and more money than our whole family could have possibly spent in a lifetime. Money bulged from every crack, hole, and panel. It was under our feet, above our heads, and in our bedding. Only after midnight would we count the money and separate the counterfeit from the real stuff. In time it became easy to distinguish them. The counterfeiters used thicker paper, and if one handled the counterfeit too long, the ink left stains on one's hands. The real money I stored or sent back to Pyongyang whenever I could find a trustworthy courier. I made sure Sister-in-Law and the household lived luxuriously. I also took it upon myself to see to my aging parent's comfort. Often I worried about them, though I knew Older Brother would tend to their needs.

On Husband's suggestion we deposited our profits in various banks around the city under Dukwah's Japanese and Korean names. She was the richest little girl in all of China, I think. Then we began to solicit names of friends; unfortunately, this proved costly because these same friends emptied their accounts and fled before we figured out their scheme. Other times complete strangers would enter a bank, give the correct name, and drain off our money without any proper documentation.

"Let them have it if they are bold enough to steal from us. Our family is still by far the wealthiest."

Husband did not take the thefts as lightly. He despised the fact that we were powerless against anyone who wanted to rob us. The police, after all, were our enemies. I knew I had to act quickly in order to keep my family and myself out of danger.

If money got us into this predicament, then money will buy us out, I reasoned. I bribed everyone from lowly patrolmen to military soldiers to high-ranking government officials. I paid off anyone who had to be bought. Soon the Japanese were providing us personalized protection. I was safe, my family was safe, and my business prospered.

A MAN

MUST

ALWAYS

EAT

Right before my eyes, my baby-faced husband blossomed into a robust and elegant man. I admired the way he wore his fine new tailored clothes. His hair was polished and silky, his shoulders even and wide. His skin was pale and clean-shaven. He always smelled of expensive foreign cigarettes, the kind that could be purchased only on the black market. He was so desirable that my heart ached; no man equaled him in style or splendor.

Soon, though, he grew restless. I tried to devise ways for him to pass his days, encouraging the children to play with their father, but even their demanding attention left a void inside him. Eventually he began to roam the streets, and on one of his jaunts he came to a building with enormous lanterns in the windows, a house of *kisaengs*. Here a man of wealth could drink exotic teas and liquor, engage in gambling, hear poetry and songs, and indulge in the most delicate of women. *Kisaengs*, with their honeyed words and cultivated talents, created an oasis of entertainment and pleasure for men.

From that day forward, Husband regularly visited the house of Lovely Blossoms once a week, then three times a week, soon every day. Recklessly, he learned to spend our good money. He would leave right after the morning meal and stumble home past dark, reeking of another woman's perfume. Always I swallowed my tears; it was my duty to accept fate as First Wife had done.

"A woman has to endure much suffering to show her husband she is a good wife," Mother once said, after I asked why First Wife seemed so unhappy. "But she must never express her unhappiness."

Those words barbed my heart each time Husband left the house. I tried to convince myself that I was fortunate because he always returned to the warmth of our bed, molding his body around mine. Naively I wanted to believe Husband's love for me soared above any temptation. Alas, I was miserably wrong. Making babies and money was no match for beauty and lust. He would scrutinize my appearance, comparing my flat features with those of the *kisaengs*. He had no tolerance for dull and common things any longer. My insecurities gushed out because I knew my hair was rough and unoiled, my eyebrows scattered, my lips dark, my hands coarse, and my breasts saggy.

One evening Husband barged in as I was unwinding my braid. He stared for a long while, critically eyeing my hair.

"You would not be a bad-looking woman if you cut your hair."

"It suits me fine," I replied with a hint of defiance.

"The new fashion is to take off the braid."

"But I have always worn it braided and coiled."

"These are new times. All the modern women in the city have their hair cut short. They will think you are old-fashioned."

"I serve only you; why should I concern myself with how others judge me?"

"Then you will not cut off that monkey tail?!"

"It suits me fine," I repeated tersely.

"So be it. Do as you wish again, but I shall trim my hair short in the latest style," he snapped.

Anger surged through me. Before we fled Korea our Japanese imperial ruler commanded all males to trim their hair. Husband refused, keeping his bangs and sideburns long as a sign of protest. Now he was willing to cut it all off for vanity. He waited for me to berate him so he could defend himself. I would not give him the satisfaction.

Pouting, he stormed out of the house. Hours later, he returned, looking totally different. The hair on the sides and back of his head were shaved closely to the scalp and the bangs were newly parted in the middle.

"I do not wish to be a country fool forever!" he exclaimed, as his lower lip trembled. No matter how mature and tall Husband had grown he was still like a little child who needed my approval. Though my stubbornness would never have allowed me to admit it, his new style appealed to me. He appeared more handsome, if that was possible.

Several weeks later I, too, chopped off my braid, simply because he desired it. Tears formed in my eyes as I took a butcher knife to it just below the ear. When I saw the long braid on the ground, I regretted what I had done, for I was convinced I had placed a curse on myself.

Delighted, Husband insisted that he treat me to a professional hairstylist. The young woman who teased and tortured my hair boasted it would be fashioned after a photo of a Western lady she once saw. That explained why I did not look anything like myself. The hair was parted deep on one side and the rest was combed behind my ears. She attempted to curl the ends, using metal clips. The clips had small pockets with lids where bits of hot coal were placed to heat the hair. Because her hands were too slow and her mouth too busy, the ends sizzled and turned brown, eventually flaking off, curl by curl. Regardless, Husband was so thrilled that we were a modern couple he failed to notice that I was practically bald.

All this I did for him, and more, in hopes that he would stay home and desire only me. Wishful thinking: his appetite for pretty women only swelled. I saw less and less of my husband— an hour here, a few minutes there. Then one night he did not return. I did not want to believe it, but the more I thought about it, the more it seemed possible. Alone I lay on the bedding and agonized quietly, the anger clenching me awake. The jealous tiger within me raged, and I wanted to scratch at their pretty powdered faces and sew them up between their legs.

"A noble woman controls her emotions." I heard Mother's words bang around in my head. I despised that word "noble." It had no meaning, no worth without my husband's love. I was still a youthful woman with years ahead of me, yet I was expected to act indifferent to his betrayal. Why had I been so stupid to fall in love with him? My heart skipped beats when I imagined Husband taking a second wife, someone blessed with white milky skin and perfectly delicate features. All at once my breath faltered as another thought raced madly through my mind. What if he never came back? The torment of my loss squeezed my chest tight. The pain blurred my vision and my eyes closed. In the darkness, I could see Husband clearly in my mind's eye. I could not bear the thought of losing him. I would rather see us both dead.

I paced around the room. The place seemed particularly damp and drafty. Compelled by an urge to see our children, I went into their room. Carefully I moved to where they slept, knelt, and kissed them lightly.

Drained, I returned to my empty quarters. The remainder of the night I stayed awake watching the moon rise deep into the night, then slowly settle. By morning, a strange powerful creature coiled in my body, ready to attack him at first sight. Unable to lie still any longer, I worked steadily through the new day into the afternoon. The hours wore on endlessly long, yet I refused to rest.

Then I heard his slow, cautious footsteps as he mounted the stairs. Crazed and relieved, I trembled all over. Every line on my face must have borne the bitter look of loathing, but when I saw his magnificent form, my anger dwindled away. He was wearing foreign attire cut neatly to his exact size. It appeared to be a suit made from a light brownish wool: the tailored pants matched the tailored jacket that matched the tailored vest. Inside the vest, he wore a starched shirt that buttoned all the way to his neck, and a rope went under the collar and tied like a noose at the base of his throat. It looked uncomfortable, though oddly enough, it fit him well.

Silence fell between us. I needed him to speak first, but he neither explained nor apologized. His gaze roamed over my face. After a few lingering moments, my anger was about to spill all over him. When he reached out to caress my cheek I snatched his hand and shoved it aside. Unnerved by my hostility, he ran his fingers through his hair, then pulled out of his pocket a handful of tissue paper from which he unwrapped a gift, a pair of jade and pearl earrings chiseled in the shape of a flower. Once again rage rose in my heart. I wanted to maim him as he had hurt me. How dare he think he could buy my forgiveness so cheaply? My face flushed.

"They made me think of you," he said meekly, avoiding my glare.

"I forbid you to bring me into your thoughts when you are with another," I threw at him. "I would rather hang myself than accept a second wife into my home, especially a *kisaeng*."

He looked so pathetic standing there, his head hung low. "I do not wish to take another wife. You are the only one I truly desire. There is no other woman that compares with you," he answered.

As much as I wanted to hate him forever, I forgave him. That night and every night thereafter, I pitched in my bed, unable to release the pain. I was desperate for some kind of escape to help me ease the agony of betrayal, and even contemplated the powerful smoke of opium, but the many long drawn faces of those victims of the pipe haunted me. Their kind sold their wives and children when they ran out of funds to support their addiction. I could never sell one of my children, even the girl.

Then I found a way to keep Husband's affections at home and not scattered all over the Orient. Slyly I suggested we go into the restaurant business. Mother used to tell me, "A man easily loses his taste for one woman or another, but he never loses his taste for food. A man must always eat."

From the grimace on his face, I knew Husband detested the thought of labor.

"Let us do something more befitting our status."

"I choose to do this for you. Do not think of it as degrading work, *Yobo*. We will be entertaining the most prominent and powerful people at our restaurant. It will be a place where everyone will want to dine, drink, and gossip. Your name will be famous, for you will be the man who owns the largest restaurant in town."

Husband clucked his tongue repeatedly in defeat. "I should have married a gentle woman of China. Korean women are much too stubborn and independent from their husbands."

The notion of Husband regretting our marriage jolted me.

He continued: "You have the will of a man . . . and the cleverness of a woman. Proceed if this is what you wish." His flirtatious smile told me I had won his confidence and approval.

"Thank you, *Yobo*," I said with a touch of light sarcasm, knowing full well he would pursue the restaurant business solely for his own fame.

Our red-brick two-story home was ideal. We kept the upper level for living quarters and the downstairs we filled with great round tables and chairs. The place was so spacious, a dozen or so separate rooms and a banquet area were sectioned off for customers who wanted privacy.

Yellow paper lanterns glowed from every corner and beam. Outside, a large sign over the door read simply "RESTAURANT"— in Chinese, Japanese, and Korean because all who could afford to eat were welcome. And they did come as soon as our doors opened.

The cooks started prepping around nine or ten in the morning and we closed only when all the drunken laughter subsided. Sometimes, the next morning we would find customers left over from the night before, snoring loudly from too much wine.

I personally sampled our diverse menu daily, which included something to delight every palate. There were many odd dishes and odors that were distinctive to the native people, like broccoli, oyster sauce, and duck. Hard as I tried, though, I never developed an appreciation for thousand-year-old eggs. They smelled rotten and were black and dirty on the outside; inside, they were purple and gooey. Nevertheless, we pickled plenty of them, for they were popular.

Also, these people enjoyed their food saturated in pork fat. If it could be fried, our cooks tossed, flipped, and stirred it in large black iron woks. Grease splattered as the food hissed and sizzled. In one day alone, whole fifty-gallon barrels of fat were consumed. I made it my job to go to the slaughterhouse and pick out the snorting pigs myself. I trusted no one else to select the prize ingredient that made our restaurant so famous. I took my time inspecting their ankles, snouts, bellies, and asses because not one part of that pig ever went to waste. The whole pig, eyeballs and all, was spit-roasted over hot coals until the last drop of fat dripped free, then the fat was poured into large barrels, where it settled and hardened into lard.

People lounged around for hours. The sound of clicking silver chopsticks was the rustle of money to my ears. In a short period of time, as with everything else I did, the business grew prosperous. Each week I had to hire more Chinese workers, but good help was hard to find. Their work ethic was so different from the Korean ways. The doorman would only open and close the door. The slaughterer would only gut the pigs and poultry. On many occasions I hollered at them to do other chores beyond the realm of their specific duties, but they simply stared blankly at me.

The only time I saw them get excited about anything was when Dukwah came around, because they knew she was her father's favorite, his princess. The doorman would announce her arrival to the others, who would cheer her name. Before she even reached the doors, the workers clustered around the entrance as if they were waiting for the return of a great hero. At their insistence, Dukwah celebrated her fifth birthday at the restaurant. It was the liveliest and grandest party the town had ever seen. The room was strewn with wildflowers and colorful paper laterns, and food and drink flowed freely for all. On that special day, her father rolled the noodles especially long, as they symbolized long life.

The news of the party spread far and wide. Soon even our enemies patronized our restaurant. High-ranking Japanese officials, in their black uniforms, regularly dined at our tables, officials I paid off to keep my opium business operating smoothly. Whatever they craved was given to them free of charge and in exchange they kept the restaurant fully stocked with supplies while the general public suffered shortages of meat, sugar, and rice. The sight of the enemy's uniforms disturbed Husband and me at first, but in time a curious thing happened. We cultivated friendships, whether we wished it or not. To eat, drink, joke, share family tales naturally drew even longtime enemies closer. This friendship contradicted all the reasons why we left our homeland. From our earliest memories, we were taught to despise the Japanese. They were pirates and sadistic cultural rapists. And we were told they, too, loathed us just as much. To them, Koreans were backward and coarse. One thing we did share throughout our history was our dislike for the Chinese, and the Chinese, in turn, detested us. So much hatred between our three neighboring countries.

Then I remembered hearing that many, many centuries ago our three countries were once the same. Suddenly it made sense. The most bitter battles raged between brothers, because love soured turned to bitter hate. There was no emotion more powerful, more destructive, and more painful than love.

The restaurant initially accomplished my goal: Husband no longer harbored any thoughts of wandering off. He mingled and drank as much as any customer, content with his life as a restaurateur, until some of the painted women dared to pass by our large opened windows on thinly veiled errands. They fluttered their long lashes and wiggled their slender hips as they sashayed slowly by. Their chests swelled beneath form-fitting robes of silk when they saw that they caught Husband's glance. Long after they were gone their perfumed scents lingered, poisoning the food and the appetites of all the men, who were reminded of their other hunger. I knew the women did not come for those fat greasy ones; they desired my husband. When he left a room, his absence was felt in the farthest corner.

It tormented me to watch him gradually return to his lustful habits. Acquaintances and customers began to question his whereabouts. I had to bury my sorrow and answer with excuses and lies. "I would rather hang myself on a beam with a rope before I would allow him to take another wife into our home," I swore. After all, I had fulfilled all my wifely responsibilities. I had given him sons and lined his pockets with gold.

Jealousy prickled my skin. As the strain became unbearable, a will drove me out the door. I ran and ran, knowing exactly where the *kisaeng* teahouses were, though I had never chased after Husband before. The first building I came to had music streaming out of it. I stood outside contemplating whether this was the type of place he would patronize. I concluded it was, because it looked expensive.

Before entering, I peered around to see if anyone saw my shame. Instantly I narrowed my eyes against the smoke-shrouded dimness. I saw it was a great hall with a high ceiling. Upon the walls hung scrolls made of cream silk and painted with figures of naked women. And in the center, on top of a podium, a beautiful woman sang soprano as she plucked a four-stringed lute, accompanied by another beating a drum to mark the time. Subtle webs of light illuminated their silky hair and pearl-smooth faces. No wonder Husband returned to this hidden den of evil. These women, clustered here like a bouquet of budding flowers, were more intoxicating than any wine I could ever possibly serve at the restaurant.

The smell of desire wafted through the heavily perfumed air. It sickened me to witness rich portly men shamelessly smiling as they descended the stairs after enjoying themselves in the private rooms. The thought of how much money and hours were wasted here filled me with loathing. I spilled through the rooms, inspecting each male face, trying to ignore the clatter of men drinking and wagering bets as they shuffled tiny wooden dice upon tables. Then all at once my heart contracted.

There in a partitioned corner, I saw Husband slouched at an intimate table for two. His head was tossed back as cigarette smoke floated out like rings from his mouth. With his free hand he held tightly to a lean young woman. She must have been no older than seventeen, but her face was meticulously designed by pencil and lipstick to appear more mature. Those red lips of hers composed poetry as her hand fanned him. He devoured every verse.

> *The lotus flower sings to her beloved.*
> *Come lay down your worries,*
> *toss aside your tireless burdens.*
> *Forever and eternally,*
> *we shall blossom,*
> *even among the muddy waters.*

Completely oblivious, neither one of them noticed that I was standing before them. I could bear no more, and jarred him from his reverie. Our eyes locked. It was as if there was no one in that room except him, me, and the wench. The smoke, the noise, the crowd—all dissolved as my hands tightened into fists. My lips curled, exposing my teeth in a snarl. As I swung around to pound the wench with my fists, Husband escaped through the back door.

"Catch him! Thief, thief!" I yelled, knowing quite well these cheating husbands would more likely rescue a woman who was robbed before assisting a disgruntled wife.

I bolted after Husband, only to lose him. In a rage, I stormed into every teahouse and gambling hall. Not one establishment went undisturbed, I made sure of that. Defeated, I returned home, dragging my feet. There I found Husband cowering beneath blankets, his face red with wine and worry. At once, my hands flew wildly all over him, and again with greater force.

"I will not allow you to break my heart any longer!" I hissed at him, my breath wheezing through parted lips. Sweat poured out of me as though I was struck with a fatal illness. In the olden days, a woman who hit her husband could be beaten one hundred times with a stick by him if he wished it. I did not care, for my heart was already shattered.

CHIRYO

All the opium and gold in China could not cure my child-hood illness. The demons had returned to torment me. It became increasingly more difficult to breathe and all I could smell was the rotting odor of my guts. On Husband's advice I checked myself into a foreign hospital built by Christian missionaries, my last alternative since herbal remedies and exorcisms had proven useless. It was said foreigners were quick to cut people open with the knife, killing them more often than saving them. Thus, I was stunned to find the walls sparkling clean and white, and the scene appeared calm and orderly. No one lay dead in the hallway with their insides slashed open.

A Chinese nurse, in her late twenties, greeted me in her language, and led me into one of the rooms. Eight other women already occupied the available cots. An extra cot had to be brought out just for me.

I was instructed to undress completely and don a thin cotton gown. It had no shape and hardly any fabric. "Dress wear," I answered back choppily in her language.

"These are the rules. You must wear the gown before a doctor can examine you."

The thought of baring myself in front of complete strangers only added to my discomfort. I was a woman of great wealth and power, did she not realize? Apparently she could not care less, judging by her indifference. To her, I was no richer, sicker, or more deserving than any of my other roommates.

"If you refuse to cooperate, I will be forced to assist you." Her tone was slightly threatening.

I was not about to be violated by this woman, so I turned my back to them all and undressed myself, humiliated to the core. I sat on the edge of the cot with the sheet pulled around my shoulders like a cape until the nurse returned with a man, who rolled me away into the operating room.

My jaw sagged at the sight of the tallest foreign man I had ever seen. Now I understood why the doors and ceiling in this building were so high. His hair was short like Husband's, and slightly thin on top. His long, straight nose looked like two of mine molded together, except his had a small butt at the tip. The eyes were large and bright blue, cupped by deep sockets.

He held out his enormous watermelon hand to me. The skin was pink like the skin on his face. I knew what he wanted, for I had witnessed other men with large eyes and pink skin perform this exact ritual. I joined my hand to his and he pumped it up and down, three quick times. His powerful grip swallowed mine. I wondered how he could be a doctor with such awkwardly large hands.

"Do not be afraid. I am here to help you." He spoke these people's language with such ease that I was embarrassed to attempt my Mandarin, although his intonations sounded more like a tone-deaf crow than a hummingbird. Painstakingly he explained what he intended to do. As I feared, he wanted to carve the infection from my nose. The infection, he stressed, also caused the tearing of the eyes and the buzzing in the ears. He assured me he had successfully performed the surgery many times before.

The nurse instructed me to lie down on the operating table, then covered my nose with a cloth. Within minutes I slipped into a relaxing sleep. The last conscious memory I had was of the bright hypnotic lights aimed at my face and the metallic clinking of sharp instruments. When I awoke, I was amazed to see that the whole day had gone by and that I was back in the other room. My face was heavy with bandages, but I felt no pain, only a slight pinch between my eyes. I discovered later the doctor had cut through my upper lip, peeling back my face over my nose to drain out the infection. That explained why I had stitches between the gum and upper lip. Every time my tongue accidentally brushed the threads I felt squeamish.

A month later I returned to the hospital to have the last of the bandages removed. What I saw in the mirror shocked me completely. The doctor had stolen the bridge of my nose, flattening it. I was hesitant to go home, afraid that Husband would reject me totally. How could I possibly hide something that obvious in the middle of my face?

I gathered my courage and went home. Just the anticipation of Husband's disgust made me want to hide under the blankets. But before I lost my nerve, I walked right up to him.

He looked at me steadily and asked if it hurt.

"No," I mumbled softly. "It is not the pain I am concerned about. I am afraid I am completely ugly now." I felt the tears leak through my lashes.

"Nonsense. Soon the bruises around your eyes will heal and you will be yourself again," he said swiftly, easing my insecurities.

The operation stopped the dripping, as the foreign doctor had assured me. I decided the family and I would celebrate with a big meal, Korean style. I did all the cooking myself, blending and adding various spices unique to our countrymen. Soon I had prepared enough good food for a whole kingdom. I watched with pride as everyone crowded around the table in awe. One by one they spooned *ozinguh chae*, cooked squid; *kalbi kui*, short ribs in sweet sauce; *sokkori chim*, oxtail stew; *tubu bokum*, bean curd sauté; *kosari*, royal fern vegetable; and *na bak kimchee*, water *kimchee*, into their eager mouths. One by one I watched their faces turn sour and spit out the food.

"Is something wrong?" I frowned.

Husband coughed out a reply: "It is too salty, everything is too salty."

"But how could that be?" I asked, bewildered. "I measured all the ingredients myself."

That was when I realized the surgery had removed my sense of smell. From that day forward, everything tasted bland.

Western medicine, my last hope for a healthier life, had failed to cure me. Not only did the operation rob me of my smell, it gradually worsened my condition. On the outside I appeared well, but inside I was deteriorating at a quicker rate and no one could do anything to rescue me from an early grave. Each morning I was mortified to discover blood and tiny living worms in my stool again. I was sure the worms had caused my bloating stomach. Out of sheer desperation I returned to the foreign doctor, who diagnosed that I was actually pregnant. I received the news badly, because I knew I was not fit enough to carry the baby. And I was right. The infant arrived after only three short months. Then, as if I had not suffered enough, I became pregnant again, and like the one before, it ripped itself from my womb and landed at the bottom of the chamber pot. Two more babes lost. I mourned silently.

Still Husband planted another seed. Each day I worried for the tiny child that clung to my inner walls. "Just a little longer you must stay inside. Fight for your life, because your family is anxious to greet you. Hold on, hold on, hold on . . ." I coaxed softly. And he did listen, he held on and came out when nature dictated that it was safe to show himself.

The Chinese character meaning "good" was a woman on the left and a son on the right. Now I had three and I was determined to give this son, Kunsam, healthy third, a healthy chance. I hired a wet nurse to feed him her breast milk. I chose this particular Chinese woman because of her pink cheeks and full breasts. I envied her two boys. Even under all the dirt I could see they were plump and rosy with fitness.

"I want you to feed my son whenever he desires and always before you feed yours," I made clear.

"He will always be fed before my own children, even if mine are crying," she assured me in Korean.

Her eagerness to please me was a comfort. I was surprised, though, that there was no jealousy in me, knowing my child would suck on her nipple and sleep in her arms. I would let her keep him for now, but when it was time to wean him away I would offer him my breast to play with.

I gave her a pouch full of money as incentive to keep her word. Her slitted eyes opened wide: the amount was far more than any wet nurse ever expected to earn, but her milk was worth every bit of gold. "And if he grows strong and sound, I will reward you again," I promised.

Husband, though, was troubled. "Is it not better to feed our son his own mother's milk?" he asked, dismayed.

"Not if you wish Kunsam to survive." I drew a breath, adding with great difficulty, "Because our second son drank from my breasts, he battles for his very life. He has swallowed all that is sickly in me. I cannot bear to watch him suffer so, and I blame myself every day for what I have done to him."

This was a hard thing for a mother to admit, but it was true. Instead of growing hardy, our second son withered. His tiny hands and feet bloated with blood, turning the flesh deep purple, while the rest of his body suffered. It wounded me to hear the poor child cry for hours because his skin was so cold. The only thing I could do was to wrap him in layers of silk blankets and place him in the warmest spot in the house.

"Do what you think is best, *Yobo*." Husband gave his consent.

This Chinese woman accomplished all that she had promised. Kunsam was healthier and plumper than all my other children. It was comforting having her around the large house, although she was quite mysterious. Often I would cock an ear up the staircase and hear a steady flow of clapping. What could she be doing? I wondered. But every time I went upstairs to investigate, the clapping stopped. At first I thought she might have been beating my son, so I examined him thoroughly and found no traces of abuse. Gradually the clapping blended with all the other sounds of the household, and I forgot about it entirely. Then one blinding morning when the winds were blowing heavy clouds of yellow dust and black smoke, and funneling into every crack and opening in the house, I collapsed, struck down by the worst pain I had ever suffered.

"Fetch Yongwoon's father, I must go to the foreign hospital." I gasped for air.

"I can treat you," she replied.

"Do not be foolish. I am too old for your milk."

"It is not my milk that will heal you, but my hands."

"How can your hands help me? You are nothing but a farmer's wife."

"True, we are only peasants; however, our men and women live long lives. This year my husband's grandfather will celebrate his eighty-ninth year."

"I do not wish to live to be that old and brittle."

"But you do wish to live long enough to see your children's marriages arranged and your grandsons born, do you not?"

I paused for an agonizing moment before I asked, "Will you circle a knife above my head and yell out Buddhist chants or will you cut me open?"

"Neither. You must trust me when I say my hands are all that I need."

"I trust no one except my family, because I am a woman of great wealth . . . but I will let you treat me. Do not fail in your claims or there will be severe consequences."

Swiftly she prepared a place for me to lie before her. After another moment of resistance, I peeled off my waist jacket and skirt, and lifted the slip up to my chest as she requested.

Instead of clapping, as I had imagined, she began to slap the skin around my lower stomach. As the speed and pressure intensified, her palm felt hot against my stinging flesh. I flinched and cursed, but her free hand and legs pinned me down. Steadily she slapped on, moving with more power, as if her hand possessed some mystical force.

For two hours I endured the torture. When she finally released me, there was no more pain, only numbness. I was speechless. Black-and-blue marks ribboned my belly. I wanted to have her whipped and banished for what she had done to me. Sensing my mood, she fled my sight. Day after day I waited for her to show her face so I could lash her with the rod.

On the third day, the soreness ebbed. Even Husband commented on how effortlessly I rose in the mornings.

"Yongwoon's mother, is it not better to try her way than to be carved open again? Perhaps next time you will not be as fortunate. What use are you to me and the children if you are dead?"

I knew he was right, but I hesitated for a few more days before I sent a messenger to her husband's field, where, I heard, she was working by his side, plowing the soil.

"What is it you call this thing you do with your hands?" I asked sharply, still clenched with anger.

"*Chiryo.*"

"And how does your *chiryo* work?"

"When you went to that foreign doctor he cut out the problem but he failed to treat the cause. I have always been taught you must treat the source with massage, and the source is the circulation. Western medicine only weakens the problem to make the ill believe they are cured."

I listened intently as she went on to explain about the blood that surged through all my veins. "Blood is the food of life. It must flow like water. If it becomes polluted and muddy it will slow the body and eventually shut down. By slapping or pinching the flesh over and over again, it generates heat and energy and draws the bad blood to rise to the surface, thus the bruises. When this happens, the blood is cleansed, making it easier to travel freely throughout the body."

"You mention the blood being the source, and if it travels through the entire body, do you have to slap every inch of the flesh?"

"That is not necessary, because the heart is where every drop of blood must pass. It is nature's filter system and *chiryo* helps to unclog the valves so it may function properly. That is why it is essential to always treat the areas around the heart and neck as well."

For some unknown reason, I finally felt I could trust her odd method of treatment. This time I held my tongue and endured the pain as her hand attacked the fatty flesh around the heart area. Using her index finger and middle finger, she pinched the skin, making long red marks that fanned out from the edge of each nipple. And all around my neck, parallel marks ran from the tip of the chin to the base of the collarbone, forming a strange necklace.

She halted the treatment only after the sun set and it was time for the household to retire for the night. Her swollen hands throbbed. I urged her to get a good night's rest so that we could resume bright and early in the morning. For weeks she diligently worked on me, stopping only to breast-feed Kunsam.

After a month of this intense treatment, wonderful changes started to occur. I felt stronger and taller, and I no longer hunched over in constant suffering. The burning sensation completely vanished, along with the fever and worms. It was as if I had just discovered the fountain of health. Before, the only awareness I had of my body was the ripples of pleasure and the strain of childbirth. Now I wanted to learn more about her *chiryo*.

"Teach me," I requested.

"There is nothing to be taught. Just use your hands and begin."

I took her simple advice and began to treat myself, hitting here, pinching there, targeting the heart and neck. Eventually I began to experiment with other parts of my body. Miraculously, everywhere I kneaded the skin it grew firm, vibrant, elastic, youthful. I wanted to share my discovery with the family. Husband, my first patient, sprang to his feet, swearing loudly. The children, on the other hand, had no choice. They screamed and kicked under my sturdy hands. It was a shame Husband could not be restrained as well; it would have eased my work.

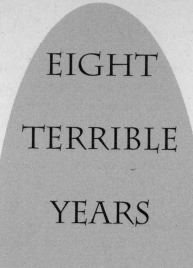

EIGHT
TERRIBLE
YEARS

After eight terrible years of marriage, Baby Sister walked out on her cheating, stealing husband, taking their young son and two daughters. The old woman silently glared as Baby Sister packed their meager belongings into a sack, unwilling to call them back, for there was no affection or bond between mother and daughter-in-law.

The morning Baby Sister arrived on our doorstep there was a loud commotion in the restaurant. Huge flames flicked from the cook's wok, and the staff ran around in a frantic panic. During all the confusion, I collided into Baby Sister and her three small children. She was stunned to see me with my butchered hair, formfitting Chinese robe, and shimmering gold earrings. The years in Soju had changed us. Little by little we had become Chinese-like. We even ate like them, lifting rice bowls to our mouths. If we did not speak, we easily passed as them.

"Is that you, Older Sister?"

"Yes," I assured her. "Where is your husband?" I asked, peering around to see if he was swept up in all the excitement.

"I left him," she stated calmly.

"That is not your choice to make."

"I have no need for him," she snorted, spitting out the words as though they left a foul taste in her mouth.

My head spun with alarm. Who ever heard of such a disgraceful thing? "There is not much for a woman outside her husband's house. You must go back to him for the sake of your children's future," I warned.

"I refuse. I wish to be free of him."

"Can you ever be truly free? Without a husband, a woman becomes an outcast with no rights of her own. Only through man and son is she made free."

"I will not return to that horrible house." She lifted her chin.

I felt tremendous pity for her. Even Crippled Sister had found happiness in her marriage, but not this one. Somehow, without her mentioning anything, I sensed he had truly wronged her beyond his fondness for *kisaengs* and gambling.

"So be it. There is no changing your mind, I see. You will stay here with us."

"I do not want to be a burden to you and your family. I will find another place for my children and me to live."

"A burden!" I was insulted. "We are a very rich family. Do you not see our business and my jewelry? We have enough for us and yours and plenty more."

"I wish to be on my own. I will find a job and support my own children. That is the only way I can be free."

"Free, free! Freedom does not feed your children. How will you keep them alive?"

"I can sew clothes and sell them for a small profit."

Since childhood, when Mother had forced each of us to learn the art of sewing, we had all despised it, especially Baby Sister. And now she was willing to do anything, even sew, to feed her children.

"Then you must let me help you set up your shop. I insist."

At last she agreed to let me assist her. I knew this was a very difficult thing for her to do, for Baby Sister shared the same headstrong streak of pride that ran through my bones and Crippled Sister's bones. Mother blamed Father for cultivating within us regal dignity to match any son's. And I knew that alone would give her the resilience to rebuild her life.

To keep her near, I purchased a two-room house down the road. I gave her a sewing machine, plenty of fabric, and ready customers, who were personal friends of mine from the restaurant and the opium business. Although her skills as a seamstress were nothing to boast about, the silk padded winter coats which she designed herself were quite popular. They were patterned after the Korean *chogori*, waist jacket, with the traditional full curved sleeves, except that the bodice brushed the floor. For extra warmth she cleverly lined the coats with chicken and duck feathers she swept up from the restaurant floor. Each week she toted away more and more sacks stuffed with feathers. Relieved, I watched her orders grow and her spirit heal.

TEN THOUSAND YEARS

The day I watched a woman lose her head for stealing a chicken to feed her child, I realized justice was vicious and unfair.

"Today is the day! Today is the day!" The news spread from one mouth to the next. The countryside buzzed, nervous, excited. Villagers and townspeople rushed off to see for themselves what all the fuss was about. Baby Sister also caught the fever. She came to fetch me with her son strapped on her back and her two daughters holding each hand.

"Come on, Older Sister. Today is the day of the great beheading!" she exclaimed, as if I had not heard the news.

"There is too much work to be done," I lied.

"It will not take too long. Hurry or we shall miss it."

A slave to curiosity, I followed her to the town's center. In the early-morning light many were already waiting. It was like a great festival where parents brought their children. Young boys performed their own mock executions in the street. The smaller ones clung tightly to their parents in anticipation of some grisly thing they did not know. Babies cried out and were hushed.

I found myself at the front, looking down at five men on their knees with their wrists bound behind their backs with hempen thongs. Before them was a freshly dug grave and on either ends stood Japanese policemen wearing long swords at their sides. The leader sat high on his white horse, and a young man, in his teens, clutched the horse's reins. The young man looked like the others, stone-faced, but I knew he was one of us by his gestures. Koreans like him were more terrible than the Japanese. They abandoned the country of their birth and were loyal to Japan. They betrayed our people and pursued our compatriot freedom fighters even more zealously than the Japanese police.

"Let their deaths be your warning against crimes committed against your emperor ruler . . ." the leader proclaimed.

Mothers and wives rushed forward to their sons and husbands, falling at their feet, crying out their names. The policemen sprang on them, picked up the women, and hurled them roughly back into the crowd.

I peered to see if I recognized a familiar face, for each one belonged to my countrymen. I searched them all. At first they appeared the same with their swollen, beaten faces, and then I was startled to see one woman among the condemned. Even camouflaged under all those bruises and cuts and men's clothing, her bold composure set her apart.

Just when I began to wonder what wrong she could have committed to deserve death, the leader announced their crimes. He spoke in a flat tone that sickened me.

"Prisoner . . . treason . . . guerrilla fighter . . . therefore . . . sentence to death . . . according to the law . . . in the name of the emperor . . . of Japan . . . Prisoner . . . stole . . ."

It was difficult for me to grasp all that he said, for his words were too official.

"The monster lies," I heard a voice whisper to another spectator. "She is no fighter. She is merely guilty of stealing a chicken to feed her child. What mother would not?"

A heavyset man with a black hood pulled over his head marched forward. His long sword glistened. No one moved as he swigged liquor from a bottle. I could feel my heart pounding as he removed the sword from its belt holster and spat on it.

The first prisoner's name was called out, and all watched as he scooted forward on his knees. The executioner held out a blindfold to cover the man's eyes, but he refused. He remained calm and dignified. The sword's shadow cut across his face as his lips moved in a secret prayer, but before he could finish, the sword swooped down. Without passion, without haste, the masked executioner chopped off the man's head and ended his young life. The head rolled once, twice, three times, then plunged into the pit. A great roar went up as blood spurted into the crowd.

One by one the men's heads fell until it came time for the woman. She crawled to the same spot. Only her eyes showed any signs of emotion as she shot her executioner a final cold glare before closing them.

"Mommy! Mommy!" a small voice cried.

The woman turned suddenly pale. She looked out toward the weeping child. Now her face erupted.

"Mommy! Mommy!" The girl tried to wriggle out from hands that restrained her.

The woman's lower lip quivered and she was no longer calm. She fought to free her bound wrists. The two policemen lunged forward and forced her face down on the ground, smearing her pale cheeks in a thick puddle of blood.

The executioner seemed a little less steady than before. His hands trembled as he brought the sword down. He missed his mark and sliced the side of her neck. Blood squirted up like a fountain from the large gash. He quickly raised his sword a second time and put her out of her misery. A few stray drops of blood splashed my face and jacket. One landed in my mouth. I wanted to vomit, but I forced the food back down.

Unable to stomach more, I turned my head away. Why did we Koreans have to lose our country only to suffer some more in a foreign place like this?

After the last head fell, the slaughter carnival was officially closed. Family members of the victims returned to their homes empty-handed, because the punishment did not end with the beheading. Instead, the heads were collected and piled into one stack, then mounted on wooden stakes and labeled with their exaggerated crimes. During the day they were displayed along the main road and at night they were locked away from do-gooders, who might reunite the heads with the bodies which lay in the shallow grave hastily sprinkled with a thin layer of dirt.

On the way home, I could not hold down my emotions any longer and I vomited all over the street, wanting to purge myself of death's sickly taste. As long as I live I would remember those bodiless heads, the eyes frozen open in horror and lolling tongues that licked the dirt. I longed to weep but was too frightened to show my tears.

Days later, I learned about the fate of the little girl. My heart ached for the pitiful child, whose mother lost her life for stealing a chicken and then bribing the police official who had caught her. Something I did every day. No doubt the bribe was not substantial enough to spare her life. With no one brave enough to claim the orphan, she was placed inside a circle of rocks and tied to a post, then a group of ravenous dogs were released on her. I heard that her tiny white dress was ripped violently from her body as they gnawed her tender flesh. I wept then.

The lingering metallic taste of fresh blood constantly reminded me of the painful contradiction I lived every day. I was making friends with the enemy, and because that enemy was losing the war, many innocent people were being massacred in Shanghai, Nanking, Hankow, Chungking, and all over Manchuria.

Secretly I supported the Korean Independence fighters exiled in China. I generously gave the guerrilla fighters food supplies and gold when they came, but they came often and always after dark. Soon I discovered that these gangs of outcasts were greedy for money. If people refused to donate to the cause, they would be executed on the spot. I did not know whom to trust anymore. Here, friends and countrymen were my enemies as well. I did not feel safe.

Gory nightmares of mutilated corpses and the little white

bloody dress played over and over in my sleep. Gradually the nightmares became worse, as I saw my family's heads rolling at the bottom of the pit. Their crimes were my crimes. The leader pronounced me the "Opium Madam." I tried to run to my children and Husband, picking up my feet as fast as I could, but the same plot of earth stayed below me. Then I felt the executioner's hand sweep me up and shove my ear down on the ground, dripping with my family's blood. I pressed my eyes closed, but still I saw the sword high above my head. The blade was dull and tarnished, and the executioner's spit dripped from the tip. One night I felt the edge pierce my neck. This dream finally convinced me it was time to return home to Korea, to be among those who truly cared about our safety and not about our money.

"Husband, let us leave this place and go back to our own country."

"Our opportunities are better here."

"They may be; however, we are still in danger. At least back in Korea, we will be near our families. It has been so long since we have seen them. I regret I was not there to properly grieve the passing of my father and older brother. I wish to be near my mother and grandmother when their times also come."

The sense of loss was so sharp that my throat ached. Until now I had hidden my feeling from Husband, not wanting to burden him, but the news of Father's passing affected me deeply. He had suffered greatly during his last moments of life, choking for air his lungs could not hold. If only I could have been there to treat him with *chiryo*. It pleased me to know, though, that he was buried in his favorite *jogori*, with his hair coiled beneath his black horsehair hat. When other elderly men his age felt pressured to cut their topknots, Father kept his because it symbolized everything he was—a Korean man. And that was what we were, Koreans. Koreans believed it was the duty of the surviving relatives to comfort and to pay tribute to the dying.

Husband understood the depth of my loss for the first time. He carefully thought over everything I had said before answering. "As always, you are right, *Yobo*. Thank you for reminding me of our obligations."

"Thank you," I breathed, the tightness in my chest gone.

"But I do not wish to return to my father's home. Let my older sister and her family continue to live there with Grandmother. Over the years I have become accustomed to more luxury. We shall buy a great piece of land and build our new home on it. It shall be twice as spacious and grand."

"As you please," I agreed to pacify him. "The South has plenty of land. Shall we build there?"

"The South has only oxen and cows."

"We can buy a farm and plant crops. I have heard the future is in the South where the soil is rich. The dirt will never run out. Its value will surely multiply."

"You have heard incorrectly. South Korean land is just like a woman's legs. Nothing grows on that soil, but the North has heavy industries and rich mines. We shall find a place near Pyongyang, among the civilized townspeople."

I had learned over the years that it was useless to argue with Husband. With maturity he had inherited my stubbornness. "If that is your wish, near Pyongyang it is." I gave in, wanting to leave as soon as possible.

"I shall go at the end of the month and find us a home befitting our wealth." His voice sounded a little too eager.

"How long will it be before you send for us?" I asked suspiciously.

"No more than a month or two," he answered. "It is an important mission I go on. It must not be done in haste."

I worried that entire morning before he left, and every hour he was absent. Three months and seven days later Husband returned, his sack empty and with no deed of ownership. He had frivolously spent all the money in *kisaeng* houses all over northern China, Manchuria, and Korea, forgetting the time and his purpose. I was more furious than jealous. The money he took was enough to buy a whole province and a houseful of servants. But there was no time to sulk over wasted money; land had to be bought quickly, for more rumors were circulating. Rumors of freedom for Korea. The gossip told of three powerful nations, America, China, and the United Kingdom, announcing their support for Korean Independence in the Cairo Declaration on December 1, 1943. Hope swelled in my heart, for I knew it was only a matter of time before the Japanese were defeated.

A few months later, I went myself, wrapping Kunsam on my back because an adulterer could not be trusted with large amounts of money.

The train carried me across the Yalu River and down through the picturesque mountain ranges of our beautiful country. As we were passing through the neighborhood of Dolsandong in Chengungni, the morning rays set fire to the sky in a way I had never seen before. This was the place. On this piece of earth I had witnessed the essence of Korea. "The Land of the Morning Calm." I had found what I had been searching for. Here, Husband's legacy, our sons' sons, would forever inherit richness and status long after we were buried. With this in mind, I bought it all. All forty square *ri*, two hundred and thirty-eight square miles of it. As far as the eye could see in every direction, the land was ours.

In early August I returned home, pleased with what I had accomplished. And exactly a year later, on August 6 and 9, 1945, the Americans dropped the atomic bomb on Japan. The unbelievable news spread wildly. Fellow Koreans spilled into the streets, crying with joy. We had a country to return to! We had our home again!

That day I rushed to all the banks to empty our accounts, but the banks were closed. Husband and I decided not to wait for their doors to reopen, and instead we retrieved the fortune still hidden in our floors, walls, and ceilings.

Later that evening we stood in a stack of paper money carefully sorting the larger bills and packing them with the gold. What could not be safely carried across the border was stuffed back into the secret panels in the house, never to be counted again, at least not by our hands.

The following morning, I rose before the others and hurried to the train station, because tickets had to be bought that same day. The ticket office was engulfed by rushing bodies. Practically every Korean in Soju was returning home. All I could hear were excited voices and curses. A shoving match broke out. I felt the air squeezed out of me as I fought to hold my place in the crowd. The harder I struggled, though, the farther back I was driven.

Fed up, I glanced around for the tallest, strongest-looking

brute in the crowd of black-top heads. I found him off to the side, tearing at a whole duck with his teeth.

"Look here," I shouted, drawing his attention. "I want you to buy ten tickets for me."

"Do it yourself. Can you not see I am busy?"

I would not let him intimidate me. "If you do as I ask, I will serve you as many ducks as you can eat and anything else you desire at my restaurant."

He torpedoed through the crowd. The bodies toppled to the side as he led me to the very front. It was a smart thing I did and it only cost me five roasted ducks, seven bowls of rice, three yams, and two yellow melons—a price well worth paying.

First, I rushed to Baby Sister's house to give her four tickets. She acted as though it was any other workday, hovering over her sewing machine intently.

"Take these." I fanned them under her nose. "Bring what you must and meet us at the train station quickly."

"Save your money. Here I will remain."

"Nonsense. Our country is ours once again. It is safe to go back."

"I am staying."

"This is not your home. You are not Chinese. You must come back with us," I insisted, shoving the tickets into her hand.

"I told you once I will never return to that horrible house. That worthless, cheating husband of mine cannot find me here."

"What about our elderly mother? It is our duty to be near her now that Father and Older Brother have passed away."

"I am sure our nephew is taking good care of Mother."

"She will be worried about you and the children. Do not cause her any more grief."

"Tell her we are doing fine." She resumed her sewing. I left the tickets behind, hoping that she might reconsider and join us at the station.

I ran all the way home. When I arrived, our belongings were packed and ready to go. Husband had secured several rickshas to take us and our luggage to the train station. There were no regrets at leaving our large red-brick house and the restaurant business. To me, it was only a house on borrowed land. Husband, on the other hand, could not tear his eyes away from it as we drove away. Here in this house, in this country, he had grown into his manhood.

Although it was still early, an enormous mob had already gathered. Even with our tickets, boarding the train was a battle. Husband and I locked our arms around the children, protecting them from frantic passengers. We clung together, afraid to be separated.

Somehow we clambered aboard the train and found a spot to sit on the floor. As the train heaved forward, I felt for the first time that day a sad loss. We were leaving without Baby Sister and her children. I searched for her frantically on the platform, but she never appeared. For hours I thought about her, because thinking was all there was room to do. Cramped, Husband and I sat back to back, using the other for support. The younger boys sprawled across our laps, and Yongwoon and Dukwah leaned together, foreheads locked, whispering secrets. I watched them, admiring their close relationship, something I was never allowed to share with my own brother. Their friendship comforted me; I knew that they would entertain each other. But for my two youngest boys, the restricted space and boredom drained them of all their youthful energy. They remained idle, dozing in and out of sleep.

Besides eating, visiting the toilet was the only activity. People blocked the aisles waiting to relieve themselves. I did not mind the long lines; it offered an opportunity to extend my legs. Most people waited their turn in an orderly manner; however, those with weaker bladders pushed to the front. Sometimes I stood for an hour or more. Unfortunately, the wait was disappointing. Although I had lost my sense of smell, the poignant stench of human waste piqued my taste buds. Traces of excrement covered the floor, the door handle, and all the walls of the sealed-off stall. Having ridden the train before, I was prepared with sheets of torn paper. Others preferred hankies they washed and hung out to dry behind their seats. Those who did not even have old newspapers to wipe themselves with left their brown fingerprints smudged on the walls. There was no window for ventilation, just a single round hole between my feet that showed the moving tracks below. Only the muscles in my legs kept me from falling to my death as I squatted.

The train halted suddenly at the Yalu River. It would not cross over the border. We had to get off and walk over the bridge ourselves. People cheered and cried for our motherland. I looked at my children, who knew nothing of the beauty of their own country. Yongwoon and Dukwah, my two eldest, were so young when we had left; their memories were lost in images of China. And my two youngest, who were born on Chinese soil, would now take their first steps on our people's land. Choked with emotion, I was returning home a rich woman with four healthy children, three of whom were sons. Home!

We boarded another train, which would carry us safely through the Korean highlands. In the city of Bonchung, the train was delayed to refuel at the station. The children begged to be allowed to explore the new sights; their pleading faces looked so endearing that Husband spoke up. "Let them go. Let them discover for themselves the greatness of our country."

"It is too dangerous. They may get lost."

"We are home. Let them have a look," he said, and handed each child some coins to spend.

"You spoil them." My voice was light with pleasure.

"And why not? They are worth spoiling."

The children giggled and eyed their money, anxious to buy sweets.

"Be careful," I warned. "Stay close to the tracks and be back when the whistle sounds."

"Yes, Mother," they echoed happily as they jumped off the train and scurried about, inspecting the vendors' carts. I watched as long as I could, until their black heads blended into the crowd. The first whistle blew loudly and they did not come running back. Panic overcame my cool composure and I leapt off the train and went hunting for them. I scanned the entire area, afraid to blink. When I reached the end of the long platform, my eyes locked on to a group of Japanese soldiers stripped of their long swords and emblems. They sat along the margins of the tracks, drowning their defeat in liquor. Tears streamed down their distraught faces. One after another, they finished their drinks, then slammed the empty glass bottle on the ground and plunged the sharp jagged edge into their guts.

Afraid, I dashed back to the train and there I found my family in the middle of a vast throng of exuberant Koreans, all milling around together, holding hands.

"At last," a voice cried out, and others followed and waved their hands in solidarity.

"Yongwoon's father, what is happening?"

"We are free! The Japanese have surrendered."

I could not believe my ears. On that day—August 15, 1945—thirty-six years of colonial oppression had come to an end with Japan's unconditional surrender. "*Mansei!*" The tiny car thundered as the call was taken up again and again in unison by hundreds of voices. "*Mansei! Mansei!*" No other word embodied our spirits and the spirit of our nation better, for it meant ten thousand years. The word was filled with a hope of a new tomorrow and a new free people.

"*Mansei!*" I joined in, charged with elation. I had never hollered so loudly in my life and it felt incredible.

Energized, the Koreans on the train began beating the Japanese civilians, dragging them from their seats and forcing them onto the roof. The gentleman beside us was brutally kicked and pushed out. I had only noticed him when he offered the children candy from his pack. Dukwah sobbed uncontrollably.

"Dukwah-yah, be silent. Hold your tears." Husband tried to soothe her, but she could not stop her weeping. And the more she wept, the more the others glared at us as if we had committed treason.

"Oh, a Japanese sympathizer!" The angry voices moved in on her.

I was afraid for her safety, and I acted quickly. "Foolish girl, you shame us!" I said sharply, then raised my hand high in the air and slapped her hard across the face for everyone to see. I had to do it, though it pained me to hit her. I knew she was only a child and did not, could not, see beyond the gentleman's kindness. For most of her life, she had lived among Japanese officers and soldiers whose generosity spilled over her daily. How could she be made to comprehend that those same men were her oppressors? Nor could I explain to the others how we had lived among the Japanese, who had provided security and favors. Neither side could be explained, so I did what was necessary, what was required of me. I had to show the others the depth of our nationalism. They began to cheer again.

For a long time, Dukwah sat with her face buried between her knees, crying silently to herself.

"If you show them your pity, you will bring trouble on all of us. Your tears cannot save him now," I whispered lovingly in her ear, but she refused to look up at me.

"Dry your eyes, pretty girl. This is a day of celebration." Husband always knew how to cheer her up. He tore a rice sack into ten equal squares and drew our *Taekuk*, Korean flag, on each one, using a piece of black charcoal to draw out the long and short broken lines and center circle of *yin* and *yang* divisions. He gave the first one to Dukwah, who stopped sobbing. The rest he passed out among the passengers. When others begged for more, I took off my silk slip and ripped it into squares for him to draw on. Soon flags flew from every hand, every window. For the first time, men, women, old, young, embraced each other freely and openly. A wave of patriotism bonded us all. Then all at once, voices rose into a chorus of traditional folk songs, songs of our nation that had for so long been sealed inside our hearts.

A few times we had to walk alongside the train as it huffed its way up the steep paths, for there were so many passengers. Along the tracks our people were dressed in the clothes of our forefathers, chanting "*Mansei!*" They had thrown off their drab, ungainly Japanese-imposed garments and proudly displayed our snow-white dress. As the train chugged on by, their fluttering sleeves saluted our return—a glorious sight. How ironic: the railroad, which served the Japanese military and which symbolized abuse and forced Korean labor, was the very thing that carried out *Taekuk* from one liberated town to the next for all to see.

With family and land, I happily embarked on this perfect life, this splendid time. We were free to dress, act, and speak Korean openly in our homes and on the streets, and the Russian troops would help us maintain our culture on the north side of the 38th parallel. The Americans would assist our people on the south. We welcomed our liberators because we believed and trusted in them. Tragically, none of us knew then that this imaginary line drawn by a single stoke of someone's pen would forever divide our country and destroy 1,277 years of unity, something even the Japanese were not bold enough to do.

Husband moved us into the former landlord's house, a kind of castle perched high on a hill, overlooking the crops of the laborers. In each room, servants were poised to please our every whim. We lived a fairy-tale life with Husband as the king and me as the queen. And as we were the supreme rulers, our laws were absolute over those who dwelled within our kingdom. We taxed the farmers and lived richly off their crops. I looked forward to a life of early leisure—to be a wife, mother, and queen was enough again.

Then our castle cracked at the foundation. The Russians installed Korean Communists to assume control over the government. By February 1946, a well-known freedom fighter named Kim, Ilsung was chosen by the Soviets to lead the so-called People's Committee. The legendary hero Kim, Ilsung was known to be in his sixties with gray hair. This one who now appeared was only in his early thirties—an impostor.

I was neither for nor against the Reds, but they demanded all that I had. In March of that year, the Land Reform Ordinance was passed. All factories and other enterprises formerly belonging to the Japanese, pro-Japanese elements, national traitors, churches, landlords, were confiscated and redistributed. And any other undesirables who did not fall under one of these categories were lumped together as anti-Communist.

Conveniently, we were labeled and all forty square *ri* of our precious land was seized after we lived there barely a year. They simply took it one day. We were told it was part of the new government's way of establishing itself since a large percentage of North Korea was farmland. There was nothing we could do. We had no choice but to accept our loss and start over. Using the remainder of the money we had smuggled in from China, we bought another plot of land. It lacked the breathtaking scenery, but at least it belonged to us.

Before we had a chance to settle in, our land was stolen

from us again. We had nothing left, and nothing made sense anymore. We had our country back but no home. The People's Committees handed over our property to landless peasants, but kept the title for themselves because only the state had the right to own land. Although these peasants enthusiastically joined the Reds, the harder they worked, the more taxes they were required to pay. Now they languished in worse economic hardship than before the "reforms."

Soon, many former landowners, farmers, and city people fled south across the 38th parallel to find refuge. Although the border was secured by the Soviet command in late 1945, it was still possible to find a way to South Korea up until late 1947. Husband refused to abandon the North; thus he took the family back to his childhood home against my wishes. Stubbornly he held on to the hope that conditions would improve.

Eight years had passed since we departed for China, leaving Husband's older sister to care for Grandmother. We walked down streets I had not seen for so long, noting many changes. Merchant shops and buildings erected by the previous Japanese owners were now vacant.

When we arrived at the gate, I noticed the house was well kept and clean. No doubt the money I faithfully sent over the years had sustained Grandmother and the household in our absence. Inside, an old waxen-faced man was sitting with Grandmother in the courtyard. I was stunned. Had Grandmother found herself a husband in her old age?

"Sister-in-Law, who is that old man?" I inquired.

"Ah, he is Grandmother's younger cousin. He came to live with us two years ago," she informed me.

Grandfather was seventy-five years old, thirteen years younger than Grandmother, but he looked her senior. Old age had chipped away their ancient memories. Grandmother was especially pitiful; she no longer recognized her grandson or her great-grandchildren. All she cared about was polishing her small silver knife. And when she tired of cleaning it, she provoked turmoil in the house.

Peace deteriorated when Husband's sister and her family fled to Seoul, for the twelve of us could not all fit into the main room, the only chamber we could afford to heat. Grandmother fell into a rage. Just the sight of my children sparked fury in the old woman.

"Where are my grandchildren!" She snapped her toothless jaw.

"They are right here, Grandmother."

"What are they doing in my house?! Who are these little *gae secki*, dog children?!"

"Do not call them that." I came to their defense, restraining my temper.

"*Gae secki! Gae secki!* I should kill them all and eat them up." She clawed for a chunk of their flesh.

I fought with her endlessly but could not tame her tongue, as the house became a battlefield. She refused to use the outhouse, so the children and I called her *Dong*, doo-doo, Grandmother. She would purposely wait until we were all out of the room, then defecate, dragging her bare bottom around, leaving a curve of excrement to bake on the warm *ondul* floor. It left the foulest stench, forcing me to let the cold air blow into every corner of the house, purifying it.

Unable to tolerate the bickering, Husband spent the last of our coins on liquor. He drank more than ever. I blamed the decrepit man and woman for all my misery, and out of sheer desperation, I isolated them from the rest of the household. I carried her into the innermost room and bolted the door shut. I tried locking Grandfather away, too, but he could still unlatch the door.

"You wicked whore." His hands whacked my head.

"Be quiet, old fool, or I will toss you in the well," I threatened.

"You will not!" He pulled my hair, and then he grabbed one of my good plates and smashed it over his bald head. Blood dribbled down his forehead. "I do not want to be thrown in a well. No, no."

He threatened the air with a chipped piece of glass. Tidal waves of sobs poured from him. The blood rolled down his cheeks, giving the impression he was shedding tears of red. His deranged sight was too much for even my hardened heart, so I let him be. But as far as I was concerned, he and *Dong* Grandmother did not exist. I stopped bathing and grooming them. I wanted their foul crusty nature to be worn on the outside for everyone to see. I could not wait to bury these two barely living shells deep in the ground with a mound of dirt so high above them that their spiteful spirits could not escape and haunt us.

"Why should I break my back caring for people who want to eat my children?" I reasoned.

Day after day, week after week, *Dong* Grandmother's shrill voice vibrated through the walls.

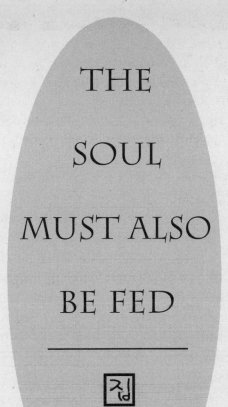

THE
SOUL
MUST ALSO
BE FED

When I was growing up, the stink of burning incense greeted each morning. For a long time, Mother would sit erect before the jade Buddha, rubbing her string of beads and chanting the same ritual prayers. She would stay until the end of the incense reddened and fell, because if the fallen ash broke it would bring a bad omen.

I chanted, too, more out of fear than anything else. To me, religion was all about evil omens, demons, and ghosts. I chanted for them to leave me alone. I was careful not to ask for too much, because for each wish a person had to bow one hundred times. No wonder the monks at Mother's temple were so frail and hollow.

Father, on the other hand, followed the Confucian ethic system, which was, in a way, his religion. He left the superstitious nonsense to his wife and daughters. He had no use for them, especially the white man's God. Father despised the Big Nose Christian missionaries, who preached their white God to our people. They threatened the very foundation of our social system that separated the rich from the poor and the men from the women. Their scriptures promised equality and their free Sunday-school classes offered the means. For the first time it gave the *sangnoms*, unpersons, and women a chance to change their miserable destiny.

"They are vulgar intruders and we are cultured people," Father warned us. "It is the religion of beasts. Why else would their language be so harsh to listen to?"

Long after I had left Father's house, I heeded his warning about the Big Noses. Whenever I heard someone yell, "Big Nose," I barred the gate. I managed to keep them out until one came knocking disguised as one of us.

She was a *kwonsaneem*, woman elder, from the Changjungnee church. Her salt-and-pepper hair was pulled tight in a bun, revealing her square expressive face. She wore a dress that was patched along the seams, though well mended and clean. She clutched a leather-bound black book next to her heart and around her neck she wore a golden cross on a delicate chain. It was the symbol of the Christians and she was on a mission to spread the praises of her adopted religion.

An idiot, I thought. Only idiots worked for free. Happy to be poor. Content in their tattered clothes. And for what? To serve a foreign man who was not her husband. Her disposition intrigued me, though, and yet at the same time annoyed me. She was full of goodness, her words always positive and kind, unlike the monks with their solemn mood and drawn faces. It made me trust her less.

"Yongwoon's mother?" Her sweet voice floated into the courtyard.

I crouched low behind the great cauldrons filled with *kimchee* as Dukwah stalled her at the gate.

"My mother is not home. She walked to the market at the edge of town," I coached her to say.

"When will she return?" *Kwonsaneem* asked, her tone bright.

"She usually returns at night," Dukwah answered.

"Well, tell your mother I will visit again."

And she went away peacefully till the next Sunday, the Sunday after that, and the Sunday after that. There was no escape from her unwanted persistence.

"Yongwoon's mother!"

"My mother had to leave," Dukwah apologized.

"Then I shall wait for her," she announced.

"But I fear it will be way after dark before she returns." Dukwah stumbled over her words.

"You have a lovely house." *Kwonsaneem*'s voice sounded nearer.

I sat quietly behind the cauldrons. A small stool was permanently installed for my convenience since it had become a weekly hide-and-seek game.

"Ah! Yongwoon's mother, there you are." Her voice boomed above my head. I was discovered. "Shall we go?" She smiled broadly.

"Thank you, but I have no time for your God or any other Gods. My children must be fed."

"Good woman, you cannot feed just the body. The soul must also be fed."

"But your Christianity is the religion of beasts."

"Do I look beastly to you?"

"No," I answered hesitantly.

"Our God teaches love and justice. Through Him I have learned to love all His creatures."

"I do not wish to love freely. That is the trade of whores."

"A whore who accepts Christ into her heart is a far better person than one who denies His name."

"Are you claiming I am below a whore?" I asked hotly.

"Those are your words, not mine."

"Out of my house."

"Do not pretend anger, because you are afraid. I was once like you." Her voice was calm and controlled, unlike mine.

"I do not fear you or your religion."

"Then come with me."

Out of sheer frustration I followed her. The road leading to the church was crowded with people on rooftops and in trees. They had all come to hear the famous Reverend Kim, Ikdo. Many traveled from far-off provinces to hear his sermon.

The first thing I noticed was the raised cross, its sharp ends jabbed toward earth, sky, and oceans on either side. For so many years I had looked upon these two crossed sticks as symbols of seduction and imported corruption. Now I was allowing this bothersome woman to infect me with its poisonous venom.

Inside, I expected to see carved faces of demonic ogres with horns, grotesquely stretched lips, and flared snouts like the ones I chanted under as a child. Instead, I saw lavish stained-glass windows, a choir, benches, and a prominent brass cross. To my dismay, she led me to the front row. All around us men and women sat with their heads sunk on their breasts and their eyes closed. Were they sleeping? No, lips were moving.

From the back a wave of voices rose as Reverend Kim made his way to the podium, the hem of his black gown billowed with air. It seemed unlikely that this ordinary man had a direct line to the heavens. No halo illuminated him. He looked like every other man in his early forties, perhaps better fed. He removed the small black Bible from under his armpit and stroked it fondly before placing it on the podium. The only other item I noticed was a glass of boiled barley tea, which he sipped occasionally.

"Let us pray." His voice rang clear.

The congregation closed their eyes and bowed their heads as he fanned his arms above us. I kept my eyes open to study everyone's face, to see if anyone would slip into a trance. His voice overpowered the room as he gave thanks again and again.

"Amen," all repeated on cue when he finished.

The entire morning I listened to him speak fervently of a mysterious man named Jesus Christ, whose face sprouted a thick, full brown beard. Somehow his mother was a virgin and he died for my sins. Being a mother myself, I knew that was impossible. What nonsense. The stained-glass windows intrigued me more; their jeweled colored rays danced on the floor.

As we were leaving, *Kwonsaneem* asked me, "Do you feel changed?"

"I cannot say I do." I yawned.

"Do you not wish to go to heaven when you die?"

"When I die, I die. Where can I go but in the ground? I cannot do anything about it."

I was certain that was the last I would ever see of her, but *Kwonsaneem* intended to save my soul. The following week she dragged me back, to the same front seat. As before, the colored rays held my attention.

"Did His words touch your heart?" she inquired as we left the church.

"No," I answered.

"Do not fret. God has His own time for you and—"

"But I do not have time for Him." I stepped over her words. "I beg you not to come calling on me again."

The next Sunday, I found myself sitting beside her in that church again, itching with annoyance at her determination and loathing myself for being weak. Why me? Why was she so eager to convert me?

That morning the clouds clung tightly to the sun, preventing the stained-glass lights from sparkling. I gazed around the room completely bored, wishing something amusing would happen. Reverend Kim's voice swelled and fell. Sobs and sighs sounded from the whole congregation. It was as if he was bewitching them. As a game, I concentrated intently on his every word, willing his voice to crack; then it struck me that he was a cultivated man and not a peasant's son. I had always believed that Christians were bred from the lower class. Perplexed, I listened further, for he spoke very well. Without my being aware of it, his gentle wisdom and goodness weakened my resistance. Not once did he invoke demons or mention ghosts. Instead he spoke about his Jesus with relish and sincerity. Every passage he read from his black book was uplifting and enlightening. My ears opened to his teachings.

"God gave His only son to die on the cross for us, so that we may be reborn and our sins forgiven," he proclaimed.

These were the same words I had heard before. As I listened to them once more, drinking in their profound meaning, I felt some unseen force inside me, massaging, softening my callused heart. Instantly thirty-five years of jealousy, dishonesty, lust, and pride were exposed. I saw the person I had been and the sins I had committed against others. My heart felt heavy, I wanted to be purged of my burden. I wanted this Jesus to help me. At that moment when I asked to be saved, the light of the sun seemed to flood the room. Before I knew it, my legs carried me before Reverend Kim.

"Forgive me, for I am a sinner," I cried.

He stepped from his podium and brushed his hand across my forehead. Even in my pool of misery and guilt, the electric charge of God passed through him and into my soul, sending it soaring over the whole earth. I saw people of different races, animals of various shapes, and oceans filled with exotic creatures.

There is His house, among many witnesses, I accepted Jesus Christ as my savior. Dropping to my knees, I confessed to hiding Crippled Sister in the bushes, dealing opium, hoarding money, jealousy of *kisaengs*, locking *Dong* Grandmother away, threatening Grandfather . . . I cried for what seemed like hours. Tears flowed from my eyes and nose, so many salty tears.

"Forgive me, Jesus, forgive me, Jesus," I repented.

"He has already forgiven you."

Nothing in my life had been as sweet as those glorious moments when I had known freedom and clarity. I was completely free of desire, free of temptation, free of greed, and free of myself. I never felt more alive or more blessed. The old me had long ago lost the capacity to feel true compassion for anyone besides my own. Wealth and power had twisted my mind into believing I was above others. Now I was filled with boundless affection for all God's creatures. How I longed to see heaven, but I knew God had a greater purpose for me on earth. In the meantime, I had to make amends to the two old neglected folks I had mistreated.

When I arrived home my face was still flushed and my blood boiled with new energy. I threw the door wide open to the inner room where *Dong* Grandmother was forgotten. Spiders had knit winter blankets in the corners of the ceiling. Although it was only a few hours past noon, darkness engulfed the room. I had long removed the oil lamp and bolted the windows shut to muffle her threats.

There in the blackness, a human animal slept in her own excrement. A pang of remorse stabbed my heart at the sight of the eighty-pound invalid. I swept *Dong* Grandmother out of her dingy, filthy prison, and I lowered her into a pool of warm water. I washed her with much care until the sallow face was again recognizable. Only a few tufts of long gray straggly hair clung to her scalp and not a tooth remained in her shriveled old mouth.

I cloaked her in my best cotton slip and I cut up a fine blanket to make her a diaper. Massaging her threadlike muscles, I begged for forgiveness, but it was too late. She was lost in the private mazes of her mind.

"Hurt, hurt." She sucked on her lower lip like an infant, her dry tongue slipping in and out. It was shrunken so small, no doubt from years of hurling many curses. However, none of that mattered any longer. All was forgotten. That night I laid the two old ones over the warmest spot on the heated floor. Husband and the children looked on, confused.

"Why are you being so kind to Grandmother and Grandfather?" Husband inquired suspiciously.

"I found Jesus," I replied.

Husband reacted as if I had said I found a stray dog. He did not ask any questions, but I expected it. Over the last few years, we hardly spoke, and when we did we fought about *kisaengs* or his drinking or my sharp tongue. In my prayers, I asked just one thing for myself. I asked God to give me back my husband. Though he was in my presence every night, I missed him.

Meanwhile, I waited on the old folks endlessly. I coaxed the children to do the same. "Children, come rub *Dong* Grandmother's shoulders and I will buy you rice cakes," I would bribe them.

"No, she will fry us up and eat us," Kunil cried.

"Come see, she has no teeth to eat you with."

"No," they protested, then skittered away.

As hard as I tried, nothing worked, so I alone tended to the old people. From memory, I recited past sermons into their deaf ears before they drifted to sleep. I was determined to reach their souls somehow before death claimed their bodies.

"God's love is sweeter than a mother's milk." I used food references to capture *Dong* Grandmother's attention, for food was the only thing she still responded to. Occasionally I would hear a sigh or the same gummed response: "Hurt, hurt."

In the middle of one of the Ten Commandments, "Thou shalt not steal," she spoke at last.

"Fetch your reverend," she said weakly, reaching out for my hand. Her small frail fingers were cold and dry.

"Yes, I will bring him in the morning."

She paused to fill her failing lungs again to speak. "Tomorrow will be too late. I am dying, Hongyong-yah."

It took me a moment to swallow the lump in my throat. She had never called me by my name before. "Nonsense. You have just come back to us."

"Please, my time is here." Tears filmed in her eyes.

"*Yobo*, we must do as she asks." I shook Husband up from his sleep.

"She does not know the time of her own death."

"I beg you, *Yobo*, do as she requests."

I pleaded and pleaded until his ears burned. Finally, he went out with his shoulders bent forward. While he was gone, I propped *Dong* Grandmother's head on my lap.

"Rest yourself; the reverend will be here shortly."

"Have you seen this place called heaven?" she questioned, fear ringing in her voice.

I knew why she was asking. All her life she had lived entirely in her flesh. Now with death upon her and the body betraying her, she was terrified of the unknown.

"It is a wonderful place. A place where there is no pain or fear or loneliness." I repeated what I had heard.

She hesitated a moment before asking, "Can anyone go?"

"Yes." I clutched her hand tightly. "His gates are always opened to those who wish to enter."

"Yes . . . yes . . . I think I would like to visit that place." She sighed, relieved. For a long time she lay so still with her eyes shut, I wondered if she was gone. Then her lids fluttered at the sound of approaching footsteps. Reverend Kim led the way. Husband came in next, followed by the Reverend's bronze-faced wife. The couple toted matching Bibles under their arms.

Everyone, including the smallest babe, gathered around *Dong* Grandmother. Reverend Kim read a long passage from the Bible and then together we sang hymns late into the night, waiting for *Dong* Grandmother's spirit to leave her body; instead, she fell asleep. So, with a yawn and a final inspirational word, the tired couple parted.

"See, she is not dead; she is only senile." Husband scowled and crawled into bed.

"You were right," I apologized, tucking the children under the covers beside him.

Near midnight, *Dong* Grandmother began to mutter and toss and turn her head. I sat beside her, wiping the beads of sweat from her brow with a cool cloth. She opened her dark eyes wide. As I peered into them, I could see there was an emptiness, the sign of death. I woke the family once more.

"She is leaving," I announced.

"She will outlive us all," Husband grumbled, rubbing the sleep away with his sleeve.

"What is *Dong* Grandmother looking at, Mother?" Dukwah inquired.

Dong Grandmother was staring at the ceiling as though something wonderful was there. The dullness in her eyes had dissipated and suddenly they were clear, the sharpest I had ever seen them. She flung out her arms, hugging empty space.

"Angels!" she called out, twirling her fingers before her. "Angels are dancing all around my head. They want to hold my hands." We saw only the shadow of the flickering light from the oil lamp. At once she sprang up.

"Yes, I will hold your hand." She uttered her final words as the door to her soul was opened and her spirit was free to soar. Now empty, the withered body sank back down. So tranquil. The lines on her aged brow had softened. Her smiling eyes were still wide open, gazing up at the ceiling. I did not have the heart to move her that night, so the family slept with *Dong* Grandmother one last time.

The following morning, I rose early. There were many arrangements to be made for the burial. If I had not accepted Christ, things would have been done differently for the dead. Before, the body would have been exorcised quickly to avoid bringing misfortune into the house. Now I leisurely prepared *Dong* Grandmother, comforted in the security that no wicked spirits would loosen themselves from the flesh of the dead.

As I was about the bathe her, I found a coin pouch hidden beneath her skirt. Inside I discovered the long-forgotten silver knife which *Dong* Grandmother loved to polish so diligently. All this time, she had cradled it against her feverish body. To my surprise, however, the silver glistened. There was not a trace of dull tarnish. I wondered who could have polished it for her. I questioned the children and Husband, but their faces were blank. The more I searched for an explanation, the more I was convinced that *Dong* Grandmother did dance with the angels.

TEN
TOO
MANY
DISHES

With *Dong* Grandmother's passing, I had stepped closer to my own mortality, and yet I felt like I could accomplish anything, even learn letters. This desire went against Father's strick beliefs. "A virtuous woman cannot count dishes correctly though they number fewer than ten" was one of his favorite proverbs.

My yearning for knowledge quelled any fear of punishment or mockery. Eagerly I went to church, where the members welcomed me. There were no barriers or obstacles to battle with because I was a woman; they simply handed me a book and pencil of my own to keep.

They taught me how to read and write by studying the Bible. It took all the mind power I could muster, but I listened in a euphoric state, gulping in the words as though they were pure water. Soon I discovered I had the ability to memorize the sounds of the ten vowels and fourteen consonants of *Hangul*, our Korean alphabet. A long time ago King Sejong had designed the simple alphabet. It was his wish for all his people, even the laborers, to communicate with him, because only the privileged few understood the complicated Chinese characters. A scholar himself, King Sejong studied the principles of phonetics and tailored the twenty-four letters of *Hangul* to express every possible sound of the human voice. Surely he was in heaven, and someday I look forward to thanking him myself.

The words flowed. I read aloud at home, in the streets. How I loved the way the sentences rolled off my tongue. I was so proud of my Bible and notebook, I walked the three miles to church with them in full view for everyone to see. I was never without them, in case at any moment I wanted to jot down a phrase, a quote, names of friends or flowers. There was no end to this alphabet game.

Before bed each night, I reread my notes and studied the Bible, savoring its rich lessons. Right there in bold print, for anyone to read, was the message of love. God treasured all his children equally, regardless of gender. For the first time in my life, I was truly content simply being a person, not a wife, not a mother, not a woman. A person.

This awakening drastically altered my life. Husband called me mad and stopped me before I gave away all our belongings. I was not mad, just extremely happy. It brought me much joy to see other women walk around in my donated silk dresses and warm padded coats while I modestly wore hemp and cotton.

I enjoyed giving things away. Only once did I bring something home for myself. On my way to church one morning, a strange sight captured my attention. A huge concrete trash container rattled and groaned as if possessed. I crept up to it, the ice cracking loudly under each foot. As I reached for the lid, the metal hatch popped up, causing me to jump back. A little foot poked from the trash. I peered in and saw that the foot was attached to a little girl, no older than twelve or thirteen, huddled among the stale garbage.

"Yah!" I pinched her exposed foot. "What are you doing in there?" I asked sternly, thinking the girl was playing a childish prank.

"I am sleeping."

"Why are you sleeping in there?"

"Here I sleep every night. Please close the lid." Her voice sounded nasal from the cold.

"Poor thing, you must be freezing. Will you come out so I can see you?" I asked more kindly and offered her a hand.

First she stared at my face, then the hand. After a moment of contemplation, she grasped it. Although her hand was chapped and small, it felt like she had folded it into my palm many times before. Then she stood in front of me, bent over at the waist, shivering.

"Stand up," I requested, but a large lump on her back prevented her from straightening her spine. I understood now; this unwanted hunchbacked child had been discarded.

"Please do not beat me. I will not sleep here again," she pleaded.

"I will not let anyone harm you. Do you have a name?"

"Meenah."

"That is a very nice name."

"I picked it out myself."

"Meenah-yah, I cannot feed you, but I can offer you a warm, clean place to sleep if you come live with me."

"With you?" Her downcast lids lifted.

"Yes."

"To your house, with you?"

"Yes, to my house with me," I repeated. "But first there is a place we must go."

I took Meenah to church with me, and sat her next to the burning stove while I prayed for guidance. Even the good people gossiped together, their nostrils twitching with displeasure. I wondered about Husband's reaction.

"Please forgive them, Lord, and please forgive my husband for what he might say. I feel he will reject this new addition to our family. Give me strength. Amen," I prayed.

"Now are we going home?" Her large black eyes glimmered with hope.

"Not just yet," I stalled, knowing I could not present her to the family smelling the way she did. First, I walked her to the public bathhouse for a good scrubbing and soaking. Women squatted around a large tub scouring the dead skin off each other's backs. One woman leisurely enjoyed her morning meal of *kongnamul bahp*, rice with yellow bean sprouts, and *kimchee*.

The way Meenah kicked and squirmed, I got the impression

she had never taken a bath, much less felt a washcloth against her skin.

"Now you are ready," I announced, eyeing her tattered dress with shredded strips of fabric dangling everywhere from safety pins. I tried to remove the fringes, but her face stretched into a long pout, so I let her wear her odd attire.

Her reception was less than friendly, as I had anticipated. "Why did you bring this gypsy here?" Dukwah whined.

"We have no room," Husband said.

"We always have room," I replied sweetly.

"Who is she, Mother?" Yongwoon asked.

"She is your new sister and she will care for your younger brothers."

"How can she? She cannot carry the boys on her back." Dukwah pointed an accusing finger at Meenah's lump.

"She will care for them in other ways."

"I dislike her. Her clothes smell rotten." Dukwah pouted.

"That can be fixed."

"I will not give her one of my dresses."

"Dukwah-yah, you must learn to share with your sister."

"She is not my sister—"

"Enough!" I said firmly, clucking my tongue. "She is, and you must love her like I love you."

Dukwah glared at me for a long time, blinking away the tears. When she could not hold them back, she stormed out, coatless, into the winter evening. I wanted to chase after her and bring her back into the warmth, but I let her vent her frustrations; frustrations that sprouted not from the hunchback girl, but from being thrust into poverty and ugliness. An hour later she returned, her teeth chattering uncontrollably.

"Now you know how it feels to live out in the cold," I said, warming her with my arms.

Meenah's transition into our family was uneasy and charged with constant complaints. The children refused to sleep next to her. To Dukwah's displeasure, I placed Meenah between the two of us. In the morning, we would wake up, shuddering with cold. The sliding doors had been pried open and the comforter that we all shared kicked off. And there Meenah would lie with her head stuck out into the frigid air. For so long she had lived like a vagabond, she could not endure the warmth of the heated floor.

Eventually, Meenah's devotion to the family won them over, especially the boys, whom she cared for faithfully. She cleverly tied them to her side and carried them under her armpit. And if someone wanted a glass of water, a brush, a song, she offered it gladly. When the others discovered where I had found her, it did not matter.

Meenah's joyful addition inspired me to take in a whole family next. A rail-thin man, surnamed Cheong, pushed a wheelbarrow around our neighborhood. *Ahjuhshee*, mister, came by often, rhythmically clanking his metal shears, begging for work. It was always the same desperate tune.

"Work! Work! Any work! I will work!"

In those days, there were many beggars like him—beggars who were once landowners, respectable men, honorable men, now cloaked in rags.

Cheong's wife and two sons followed him around, for they were homeless. He was puzzled when I offered his family a room in our house.

"Why should you do this for me when my own brother has turned us out?"

"On one condition. Your family must accompany us to church every Sunday."

"Are you one of those Christians?" He gestured to the far-off steeple.

"Yes," I answered proudly. "If you are willing, I welcome you and yours into my home. Here you may live freely."

"Free?"

"God is merciful. He has sent you here for a reason."

Cheong paused for a minute, his eyebrows squeezed together and his hands loosely placed on his hips. "Uhh." He scratched the side of his head. "Then I must accept."

He immediately fetched his wife, his sons, and their meager belongings, and moved into *Dong* Grandmother's inner room over Husband's fierce protest.

"Why must you always take in beggars? We have our own children to care for."

"We are all God's children. Their needs cannot be ignored.

Though we do not have much, we have too much not to share with others less fortunate."

"I am the unfortunate one. My fate is to live with a wife who disobeys her husband. You do all this to spite me."

"That is untrue."

"I know you blame me for keeping the family here on the north side. I know you blame me for losing our land because you were the one who insisted we buy in the South."

"I regret nothing as long as we still have each other."

"You lie. You do not need me. You have never needed me." His voice was husky and dry, for it had been a while since his last drink. Our money pouch was empty and so was his soul.

That was why I tried so hard to lead the heartbroken to church. Perhaps through Meenah's and the Cheongs' salvation, Husband might emulate their example. Thus I stood firmly by my conviction and opened our home to outsiders.

I rarely saw *Ahjuhshee*, except on Sundays, when everyone except Husband attended services. Then, immediately afterward, he dashed off with his wheelbarrow to find work. The poor man refused to rest. Inevitably, one afternoon while I was gone on an errand, he dragged himself home exhausted.

"I am dying!" *Ahjuhshee* moaned.

His panic-stricken wife rushed into the kitchen, convinced that food would cure all her husband's ailments. "Eat, eat," she said as she stuffed a hard-boiled egg into his mouth. "You are much too skinny."

To her horror, he dropped dead in the very chair he was sitting in. Cheong's wife shrieked and fled from the house, hitting herself on the head as if her hair was on fire. When I returned home, I found her outside the gate huddled in a circle with her children and mine. When she saw me, she began to wail loudly.

"My husband, he is dead! What shall I do?!" She clutched my hands tightly and slobbered some more.

"Are you certain?"

She jiggled her head up and down, up and down. "I should have fed him more. There is never enough food. The good man gave it all to his children . . ." Her mouth frothed with foam.

"Take me to him." I signaled her to lead the way.

She released my hands and shook her head from side to side. "No! I cannot."

"He is your husband, not mine," I scolded, but she was unwilling to step inside. I was forced to investigate alone. For an instant I thought he was napping in the courtyard. He sat with his head resting on his chest and his hands splayed on his lap. Moving closer, I tapped his shoulder gently.

"*Ahjuhshee*. Wake up, *Ahjuhshee*," I whispered.

There was no response. I tugged at his hair and his loose head lolled back in death. Someone screamed. I was shocked to discover it was me. His unshaven chin was thrust up into the air and the hard-boiled egg was still sealed between his lips. He looked like a monster with three bulging eyeballs. What a dreadful way to die and a waste of a good egg, I thought.

Husband came home late and practically stumbled over dead Cheong sitting in the chair.

"What is this?!" his voice boomed.

"*Ahjuhshee* has left us."

"Why is he sitting here?!"

"His superstitious wife refuses to come back into the house and care for her husband's body," I replied, then asked if I could have one of his coats to purchase a coffin.

"First I let you force me into sharing my home with beggars, now you ask me to give them the clothes off my back?!" He spat out his words so furiously that a river of spit trickled down his chin.

"A coffin is the least we can do. Every person deserves to be buried properly."

"I want him out now!" He jabbed his finger toward the gate. "Out!"

That night, after I tucked the spooked children and Husband in bed, I crept back into the courtyard. A puddle of urine spread beneath the chair where Cheong still sat. Immediately I cleaned it up before Husband slipped on the mess. In the early morning, I sneaked out of the house with a pair of Husband's custom-made leather shoes concealed under my skirt. I ran down to the marketplace and hunted for buyers. Many admired the fine quality, but none offered a decent price.

"Let me try them on before I decide to take them off your hands," a slender man proposed; his pant legs already rolled up, exposing his bare feet.

"How can I be certain you will not run away once they are on your feet?" I asked cautiously.

"How can I tell if they fit if I do not try them on for size?"

"I see your feet. I say they are the exact size as my husband's."

He turned and acted as if he was about to walk away, then faced me once more. "You are a troublesome woman. Take what I have."

In his palm he presented a few coins. It was the only offer I received all day, so I sold him the shoes. And with the money I purchased a plain wooden coffin without varnish—just wood hastily hammered together.

By the time I returned home with the coffin, *Ahjuhshee* was dry and stiff. I tried to lay him in the coffin, but his body had conformed to the frame of the chair. Every effort I made failed. It was like trying to flatten out a rocking chair. I would push down his legs and his head coiled out. When I held down his chest, his knees kicked me in the belly. At last, I finally laid him straight after cracking a few bones, and just to make sure he was not going to pop the lid open during the funeral, I sealed it with extra nails.

"Poor man," I sighed, remembering the look of surprise on his face. "He is not going to heaven."

"How do you know, Mother?" Dukwah inquired.

"People who die struggling are fighting to live because they fear death. Only Christians die peacefully, knowing what awaits them on the other side."

For days afterward, the stench of Cheong's rotted corpse lingered in the house. His wife wept endlessly, clutching a framed photograph of her deceased husband.

"*Ii-ee-goo. Ii-ee-goo.* I feel his restless spirit moving about the house. He has come to bring sickness and harm on us. I feel it. I must call the shaman woman to perform the *kut.*"

"Have you forgotten it is against our practices to believe in such nonsense rituals?" I reminded her.

"She must come in costume and dance to her drum. She is the only one who can convince the spirit of my dead husband to move on to the next world."

"I will not allow it," I said sternly.

That day Cheong's wife packed her bags and left our inner room without formally saying good-bye, taking her sons with her and even the chair Cheong died in. In a way I was relieved she was gone. The constant mention of Cheong's ghost roaming our house haunted Husband so much he began to imagine things, see things that were not there.

"He is here. *Ahjuhshee* has returned," Husband muttered. Fearful, he sprinkled *maiju* beans, soybeans, all over the house, commanding Cheong's spirit to leave.

"Get out!" Husband shouted, hysterically wasting more precious *maiju* beans. "Get out! Get out! Get out! Get out!" he chanted. Every vein on his neck and temple bulged.

"*Yobo*, please pray with me," I begged.

"You go to your church and believe in your God. I believe in only one God—the drinking God," he slurred.

I loved Husband deeply, but I knew my love was not enough; he needed to accept the love of Christ to heal his addictions of the flesh.

"*Ii-ee-goo!*" he cried out suddenly. "I cannot bear it any longer." His voice was a hoarse whisper. He was on the verge of breaking. He held his hand over his trembling lips to calm them, to hold back the tears, but he could not. The immense sadness that hung over our small oppressive world drove Husband to his lowest point. No longer did he have the comfort of liquor or beautiful women to numb his sorrows.

My own heart shattered at the sight of this once proud and dignified man, now dressed in the garb of common men, sobbing. He sank to the floor in a cradle position, hugging his knees. The sobs kept coming, rushing, louder and louder. To see my husband like that reminded me of the only time I saw my parents cry.

He wept and wept, and I let him continue for as long as he needed. The whole time I watched in silence and only after he had collapsed with fatigue did I go to his side. I made my voice soft, for I did not want to startle him. "I am here, *Yobo*."

When he heard my voice he laid his head on my lap and I rocked him in my enclosed arms. Though I despised drunkenness, just this once I wished he had some liquor to ease his misery.

"Open your heart to Him. He will listen and take on your sufferings."

Husband finally opened his eyes and spoke in a sobered

tone. "How can a white man's God understand my pain? Have you forgotten they are our invaders? Why should we subject ourselves to their religion, to any religion?" He wiped his eyes with his callused palms.

"Because He is real and He belongs to all people. Accept Christ and your soul will fly free from this lustful body that torments it."

"And if I do not?"

"Then no one can save you. These days life is uncertain. We may all be killed instantly. But if you accept Christ, the children and I will surely meet you in heaven."

He sat up and looked me straight in the eye. "If there is a chance to be reunited after death, I wish to go where my family is. I do not want to be separated from you," he said sadly, as though we were leaving that very instant.

"If you become a Christian nothing will separate us, ever."

"Then I wish to be a Christian."

I felt my body grow warm. Love was lost or gained at moments like this and ours was strengthened. The bitterness of the past lightened to joy. And Husband began to groom himself, wash his body, brush back his hair, revealing his handsome face, his bright eyes. Eyes that now showed a forgotten twinkle.

Husband was always the first one up and ready to go to church on Sundays. He studied the Bible earnestly. He spoke to anyone who would listen to him about the saving grace of God. His electrifying enthusiasm attracted many converts and continuously inspired the family. I will forever remember the picture of Christ's face that he sketched for us to uplift our spirits. Every detail was so realistic—the tressed hair, the mighty forehead. It was the grandest gift Husband had given me, grander than any expensive jewelry. Nothing hung near it or around it. And on every seventh day something awesome happened. The picture seemed to glow as if the face of Christ came to life.

Motivated by their father's enthusiasm, our two eldest children strove to become exemplary students of God. No other child matched their achievements. Husband received much praise from the congregation for their excellence. Needless to say, modesty was one of Husband's weaker qualities.

Their commitment to God was intense, and yet I feared they might be swayed by the Reds. I asked myself if I had made the right decision in handing over my children to these disillusioned people, for to teach a mind was to assume power over it. Already their propaganda had twisted many adults' thinking, leaving them without the ability to see the truth behind the sugarcoated promises.

If Dukwah had not insisted on remaining in school, I would have kept her safely hidden in the kitchen, because as people of religion we were being targeted. Ironically, the North Korean People's Constitution of 1948 confirmed the right to religious belief and the conducting of services. Now all religious people were being hunted down, even at the primary school level.

One day after the song and pledge of allegiance to our newly promoted Premier, General Kim, Ilsung, whose color portrait was prominently mounted in the front of every classroom, a group of ten officials circulated from class to class, unannounced, armed with pads and pencils. Their assignment was to identify all Christian students. "If you believe in God, raise your hand," Dukwah's teacher instructed.

Thirty-nine out of sixty students raised their hands, including Dukwah. Their names were recorded on the pads and in the teacher's memory. Then just as orderly as they came in, they filed out in a single line, their footsteps in perfect synchronization. The teacher waited until the last man turned the corner before slamming the door shut. The frightened students squirmed at the edge of their wooden seats.

"Even if you believe in God, do not raise your hand again. You can still believe and not raise your hand." Her voice was stern.

"Yes, Teacher," the children responded in unison.

The same ten officials arrived promptly with pads and pencils in hand the next morning. They looked more intimidating: their beady eyes peered over identical gold-rimmed glasses.

The teacher posed the same question to her young students. "If you believe in God, raise your hand."

This time only two brave students raised their hands, Dukwah and a boy, to the teacher's disbelief. Again, their names were jotted down. The teacher stood rigidly behind her desk, letting the anger steam out her ears until the men left the room. She paused as the classroom stirred; a cloud of doom hung over every child's head. In one quick swoop the teacher grabbed Dukwah's and the boy's ears and jerked them into her private office. Suddenly the tigress changed her face; she was wearing a friendly mask.

"You two are my brightest students, it would pain me to see you both expelled from school. This will greatly upset your parents." She was conniving. "I know you two will come to your senses. You do want to remain in school?"

"Yes, I want to stay in school," the boy mumbled.

"That is better." She smiled and sent him back to his seat. Then she turned to Dukwah. "What about you?" she asked cheerfully, basking in her success.

"I cannot," Dukwah replied.

"What do you mean you cannot!" the teacher bellowed, but promptly regained her composure. "I see," she said, slowly pacing behind Dukwah, who stood with her arms pinned to her side. "Dukwah-yah, you remind me a lot of myself when I was your age. I can see you were also born to lead and I want to help you. If you do not raise your hand tomorrow, I will make you class president. And because I like you very much I can also arrange it so that you will not have to take the final exam. You can go straight into the best middle school next year on a full scholarship. All this just for you."

Dukwah, at eleven, faced her hardest decision. Education was her greatest love, next to God. The temptation was so strong she came to me for advice.

"Mother," she sighed, "what shall I do? Teacher promised me a full scholarship at the best middle school if I do not raise my hand."

She was desperate; she knew her father and I were barely able to pay for this year's fees. The eldest son was our first responsibility, our first priority. Yongwoon's education rightfully came before hers.

"No, only God can promise you those things and He can easily snatch them away as well. I wish I could tell you it does not matter if you raise your hand or not as long as you believe in your heart, but that would be wrong."

"Teacher is too powerful. I cannot fight her alone."

"Do not worry about your teacher. She will not be the one to judge you in the end. In this world, God said, if you do not know my name, then I will not remember yours. Tomorrow when you raise your hand, raise it right away. Trust in Him and He will protect you."

Dukwah was silent. I could see her thoughts reaching for advice superior to mine. "I will try my best," she promised at last.

"No, Dukwah-yah, you must do your best."

She nodded in agreement, hiding her eyes behind her cropped bangs.

The following morning, I chose a pink-and-blue sweater I had knitted especially for her to wear. I wanted her to feel my presence embracing and supporting her. I watched helplessly as she went on her way to face one of her hardest tests.

All eyes were fixed on Dukwah as the firing squad marched in, pencils cocked and ready to scratch out their last target. Dukwah sat straight up on the edge of her chair, hands folded on top of the desk. The teacher cleared her throat; the students waited for her to speak. She clamped her jaw so tightly that her words were barely audible, though every student by then had memorized word for word the dreaded question.

"If you believe in God . . ." she began to say, but before she had the opportunity to complete the sentence she was abruptly cut off by Dukwah's zealous hand. Her eyes locked directly ahead, her arm was pressed to her ear, and her hand darted in the air. The teacher's face furrowed with anger.

Once again Dukwah was dragged into the private office, this time by the hair. The teacher hurled a whole new set of vocabulary at her, venomous words. During the entire ordeal, Dukwah stood upright and looked her elder boldly in the eye.

"In all of North Korea, there is only one girl like you!" the teacher roared, slapping both palms on the desktop.

Dukwah's grin grew to a full smile at the unintended compliment, which enraged her teacher. "What are you so happy about?! I will rip that smirk right off your face! Just look at you, even your clothes bear the Christian cross!" The teacher was right: Dukwah's pink sweater had a blue horizontal waistband and a vertical line down the front.

At that moment, Dukwah heard God speak to her. "You, Lee, Dukwah, are so good I will cherish and protect you from this day forward," He promised her, and He kept His word. When the national exams were being held to see which students qualified to move up a grade, He watched over her. While other students fell ill with exhaustion poring over books, Dukwah remained healthy and rested.

On the day of the exams, all sixth-graders were randomly issued test numbers. They shuffled from one exam room to the next. Stressed students buried their noses in books as they crammed in information at the last minute. Dukwah did the same. Miraculously, each room she entered, the examiner orally drilled her on the very question she had been reviewing just minutes before. The examiner would toss out a question and Dukwah would immediately volley back the correct answer, forgetting nothing.

A week later, the whole family accompanied her to school to receive her grades. We were all nervous, except Dukwah. She was so confident I worried she might be disappointed if she did not do as well as she had boasted. To my relief and pride, she scored one of the highest marks. I knew then that God truly favored her.

Yongwoon, unlike his younger sister, was by nature more soft-spoken and mild, but he had a gifted mind that churned constantly. This gift became a burden; he pondered too much the injustices all around him. He felt betrayed by the ruling People's Committee. He prayed and waited for justice to dawn, but it remained dark. And then one day that darkness entered his heart and his golden childish laughter vanished. He began to change. This soft-spoken son of mine broke the law. He rallied together his high school classmates and organized a demonstration, protesting against our leader, Kim, Ilsung. The demonstrators carried picket signs containing the hated tyrant's face with a bloody slash painted through it and marched around the campus.

"Down with Kim, Ilsung! Down with Kim, Ilsung!" they shouted for all to hear. "Christ is our true leader!"

Later that day, as I was washing turnips, I glanced up to see Yongwoon stumble over the high threshold. My whole body trembled at his mangled appearance. His torn jacket barely clung to him. I could see that the skin underneath was welted in stripes. Blood oozed from where the skin was ripped. The extent of the whipping was barbarous. I ran to him, tripping over my skirt.

"Yongwoon-yah, who did this to you?"

He could not speak, although the words formed too clearly in his heart. He was silent for some time, his eyes fixed on my face. They were large and black like his father's, but greater in depth.

"What happened?" I asked tenderly.

"I told them there is only one God and He is not our General Premier, so they beat me with my own sign."

I held him tightly against my breast. Yongwoon gnashed his teeth as tears of rage welled in his eyes. Panic filled me. I knew it was only a matter of time before the Reds arrested him. All Christian political activists and leaders were being stamped out, though worship was still tolerated.

I vowed to keep my son safe even if that meant defying the authorities.

WAR!

WAR!

WAR!

In the spring of 1950, every aspect of life got progressively worse on the north side of the 38th parallel. Hopes of eating well, living comfortably, and, most important, enjoying personal freedom were dead. And no one knew why the main roads were overrun with military trucks loaded with young soldiers or why the railroad stations were packed with more soldiers heading south. Citizens were kept ignorant. Information was guarded. And newspapers mounted a propaganda campaign to depict the South as having aggressive intentions against the North. It felt as though I were living in some strange country filled with suspicion and deception.

On June 25, 1950, the "Land of the Morning Calm" erupted. I would always remember the day when our peace-loving people were ripped apart because of clashing ideologies.

On that Sunday, my family and I attended church services as usual. At about nine-thirty in the morning, midway through the opening hymn, shouts of anger arose outside. My initial thought was that the church was going to be stormed. Apparently others arrived at the same conclusion, for the whole congregation stirred, glancing back at the double doors. Even Reverend Kim lost his train of thought and his words slurred together. The first to abandon the sermon, I slipped through a side entrance to see what was happening.

Outside, people dashed through the streets. Vendors rammed their carts into others, breaking earthenware and leaving trails of fruits and grains. Lost children cried out for their mothers. Mothers yelled for their lost children. Animals rattled in their cages. Complete chaos.

A few yards away, I saw a man squatting on the ground, head buried in his hands. I rushed to him, bumping into several dazed-faced people.

"*Ahjuhshee*, what is happening?"

"It is terrible. Who would have thought?"

"Thought what?" I hurried him along.

"Our brothers and sisters down south have attacked us," he said gravely.

"That cannot be true! You are lying; tell me it is not true," I demanded, but he just buried his face again.

I ran back into the street, collaring the first student I saw. He was wearing the required college navy blue double-breasted uniform and cap of the Reds.

"Student, what is the news?" I pleaded.

"The fascist puppet regime of Rhee, Syngman has attacked us," he shouted, and darted off to join a group of young men and women wearing the same garb. Together they marched away with upraised clenched fists, singing patriotic songs.

I was too shaken to sing, move, or cry. Could it be true? Standing erect, I closed my eyes and murmured a silent prayer, "Our Father, let it be a bad dream." Just then I felt a hand squeeze my shoulder, as Husband brought me back to the present. I turned toward him and saw my reflection in his mournful face.

"What shall happen to our people, *Yobo*?" I asked.

"I do not know," he replied weakly.

That was not the answer I wanted to hear from Husband. I needed him to be the brave one, to be the man, the leader we needed.

"Our hero is on the radio!" a girl student announced with authority.

Mobs funneled into public buildings and schools, searching for a radio. Husband and I picked up our two youngest boys and ran as fast as we could to hear the broadcast. Yongwoon and Dukwah led the way. We entered an already crowded bank where eager listeners were huddled around a single portable radio. Not a peep was heard, except for a crying child.

Then the news came over Radio Pyongyang: General Premier Kim, Ilsung himself gave his "Message to the People of Korea." We all listened grimly as he told us our fate. He called our side the "Democratic People's Republic of Korea." The title sounded so official and military, it rustled the roots of my hair. "The South Korean puppet clique has rejected all methods for peaceful reunification proposed by the Democratic People's Republic of Korea and dared to commit armed aggression . . ."

The nightmare was true! At eleven o'clock that same morning, the North declared war. War! . . . War! . . . War!

We were informed that our side counterattacked only after the Republic of Korea (ROK) attacked the Haeju district, north of the 38th parallel, plunging our nation into a civil war. Over and over again I asked God why a brother would fight his brother inside our father's home. I pitied our southern countrymen, who were being manipulated by the Big Nose American barbarians. Yet at the same time, I felt betrayed and angry. I, too, wanted to lift my clenched fist, but I remained still.

Nervously, my family and I waited for the war to reach our home. And suddenly it came. A horrible noise thundered above our heads, as if heaven was crumbling and was about to crush us all. But it was not heaven, it was the rumbling sounds of swift jets and attack bombers coming to mercilessly drop their bombs. One after another the whistles of the falling bombs were heard moments before they hit the earth and exploded, shaking everything. Instinctively, we huddled on the ground and hid our faces. *PONG! PONG! PONG!* The ground shook and shook. *PONG! PONG!*

We crouched until the last bomb did its damage and the hideous roar of flying engines faded toward the southern horizon. Everyone sat motionless, waiting for something more to happen. We waited and waited but nothing more shook or blew up. Then out of the eerie silence a siren wailed, long and clear. Slowly I staggered to my feet.

"Is it all over?" the children cried.

"No," I answered honestly, knowing we lived in the capital of the People's government. And I was right; screaming air-raid sirens became a familiar sound in our ears. Our region was under constant attack. News reports underplayed and underrated the damages and lives lost. The public was fed dubious information about victories to win our support, but it was obvious the casualties and destruction were massive. Planes swooped low, wrecking mines, electric power plants, industrial centers, railroads, and bridges.

Soldiers tore up the countryside, piece by piece, searching for new recruits to replace the dead and the injured. All men, young and old, were being abducted into the Red Army to fight for unification. No longer was there a minimum or maximum age requirement. Every family was asked to volunteer their husbands and sons, a cruel request. What woman would make such a sacrifice? I hid Husband and Yongwoon inside the house under piles of blankets as other men marched to battle. Hundreds upon hundreds, two by two, they passed by.

Husband, tired of hiding, yearned to do something useful, anything to pass the endless hours. On his own, he accepted the dangerous appointment of *jipsaneem*, deacon. It became his duty to organize secret Bible meetings for our dwindling congregation. I was torn between pride and panic. While others denounced their faith in order to keep their homes and their heads, Husband's spirit never wavered. I wanted to support his commitment, and yet save him from inevitable persecution. The Reds acted ruthlessly against Christians since Christianity threatened their very existence. As people of faith, we believed in one supreme God and the Reds believed there could only be one supreme dictator; therefore, church leaders were imprisoned. The People's Constitution that confirmed freedom of religion was now a total farce.

I, too, wanted to flee south like so many others. I hated the Reds. I begged, but Husband refused to lose hope and abandon our congregation. So we lingered, hoping the war would end. While we waited, I became pregnant again. This time Husband was not overwhelmed with joy. The thought of an additional mouth to feed triggered such an outburst that he punched the walls, crushing several knuckles.

"Another babe, how could you do this?! What am I supposed to feed it, dirt?" He smacked the wall again.

I could have blamed the child on him, but I knew the true reason for his anger. It was not that he did not want the babe; he desperately did.

I constantly worried. My belly stretched and our chances of escaping grew slimmer. I worried that the next bomb might blow us up. I worried about my elderly mother, who fled across the parallel with Nephew's family several years ago. I worried about my sisters, whom I had not heard from since the start of the war. I worried.

As the weeks wore on, Husband regretted staying behind, but we were trapped. I could barely move. The child clung on for the entire nine months. When she thrashed into the world, Husband slipped away silently into the perilous streets, aggrieved by the burden. I peered down at her tiny face; it resembled his so much, it hurt. She even had his deep frown. Somehow she must have known she was unwanted.

I waited, unsure of Husband's return. Day passed into night, then another day and another. On the third night he slipped back in. He did not ask if it was a boy or a girl, as he had done with our other four children. The gender had no importance, for life had little value in times of war.

"Please, *Yobo*, give her a name," I begged, hoping that might bond him to her.

He said nothing. He just sat next to the nameless girl, unable to comfort her or bounce her in his arms. Not until two weeks after her birth did she receive her name, Lee, Dukhae, meaning grand glory. It was an inspiring name, though we rarely used it. The family just called her *ahghee*, baby, protecting ourselves in case she did not survive the hardships.

Life got bleaker and bleaker. Gates were barred shut. Shops drew in their banners and boarded their doors. In the marketplaces, stalls were empty of food. Formerly jade-colored rice fields were aborted, yellowed, and dead. Farmers bent over their hoes riling up the soil, sons laboring beside their fathers with heavy wooden buckets slung on a bamboo pole across their shoulders were forgotten sights. Children played silently near the gates of their homes, ready to duck inside in an instant. There was no more casual talk. People were scared to greet strangers or even to speak openly to friends.

My nerves tightened at every suspicious noise outside our gate. Was it the secret police? I knew that one day they would come for both Husband and Yongwoon, and one day a loud knock did rattle our gate. I panicked and darted inside, willing them to go away.

"Is Lee, Dukpil here?! Lee, Dukpil!" a husky unfamiliar voice called through the gate.

I turned mute, giving no answer. Husband and Yongwoon popped up from behind the blankets and looked at me in terror. The silence vibrated between us.

"Lee, Dukpil, are you home?!"

Thinking quickly, I motioned to them to burrow themselves deeper. Hurriedly, I messed up my hair and rumpled my clothes before pulling back the iron bar. Two men, totally opposite in build, stood on the other side. The shorter, better-looking one spoke. His voice was unexpectedly deep and coarse.

"Sorry to bother you, but is this the house of our dear friend Lee, Dukpil?" he asked, his eyes roving over the courtyard behind me.

"He is not here." I yawned, pretending I had just awoken.

"*Ii.*" He clucked his tongue in disappointment.

"Where did you come from?" I asked casually.

"My family lived near yours in China. I am Pea, Seongchil. I am surprised my good friend has not mentioned me," he stated matter-of-factly.

I searched my memory for such a face, but none came to mind. I studied him harder and still I did not recognize him. After some hesitation, I replied, "Do you know him from our home in Chungking?" I inquired.

"Yes, that is where."

Liar. Our house was in Soju. I had outwitted him. "Oh, then

please come in. My husband stepped out to find work early this morning. I do not expect him to return till much later, but you may wait for him if you wish," I said courteously, showing them into the men's quarters.

The shorter man looked puzzled, pinching his eyebrows together in thought. He craned his head around from side to side, scanning for any signs of Husband, who was only a few yards away. Finding nothing, they bowed and excused themselves.

"Please tell my friend I look forward to calling on him later this evening."

"Yes, I will give him the message." I nodded.

I waited until they were far down the street and out of sight before barring the gate shut. "It is safe to come out now." I jiggled the blankets.

Husband emerged dripping sweat. "Have you lost your mind, *Yobo*, asking them to come in? What if they stayed?" Husband gasped for fresh air.

"I was not scared. Neither my eyes nor my voice betrayed your location. You were safe."

We all sighed with relief for a moment, but the moment became increasingly dangerous with each second. I had to find a way to sneak Husband out of the house. For now, Yongwoon was safe, I thought; they had not asked for him.

"You must go quickly, before they return. The next time they will not be so cordial."

"I cannot run off and abandon my family; I am the man of the house."

"We will be fine. It is you they want."

"The children will think I am a coward."

"For them you must go, run, hide. Whatever it takes, because they need their father to stay alive."

Reluctantly, he gave in. Together we prayed for the courage to separate our family. We had discussed this possibility many times before, but in my heart I wanted to believe it would never come to such a desperate measure. I tried to trick myself into believing Husband was simply going on an extended trip to a *kisaeng* house like in the olden days. It was less painful to surrender him to other women than to death. At least when he was with *kisaengs* he always returned, but death was final.

Using a little imagination, I disguised him as an old farmer.

He wore a large gray overcoat, baggy trousers, straw shoes, a wide-brimmed straw hat, and he leaned on a cane. Even his improvised shuffle looked authentic. But one thing troubled me: his young, handsome face.

"Dukwah-yah, bring me some flour and lard," I instructed.

"This is no time to be cooking," Husband scolded.

"I am not cooking, I assure you."

Dukwah brought over the last sack of flour and grease. I had been saving it for a special occasion and the time had arrived. First I smeared the grease all over his brows, eyes, cheeks, and chin, then dusted him with white flour. Now he was ready to walk out into daylight.

I led him to the back door. He glanced beyond into the streets, then back at our house. Without speaking, I knew his thoughts and I felt he read mine.

"We shall meet again, *Yobo*." He reached for me with both hands. I felt the warmth of his touch through my cotton jacket, savoring the intimacy, then drew back.

"Do not return until it is absolutely safe. You must not be foolish," I replied coolly. I wanted to say something sweet for him to remember me by but all my life I had been taught to be the sensible one, the strong one, and I was playing that role again.

"You are always looking after my well-being." He smiled. "I do not deserve you."

"Now you are being foolish." My mood lightened, and I could not help but return his tense smile.

"That is much nicer." He traced my lips with his finger, then went on his way, deep into the eastern mountains that bordered our region. There he would spend the next few weeks in dark, wet caves and tunnels bored into the range's slopes. Like a gopher, he would live inside the earth, avoiding artillery fire from the south.

Throughout the day I was tormented by visions of Husband—hungry, cold, maimed—being hunted down like a wild animal. I could not shake them off. I tried to busy myself with unnecessary chores, but there was no escape from what was about to happen.

A second loud knock broke the silence of the house that same day. Please, let it be my husband, I selfishly wished as I hurried across the courtyard. With hope in my heart, I cautiously asked who it was through the gate.

"Is Lee, Dukpil there?!" It was the dreaded deep voice of the shorter man.

My pulse raced as I noticed Yongwoon's tall, youthful frame hovering behind me. "Dukwah-yah, take your older brother out the back gate and close it behind him," I whispered urgently. Only after Yongwoon had safely vanished did I draw back the bar. As before, the two men snooped around.

"What a shame. My husband just left. He so wanted to greet you both."

"Where has he gone?" The shorter man's voice rumbled with suspicion.

"He waited as long as he could, but as you know, a man must journey farther outside of town to look for work these days."

"When do you expect him back?"

I pulled out a piece of torn paper from my sleeve and handed it to them. "I am such an absentminded woman; I almost forgot he asked me to give this letter to you."

The shorter man snatched it from me, slicing my finger with the paper's edge. "I have gone out of town to find work, perhaps we can meet when I return." He read each word out loud as if he wanted to strike me. "Did you not tell your husband I had come to call on him from so far away?" His fuse was shortening.

"I am only his wife, I cannot tell him to go or stay," I said evenly.

They were unimpressed with my performance. Suddenly all pretense was tossed aside and they donned their official policemen's scowls.

"We have been informed that your husband is responsible for inciting demonstrations and treasonous meetings," he said, blurting out the false charges.

"That is a lie. My husband passionately loves his country."

"Which government are you speaking of?"

"Our Korea." I kept my answer vague.

"Then why is he not here to defend himself?"

"You read his letter yourself. He has gone to find work."

"Do not deceive us or you will suffer the consequences."

Just then Dukwah came forth, cradling the baby in her arms.

"Go back inside the house!" I shrieked, my pitch a little too panicky.

"Stay right where you are!" his voice roared over mine.

Dukwah halted in mid-step.

"It is okay, Dukwah-yah," I said as calmly as I could muster. "Do as he asks. We have done nothing wrong." I bit down on my lips quickly so my harassers would not see them trembling.

"Now, that is more like it." He adjusted his collar. "Where is your eldest son? Lee, Yongwoon is his name, I believe."

The sound of his slimy voice polluting my son's name sent my heart pounding with outrage. "He is visiting his aunt up north; she had need of him since her husband had been called off to war," I said.

"You must be mistaken, Seoul is down south." He pointed his finger in that direction.

"I . . . I . . . do not know what you are talking about . . ."

War had shattered the protective barrier that once had shielded women. To my two accusers, a traitor had no gender, no rights. In their demented minds, I was a national threat who deserved to be punished.

"Teach the *ssangnyun-ah*, bitch, a lesson. Show her the People are not to be made a fool of," the shorter man ordered to the larger one.

The larger man lurched forward and grabbed my arms, mercilessly twisting them behind me. He shoved his knee into my spine, grinding my face into the gravel. The pain was great, but it was more agonizing to hear Dukwah crying out to me. "Mother! Mother!" Hearing their older sister, my two younger boys toddled in to see what was happening. The three of them stood dumb, pale as powder.

"Children, go inside!" I yelled frantically. "Go in—"

I felt a hard leather boot stomp the back of my neck, cutting off my words and rubbing my face into the dirt. "Get up!"

He screamed some other obscenities, but I did not hear him. I was desperately thinking of what to say, the perfect words to save myself and my children, who were now bawling hysterically, but my tongue failed me.

"I gave you an order, *ssangnyun-ah!*" He kicked me in the ribs again and again.

Deadened by pain, I made an attempt to raise myself, but the heel of his boot dug deeper into my back. "Get up!"

"Take anything. I have expensive silks from China. You can have it all!" I pleaded at last.

The word "expensive" caught their attention. "Show me what you have!" the shorter man demanded, his body curled over so he could shout directly in my ear.

I crawled free, clawing the ground with my fingers, before he could kick me again. I stumbled into the house and pulled out all but one bundle of silk, which I kept hidden.

"Here, it is yours." I held them out, displaying their richness on each arm. "Take it, it is yours, just leave us alone."

The shorter man felt the fabric with his callused fingers, estimating its value. "What else are you hiding?" He clasped a handful of hair and yanked my head back. "Where is the rest?"

"This is all there is," I gasped.

"We shall see for ourselves." He clopped around the house, pawing through cabinets and dressers. When he found the leather-bound Bible, worn from constant handling, he picked it up and leafed through the marked pages.

"A Christian," he spat, and began to rip its precious pages. I was speechless; it felt as though he was tearing out chunks of my flesh. On his face I saw a kind of sinister pleasure. I knew then that no amount of bribery could save me.

"Take her."

"My baby, please. She will not survive without me." I groveled at his feet.

The shorter man studied the small helpless child with narrowed eyes. Then he stared squarely at me, flashed a big smile, and stated coldly, "She will die anyway."

I knew I had to fight for her life. I resisted with all my might, kicking and screaming at the top of my lungs, but I was no match for them. They dragged me away, my knees scraping the ground, leaving a trail of skin and blood.

We arrived at the police station. I was certain they were going to take me somewhere in the dense woods and execute me. At the station my wrists were tied together with burlap cloth and all personal items confiscated. I was grateful they left my clothes untouched. Then I was led through a narrow hallway to the main questioning area. Two long lines of captives were already awaiting interrogation. A sloppily uniformed guard stood at the front, stroking a battered billy club. "Men over here!" he ordered. In any other circumstances it would have been simple to follow, but at that moment my mind was confused and I slipped into the wrong line.

"Want to be a rebel, do you?" He tapped the club against his palm. In a panic I looked around and saw that I was in the men's line and immediately hastened to the back of the correct line, hiding my face.

The wait was endless. Everyone feared a heavy blow from the guard's club. At last I stood at the head of the line. I was relieved and terrified at the same time when they called out my name. Those few steps into the interrogation room felt like they were my last. The officer, a small man with a crooked nose, sat behind an old schoolteacher's desk.

"Are you a Rhee, Syngman sympathizer?" His voice was as dull as his expression.

"I know nothing; I am just a woman," I responded.

He sat there unmoved as he recorded my statement in his slow and laborious handwriting. "Where are your husband and eldest son?"

"I do not know." I pleaded dumb again.

"Where have you hidden them? Who are their accomplices? What other crimes have you committed yourself? Will you confess your treasonous crimes against your government?" His questioning was relentless, always in the same lifeless tone.

"I deny everything. I know nothing of your politics; nor do I have the energy to commit all the crimes you unfairly accuse me of."

"Do you know what we do sometimes to traitors who refuse to cooperate?" he threatened, but still I would not betray Husband and son's whereabouts. "Are you not frightened?"

"Yes, but I am not afraid to die. If you should kill me, I shall go directly to heaven."

"You are a stupid woman. It is dangerous to take on a religion. When you join them, you inherit their burdens."

My interrogation could not have lasted more than a few minutes, though it seemed like an eternity and a half. God must have been watching over me, for my accuser never laid a hand or boot on my body. He remained seated the entire time.

As expected, I was found guilty and marched to a cell with a group of other distraught women. Quick, steady steps down a gray corridor, blocks of cells on either side. Only the sound of our footsteps echoed off the walls.

The cells were already full beyond capacity. Arms reached between the iron bars. With one whack from the guard's billy club, the limbs coiled back. A door swung open, and we were ordered to enter.

"Step in!" the guard demanded. A short, ordinary command, yet it was the worst command I was ever given.

I was the last through the heavy iron door that clicked shut in my face. I began to hyperventilate as the locking sound of freedom gone echoed in my ears.

I felt eyes staring at me; a hole was burning through the back of my head. I dreaded turning around and facing the inmates, but I knew I could not avoid them. We would be confined together for an indefinite amount of time.

"God, please make them friendly faces," I prayed. To my horror, they were faces of women who had lost all faith. Hopeless faces.

"Move along," an unknown voice demanded.

I was driven to the innermost circle, where the decaying sight of bodily waste choked me. The toilet was merely a bucket surrounded by four thin panels. Being the newest inmate in this wretched harem of women, I was forced to sit in the worst spot. Here seniority was based on length of imprisonment, not on age or social distinction. The longer you survived in this hell, the more power you gained.

"*Ahjoomah*, ma'am, you can sit by me," a meek girl mouthed.

"Thank you," I whispered gratefully, brushing my palm against her hand. With that bit of kindness, this young girl immediately clung to me. Her body pressed against mine. Up close I saw traces of gray hair, prematurely turned white by her ordeal, no doubt. She rested her head on my shoulder, and before I knew it she was sound asleep.

I looked around through sideways glances. The most senior inmate, in her dirtied clothes and oily hair, rested against the back wall in semi-comfort. That was one privilege I never wanted to earn. Suddenly the toilet did not seem so revolting, except I was uncertain how long I could last. Whenever someone used it, we all knew her business. There was no plumbing, no flush system, and no lid. The excrement just rotted in the bucket all day and all night.

Sitting in the dark windowless room, I lost track of time. A single naked bulb which dangled from a chipped hole in the ceiling provided our only patch of light. The sight of the wheelbarrow rolling in our food hinted at the dusk hour.

The meal consisted of a watery bowl of millet slop. By the time it was passed back to me, the slop was half consumed. Immediately its stink caused my stomach to retch up acid. It stung my throat as I swallowed it back down. How could they in good conscience serve us this waste? I refused a second taste, though I had not eaten since noon yesterday. I was repulsed to see the others lick their fingers, savoring every morsel.

For a long time I stared at the slop that lay in my lap. Like vultures, the other women eyed the food. The senior inmate with the oily hair was the undisputed beneficiary. I could not figure out why the others were so afraid of her; she looked more like a chipmunk, with her hairy upper lip and overbite, than a fierce tiger. I was determined not to let her intimidate me. As I passed the bowl to an old woman sitting in front of me, she covered her mouth with her skinny fingers, fearfully looking in Chipmunk's direction.

"Grandmother, if you do not take it for yourself, I will drop it in the toilet bucket." I touched her arm in a reassuring way. All ears were on me, because it was so odd to hear someone speak at a normal level.

"Be quiet!" The guard marched over from his post and drenched us with a full pail of water.

Immediately everyone hid her head, forgetting about the millet. No one wanted to get soaked again and risk getting pneumonia. It was especially easy to contract it on nights when the temperature dropped and we slept unprotected. There were no blankets or mats to prevent our buttocks from freezing to the cold concrete floor, only the lice-infested shreds we wore.

Being a newcomer, I had to squirm into a convenient sitting position in which to sleep. For the first two nights it did not bother me, because I stayed up the entire time in a daze, staring into the hallway, dreaming of life beyond the iron bars that imprisoned me. By the third morning, it mattered very little that the scanty portions of millet were mixed with stones and dirt or that it smelled of mold. I was eating anything they slopped out.

Unfortunately, the three meals a day lasted only a few precious moments. The rest of the time I had to force myself to think about other things. For many hours I watched the young girl next to me smooth out the dirt, mess it up, then smooth it out over and over again. She was so absorbed in her mindless artwork she failed to noticed my absorption in her. But that, too, got tiring. The urge to speak, to relax my compressed lips, became maddening. Silence was the worst form of torture our captors inflicted on us, for it prevented us from releasing the anxiety that was building inside. I needed to say something before I lost my sanity. So I began to use gestures to communicate with the women around me. We became very innovative and expressive with our hands, faces, feet, whatever gave us the means to express what we could not with sounds. Using our palms and index fingers, we exchanged names, how many children we had, our alleged crimes. In comparison with what the others were convicted of, my crimes seemed enormous.

Through sign language I was able to piece together the puzzle of the war. I learned North Korea was the first to pour across the 38th parallel. It never occurred to me that our side was the aggressor. We had been deceived again. I spent those long hours wondering why. Why so much hatred? Was power worth so much suffering?

In my daydreaming I pictured *ahghee*, her mouth wide open, searching for her mother's nipple. I was scared. I wanted so badly to lift my hands to the sky and call out Jesus' name, but I knew if I was caught praying, the guard might take me out to the countryside and shoot me along with the other Christians. I was torn between my survival on earth for the sake of my children and my eternal life in heaven.

Each weighed heavily on my soul. I became extremely depressed. It was because my faith was weakening. If my faith was truly pure, any hardship, regardless of how terrible the situation, could be transformed into happiness. Knowing this, I sank deeper and deeper into hopelessness.

Finally I decided to risk my physical life for a prayer before fear totally consumed my faith. I leaned on my knees, palms pressed together. "Our Father who art in heaven . . ." I prayed out loudly, but it was interrupted by sirens announcing an air raid. The guards ran for cover. The blasts of bombs and machine guns rained down near us, barely missing our prison. When the all clear sounded, our captors returned so angry they hurled curses, accusing us of being South Korean whores.

I interpreted the raid as a message from God warning me to pray only at night when it was safer. After all were asleep I clasped my hands together and prayed. And my prayers were heard. Dukwah, carrying her baby sister, miraculously appeared. Fearing for *ahghee*'s fragile condition, Dukwah walked the four miles, dodging explosions the entire way.

I thought I was hallucinating. The thin glow of light in the hallway was so faint, their figures were undistinguishable. Only when she walked right up to the bars and squeezed her forehead between the iron did I know I was not losing my mind.

"Mother. Mother, are you here?" she called, her pitch jittery.

"Dukwah-yah, Mother is here!" I whispered back, but only breath escaped. I tried to stand, but my muscles tightened from lack of exercise, forcing me to crawl and stumble to the front.

"Dukwah-yah, Mother is here!" I repeated a little louder in the same hoarse whisper, and this time they both heard me.

At the sound of my voice, the baby started to wail. The sound of her crying made the milk trickle from my breasts, forming wet circles around the nipples. They had been like two corked bottles ready to pop.

"*Ahghee*'s ears, *ahghee*'s ears!" Dukwah mumbled, her hands folded over her sister's tiny ears.

I panicked and reached my arms through the bars and grabbed the infant. Frantically I searched for wounds.

"Dukwah-yah, *ahghee* is fine," I assured her, but she still looked distressed. "*Ahghee* is fine."

"I shut my eyes and held my breath as long as I could. The bombs were so loud, Mother."

"Why did you not protect your ears?" I asked, then asked again. "Why did you not protect your ears?"

". . . I only have two hands."

That was when I realized she had sacrificed her hearing to protect her sister's. "You did good," I managed to get out before my throat tightened with emotion. Even if I had my voice I could never fully express to her my gratitude.

Without any further delay, I loosened my jacket and fed the baby as I held her through the bars. I was careful not to graze her head against the rusty iron. At first, her mouth refused the round dark nipple, forgetting its purpose. The poor little thing had had nothing but her fingers to suck: the flesh on her fingers was wrinkled and discolored. I tried again, coaxing a few drops into her drooped mouth. Tasting its sweet warm milk, her mouth tightly clamped on. For a long time she nursed until each breast was dry and the nipple sore. We were both satisfied.

"When will you come home?" Dukwah implored.

"I do not know," I answered truthfully. "You must promise to be strong and take my place until I return." I held out my right pinkie to her.

"I promise," she swore, locking her pinkie to mine, sealing the promise.

I had no doubt she was capable of taking my place even at such a young age. I thanked God again for blessing me with this daughter. From that day forth, Dukwah dodged the attacking planes and gunfire for *ahghee*'s noon feeding. I knew that the trek was dangerous but the baby's survival depended on Dukwah's courage. It was an impossible decision for a mother to make, whether to risk two lives to save the life of one. How could I possibly choose which daughter deserved a chance? I could not; it was Dukwah who ultimately made the decision.

I looked forward to those daily feedings, but it did not lessen my anxieties. Twenty-nine days and still no news of my release. Every noise, smell, movement began to irritate me. The crowdedness became unbearable. There was no longer any room to kneel and pray at nights. Suddenly I had enough. Was I not a human being deserving of some compassion and mercy?!

"I am not an animal!" I wanted to scream.

Out of sheer hopelessness I crawled into the privacy of the toilet stall. This repulsive coffin was my sanctuary. Instead of the calming scent of burning candles, feces assaulted my senses.

"Dear God, this time I do not ask for my children, I ask for myself. I fear I will not survive another day. Here a day seems like years. Give me a sign, tell me Your will, I will do anything to leave this loathsome place . . ."

The next morning, I was in the same cramped position when a loud knock jolted me from a wondrous dream.

"Are you going to stay in there all day?" Chipmunk whispered.

I walked out in a happy daze. God spoke to me in my dream; He had not forgotten about me. "I am going home," I announced for everyone to hear. I knew God would protect me from a clubbing as I told His story. And He did, for the guard on duty slept soundly through it all.

"How do you know?" one after another asked skeptically.

"In my dream, I heard an angelic voice call out my name. 'Baek, Hongyong, come with me,' it said. The calm voice drew me to a woman, cloaked all in white. It was *Kwonsaneem*. 'Come, this way,' she called again, and I followed her to a dark concrete tunnel. 'Trust me,' she said. And I did, though it was pitch-black inside. I felt my way through with my arms stretched out in front of me. *Kwonsaneem*'s voice was my only guide, but I was not afraid. As I walked deeper into the tunnel, I saw a light marking the end. When I reached the light, I came upon a lovely valley, so unreal it looked as though each detail was rendered with a faint brushstroke: the snowcapped mountain ridges; the emerald green hills; and the pristine lake nestled at its base. The freshness expanded my lungs and the blazing orange sky lifted my spirits.

" 'Go in.' She motioned toward the vast blueness of the water. Knowing that I could not swim, I stepped back. Sensing my hesitation, she walked in first. The surface of the lake reflected her inner glow and held it as she floated toward the center.

" 'It is safe.' I heard her honeyed voice speak inside my head. The water was so crisp and clear, I caught my glistening image. Step by step I entered, testing the water for coldness. The temperature was perfect. Step by step I submerged myself to the nape of my neck. Its refreshing coolness seeped into every pore, cleansing me of all my troubles. 'You are free.' "

Excitement gathered in the cell, as the story was retold and retold. Some were believers; most were skeptics.

"She is making it up." Chipmunk snickered.

"Say what you will. I am going home."

"Why should you be the first to be released? You have only been here a short while. I have been here almost a year," another said.

"I have been here nine months."

"Five months, two years . . ." They all tallied up their time.

"I have never heard of a toilet God. I think I will dump a prayer right now." Chipmunk crawled over to the stall and mimicked a gesture of prayer.

The cell ignited with tiny sparks of laughter, almost startling the guard awake. I pitied those without faith, because only faith sustained life in a place like this.

Dukwah arrived with *ahghee* that day, according to custom.

"I am coming home. Pack light bundles of clothes and rice. We will go find your father." I gave her instructions.

"How do you know, Mother?"

"I know. Just be an obedient daughter and do as I ask."

That entire afternoon believers and skeptics alike waited in anticipation. At around three, there was still no word of my release. Eventually the small handful of well-wishers also turned their heads away, disappointed. A few more grueling hours passed and around dusk I, too, started having doubts. I beat myself for being so foolish as to place all my hopes in a dream, and foolish enough to boast about it.

"I know what the problem is." Chipmunk crept over to the overflowing bucket. "Your toilet God has too much shit in his ears."

Everyone laughed themselves into further despair. I felt very tired, as though I could fall asleep forever. If only I could lay down my head, I would indeed sleep and never wake. Fatigue, fatigue, fatigue! Then, from out of nowhere, I heard my name: "Baek, Hongyong!" Not again, I thought, it is only a dream.

"Baek, Hongyong, bring yourself to the front!"

"That is you, *Ahjoomah.*" The young girl shook my shoulder.

I was not dreaming; it was truly the guard's voice. Jaws dropped in ripples of disbelief. The women scrambled for something, anything to write on.

"Please, tell my husband I am still alive," a young woman begged, handing me her address on a scrap of paper.

"Give this to my elderly parents," another pleaded, thrusting a note in my hand. Then another, and another. By the time I made it to the front, my hands were stuffed with names and addresses. I folded them into my sleeve for safekeeping.

"Who is your powerful connection?" Chipmunk snorted.

I faced her for the last time and simply replied, "How can a Christian have any government connections? Jesus is my only savior."

My heart raced as I was escorted back into the interrogation office. A grim-faced man with fleshy cheeks handed me a document to sign. He was so obese he could hardly breathe; obviously, he was the one eating all our provisions.

"What am I signing?" I questioned, because I could not read the tiny characters. My eyes had been accustomed to the darkness too long.

"Do you wish to go home or not?" the officer asked.

Because I wanted to go home more than anything, I signed it. I was glad I could not read it. Hurriedly I walked out, afraid they might discover I had scribbled the wrong name.

It was pouring outside. I welcomed the rain and let the water trickle down my face and into my stinging eyes. There were far fewer people on the streets than before. On the thirtieth day of my unjust imprisonment, I ran all the way home. The reaction from the children and Grandfather was not what I expected. They stood before me, bewilderment creasing their faces. I followed their gaze down the length of my dress and saw that the rain had made my white hemp dress translucent.

"Mother, your clothes are wet." Dukwah was blushing.

"It is wonderful. Just as it was in my dream." I laughed loudly, exposing all my teeth.

The rain, though, had ruined the pieces of paper stashed in my sleeve. My moment of joy was strangled. Those unfortunate lost women. Would their families ever find them?

I threw my arms around each child, hugging them with the urgency stored up during the long weeks they had been lost from me. When I went over to where *ahghee* napped under the mosquito net, I saw a dusty old vagabond with a tangled beard pressed next to her. Instinctively, I grabbed a knife from an empty fruit basket and crept up to the intruder like a well-trained assassin. With one swing of the knife I slashed his beard and braced its sharp tip under his throat.

"Mother!" The children screamed and Yongwoon clutched my hand.

"You, what are you doing in my house?" I demanded to know.

"Is this how you welcome me?" The bearded man grinned.

"I am not afraid to use this!"

"What is a man to think when his own wife forgets her husband's face?"

The knife slipped through my fingers and grazed Husband's cheek. He had aged, and this time without the help of a disguise.

"Why did you come back so soon? It is not safe," I asked, distressed.

"I am going to turn myself in. Why should women and children suffer in my place? The children need a mother more. I was selfish to save only myself."

"No, it was my idea," I interrupted. "You are in worse danger than we are. You must go back to your hiding place."

"I would rather die like a man, not like some frightened rodent in its little hole. A human being is not made to live under the earth. Besides, I cannot bear the thought of them harming you again. Your face . . ." His voice cracked as he brushed his hand over my unhealed cuts and discolored bruises.

"You need not worry about my face. My skin is not exquisite, nor are my features beautiful and delicate. They cannot ruin something that never existed," I replied shyly.

"That is not true," he interjected. "To me, you are the most desirable woman."

I felt my face flush red. He was so sweet, even though he was a terrible liar. Having eaten only moldy rice and runny millet slop for thirty days, I was less than a woman, just a skeleton with loose skin.

That night, when it was nearing bedtime, I was almost beside myself. I had fantasized about this moment so often in jail—the soft snores of my children; my clean white night slip; the padded mattress; plenty of room to stretch out; and, of course, Husband curled beside me. I slept straight through and could have stayed in bed for another two days if I had not been awakened by the wife of our tenant. Husband had been opposed to them moving into the inner room after Cheong's wife left, because the good woman's husband belonged to the People's

Army. He was the only man we knew who volunteered for the job.

"Dear friend, it is me, the wife of your renter."

"Thank God," I muttered, and welcomed her in. We clasped hands.

"There is no time, you must leave before my husband comes back and finds you all here. I am so ashamed, he is the one who denounced your family."

"Your husband?" I was stunned. I had hoped our Christian hospitality would lure him away from the Reds. I should have listened to Husband's warning.

She nodded in genuine regret. "I begged him not to report your husband. I am so sorry."

"We have already forgiven him," I assured her.

"Thank you. You must go immediately, for he will surely report you again to the authorities."

"We will heed your warning."

"Quickly, I hope. Now I must return before he discovers me missing."

There was much to discuss. What to do? Where to go? And who should go? This time we must keep the family together. Finally, after a lot of praying, we decided to return to our confiscated land. Some loyal tenants would hide us.

I packed a few items: three of Husband's expensive wool coats, the last bundle of silk, blankets, all the food we could carry, and some sentimental trinkets I could not bear to part with.

I sneaked out first with the four younger children, Meenah, and Grandfather. Husband and Yongwoon trailed behind through dark alleys and back roads. We could not see them, but they kept a watchful eye on us, ready to leap out at any sign of danger. Our lengthy walk carried us past long stretches of blasted fields. Debris and artillery shells blanketed the landscape where trees, flowers, and animals once thrived.

When we arrived, only a handful of families still remained on the wasted land. We had to fend for ourselves among the abandoned shacks, searching for a place that was not gutted out or completely flattened. On the northeast corner of the property, we found a moderately comfortable house. The former owners left it just as it was, removing only the doors and throwing the bucket into the well to deter squatters.

Soon after we arrived in early October, villagers gave amazing eyewitness accounts of hundreds of retreating North Korean soldiers. The United Nations forces had landed at Inchon in mid-September, recapturing the southern capital of Seoul. From there they crossed the 38th parallel, heading toward Pyongyang. Many of the Red soldiers limped along, relying on makeshift crutches and each other, their large columns now uneven and scattered. Only a few months earlier, they had pushed the UN and the ROK forces to the tip of the peninsula.

Jubilant, Husband drew up a whole batch of *Taekuk* flags, using the expensive silk. It was well worth it. The flags flapped from every rooftop, so when the UN forces came they would know our village's allegiance belonged to them.

How I missed the sight of our *Taekuk*. In 1948 the People's Committee adopted a new flag—a red flag bordered on upper and lower edges by a thin white stripe. It was an insult to our people and country to think such a molested design could replace our glorious *Taekuk*. For *Taekuk* embodied the essence of an ideal society. The center circle of *yin* and *yang* divisions represents eternal duality—heaven and earth, good and evil, male and female, dark and light, life and death. The short and long bars at all four corners stated that the weak should be protected by the strong. The more precious should be protected by the less worthy. Like should cling to like, but tolerance should sanction the grouping of unlike. Unfortunately, war had made us abandon these lessons. Strong, weak, precious, less worthy, like and unlike had turned against each other . . . become murderers.

Taekuk's brilliant bold colors of red, blue, white, and black fluttered in the wind high above our heads to welcome our liberators. They came and captured Pyongyang on October 18, then kept moving north toward the Korean-Manchurian border. In late November, we saw our liberators again. This second time they were limping in a mad retreat to escape the 400,000 marching Chinese volunteers who crossed the Yalu River on October 25. Long columns came through our streets, so many of them dressed in thick olive padded clothing, a peaked cap with a red star badge, a backpack, and a rifle. Seeing the flags, the Reds headed right to our gate after frightened villagers betrayed the artist. Fortunately, a young student had come to warn us of the approaching enemy.

The race against death began. Now there was no time for

creative disguises, only a plan. I pleaded with Husband to leave us and go as far south as he needed to be safe. He insisted we all escape together, but I knew Grandfather was too old to travel such a distance. Reluctantly, he agreed to flee alone once more.

"It is I who am always running away," he said, taking my face in both his hands and holding it for a long, tender moment.

"I will be here when you return. I swear it."

"What if this time I do not make it back?" He intended it to be light, but his voice was strained.

"Then I will search the world for you," I said, and we both laughed a little. I was pleased with my response. I made a vow to myself the last time he went away that I would not allow us to part without revealing my true heart. I had nothing to gain by concealing my emotions. It only hurt the man who meant everything to me.

"You are my love," I declared. "You are my love." I let the words trickle off my tongue again.

"Thank you. Now I am ready to part."

I watched as his figure vanished into the night. It was not any easier the second time. In fact, it was more heart-wrenching. Something told me I would not see him for a long while. But the sight of our children, his offspring, made it less lonesome. Yongwoon especially resembled Husband. At sixteen, he was already taller than his father. His face was golden and square, and still smooth, lacking as yet the signs of manhood. He had always been slim but exceedingly robust. I studied my son in silence. His mouth and eyes sullen—that was the way he always looked those days. As he was a child of war, his heart was heavy beyond its years.

"Mother, I must go, too." His words contradicted his tone, as if he hoped I would forbid him to leave me.

"I see," was all I could muster. I was relieved and dying all at the same time. I knew this eldest son of mine was torn because he loved his home and family and yet he could not live here. "And when will you go?" I asked in a calm voice.

". . . Tomorrow night with two of the older students from church."

"What are their names?" I needed to know.

"Kim Bonghwen and Kim Daekun, the Reverend's sons."

"How far will you travel?"

"As far as the war forces us, I suppose."

"When will you come back?" My throat burned.

"When it is safe to openly praise our God in the streets without fearing a bullet will strike us down."

"Yes."

No other words were spoken that entire night. Bright and early the following morning I packed a sack with clothes and what food I could spare for his journey. I struggled to conceal my agony behind a cool, assured mask, but my trembling hands betrayed me as I handed him his wrapped package.

"Good-bye, Mother." His tone was more grave.

This was the hour I had never envisioned in my wildest nightmares. I wanted to frame every detail of his face in my mind. Those big round eyes of his with their overlapping lids. That sharp nose. Those pink puffy lips. How I hated standing there unable to cradle him in my protective arms like I used to when he was a child. Instead, I caressed him with only my eyes, for he was a young man now.

It took all that I had to pry myself away from his side as he said his farewells to Grandfather and his younger brothers and sisters. Only Dukwah and Meenah were mature enough to comprehend that our family was crumbling.

"Come back to me unharmed, I beg you. I will be here waiting," I promised him, as I had promised his father only a day before.

After he was gone, I left the gate open for a long moment. Shutting it seemed so final. I sank to the ground and sat there with my back against the wall and my eyes pushed tight, water at the edges. I felt the weight of his journey on my chest, heavier than the biggest bomb and more explosive. I wanted to lash out at the futility and unfairness of war which took its greatest toll on innocent lives. I shall never forget that night, nor shall I forget the face of my broken-winged angel.

TOLL OF INNOCENCE

F or days I sat despondently on the threshold of the doorstep. And for days I watched the sun rise each morning and set at the same time each night. Always the same careless brilliance. The sky remained unchangingly normal up there while down on earth it thundered and burned. Several more days I lingered, waiting, hoping for the ground to stop shaking. I was torn between wanting to escape and needing to stay. The idea of uprooting my life and starting over again at the age of thirty-nine paralyzed me. I was not a young woman anymore. But most importantly, I had promised Yongwoon and Husband that we would greet them when they returned. Surely they would think we were captured, or worse, if the house was vacant.

More days passed and I moved about with nervous energy. It was unsafe to walk in the streets. It was unsafe to sleep in the house. Which was better, to die trying to save ourselves or to die waiting? Suddenly I had the overwhelming urge to get away. The seven of us would join Husband and Yongwoon across the river. If we did not find them there, farther south we would search.

Dukwah came in right when I made my decision, as if she read my mind. "We are going to find your older brother and Father," I informed her. "Prepare the others."

Packing was an emotionally draining task. What to carry and what to abandon were difficult choices. I had to be thrifty. Too much baggage could cost us our lives. After an hour of heart-breaking contemplation, I sacrificed everything except for a pair of gold dangling earrings; the children's twenty-four-karat-gold baby rings; a light bag of rice; the two deeds to our confiscated properties; a photo of Husband in his sporty Western suit; and three of his wool coats, into the hems of which the jewelry and deeds were carefully sewn.

Being a functioning woman, I also packed four reusable cotton pads in the event I started to menstruate again or if my twelve-year-old daughter chose this inopportune time to become a woman. The thought of washing pads along the icy trail with bombs exploding over our heads was almost funny. For this reason alone, women would never start wars. War was a man's game, but the women and children seemed to suffer the most.

I no longer thought of anything but the decision to go. "It must be done. It must be done," I repeated to myself, trying to boost my confidence.

Dukwah walked in again, toting a heavy load of schoolbooks bundled together with a thin cloth string.

"Dukwah-yah, you must leave those here; they will only weigh us down."

"But, Mother, I will die without my books. How can I get into a good middle school next year if I do not have them to study?"

"We will all perish if you bring them with you. Each of us must make sacrifices," I replied sternly. "When we reach the South, I will buy you more books. Now gather Grandfather and your brothers and sisters."

"Everyone is dressed except for Older Sister."

"Meenah-yah, where is your coat?" I called her in.

"Grandfather is too old to travel, he will only slow you down. I will stay with him and watch after the house until you return."

I looked at her, bewildered. "You two cannot stay here. It is suicide!"

"It is your only choice. I owe this to you." She paused for a moment then said, "Please let me repay your kindness, Mother."

I marveled at this wise young girl who loved us with such devotion she was willing to stay behind with Grandfather so we could have a fighting chance. I would never have asked her to do such a thing because I loved her as one of my own, but I knew she spoke the truth. Grandfather had grown very feeble, half blind and almost wholly deaf. The only movement he was capable of making on his own was to feed himself.

When I reminisce on those crucial days, my thoughts often settle on the hunchbacked girl. What ever happened to her or Grandfather, I do not know.

The children and I said our short, tearful good-byes, and then I hurried them out the gate.

"Dry your tears, children. They will only turn into icicles and freeze your face. Be brave, our journey has just begun," I warned.

We must have looked like a family of overstuffed dolls. The children were wrapped in layers of sweaters, pantaloons, and socks. I wore my winter *chogori* and *chima* quilted with cotton. Warmth was a trade-off for quickness and agility. It had to be. Careless exposure of the flesh to the sharp winter air was punished by frostbite.

My hair, now long and braided, was looped about my head to balance the bag of rice, for I needed both hands to clutch on to my six- and nine-year-old boys. Dukwah, being the older, trailed from behind, clinging to my skirt. And the baby rested securely strapped on my back under the warmth of Husband's three wool coats.

The sun was still bright outside, draping a golden glaze over the northern mountains as we began a nightmarish monthlong crossing in the midst of winter. Little did I know then that the last months of 1950 were one of the most intensive periods of UN air assaults. Hundreds of fighter-bombers flew daily, blotting out villages and townships.

We had traveled only a short distance when screams came from our house. The children and I clung together in fright as we watched scavengers viciously raid our empty storage room. Torches circled the house as the bandits carried off the remaining furniture. They were our friends of yesterday, who probably hid behind their doors waiting for a chance to loot our house. I was helpless to protect the two people who stayed behind. So we continued on.

Carefully we weaved in and around piles of debris, burned-out houses, and other mangled objects I could not identify. The light frost crunched underfoot. Ours were the only footprints to be heard. It was as though we were the last five people left. Then there they were! A great throng of people scrambled at the Taedong River. These frantic refugees hovered at the edge of the bank like ants attracted to sugar water. I had never seen it so congested before. The river stood between us and the South. It was not frozen over, so we could not simply slide across as we had done all the winters past. Now various sorts of fishing boats and junks were ferrying people across to the other side. Order had collapsed; brute strength was the law of survival. People jumped on top of and clung to one another, fighting to grab seats on the already overloaded boats. Punching. Shoving. Cursing. Struggling. Even the women, with their rough language, were acting like men. They had only one purpose—to get across. Modesty and elegance had no place in war.

"Mother, look over there." Kunil pointed in the direction of a man, in his late twenties, wearing only his underwear. He stood with his hands propped on his hips and boasted he was going to swim to freedom. All eyes were glued to him. Some hoped to follow his lead if he succeeded; others were curious to see death. From the blueness of the man's face I knew the temperature was excruciatingly cold. Inch by inch he walked in, balancing his clothes in a wrapped bundle on top of his head. When the water crept up to his shoulders, he began dog-paddling. As he approached the middle of the river, a sharp wooden plank rammed into his head. He bobbed up and down for a second or so before sinking. Only a red circle marked the fatal spot.

I kept thinking: How are we going to get across? Every time a boat rowed near, I tried to hurry the children on board, but others were quicker. They climbed over us, forcing us back onto the shore. Again and again I attempted to board a boat, but without success, receiving only more scratches and bruises. All appeared grim, until someone called out, "Yongwoon' mother." It was the short, stout woman with the cowlike eyes and sunken cheeks from church. Her brow was slicked brown with sweat. I did not recognize her at first sight, for she was dressed in a man's jacket and pantaloons, but when she smiled and I saw all her teeth were missing, I knew her right away.

"Yongwoon's mother, what are you still doing on this side?" she asked urgently.

"It is impossible. The children and I are too slow."

"Wait here. I will send a boat to you," she said, and promptly rushed off.

Minutes later a small fishing boat paddled our way. "Get in." The boatman steadied the boat with his hooked pole.

"Children, quickly," I ordered.

But as we scrambled to get on, we were rushed. Dukwah was the only one able to grab a firm hold. The boys and I were roughly lifted and tossed over the side. Stranded, we watched Dukwah sail off without us.

"What now, Mother?" the boys whined.

A tangled girder from a bridge fell from the sky farther up the river, making a loud splash. Even from a distance I could see the center section was blown away, but people were still attempting to cross it. Father hated that modern bridge which the Japanese had enslaved our people to build. So as children we were forbidden to venture across it. Now it was our only chance.

The boys and I slowly made our way up the gravel path to the bridge. A larger and more desperate mob jammed the area.

"It is my turn!"

"No, it is mine!" people shouted back and forth at the top of their lungs.

"How long have you been waiting?" I asked the strained-faced woman in front of me.

"All day!" she complained.

"All day!" I gasped. "It is nearly nightfall."

We had been standing in the back of the heap for a long time when two men with red headbands and sticks marched up and down the line, maintaining some discipline. Occasionally they swung their sticks, beating people to stop them from cutting to the front.

"That small one over there is vicious," the strained-faced woman warned as he stomped toward us.

He pointed his stick directly at me. "*Ahjoomah!* Bring your children and follow me!" he shouted, and we obeyed.

"Where are you taking us?"

He stopped in his tracks and faced me. "You do not recognize me?" he asked in a less authoritative voice.

I shook my head. "Should I?"

"Perhaps not, but I have never forgotten your kindness. You once treated my mother when doctors turned us away because we were poor," he said with genuine gratitude.

I had given so much charity since accepting Christ into my life that his face had slipped from my memory. "I still do not remember," I confessed.

"It is me, Shin, Jooseong."

"*Uh-moh-nah!*" I grabbed both his hands. He had grown so tall.

"You will cross next." He pushed the crowd aside and ushered us to the front.

"Where did she come from?! We were here first!"

Hands tore at our hair, arms, and clothes from all sides. I fell under the great pressure. Their heavy feet trampled over my back where the baby was lying.

"Mother! Mother! *Ahghee* is dying!" Kunil cried.

With all my might I tried to turn on my side to shield her, but I was helplessly pinned facedown under the many feet.

"Jooseong-yah!" I shrieked.

At my call he came bulldozing through, swinging his stick wildly. One by one, bodies were thrown off me. *Ahghee*'s face was blackened and her head drooped like a broken flower. "*Ahghee-yah!*" I shook my shoulders up and down to wake her. She was lifeless. Though I wanted to mourn, there was no time to pray for the dying. "I will bury her once we get to the other side," I sighed.

More men with red headbands and sticks patrolled the mouth of the bridge, letting only a few people pass at one time. Standing there, I was able to get a clear view of the mangled bridge and what was ahead of us. The front and end sections were still intact; however, a huge chunk of the middle was nothing but twisted steel rods and loose planks.

"They are next," Jooseong informed the front guard.

"Us?" I squeaked cowardly. "My boys, how am I going to carry them across?" I stepped back ready to retreat.

"The smaller one will ride on my back and the bigger boy and I will follow close behind," Jooseong offered courageously.

"Even if we fall, we must try," I convinced myself.

I instructed the boys not to stare down until they reached the other end. They nodded their heads obediently. It was unbearable to watch my precious sons balance themselves along the narrow wobbly beam, but I did anyway. Kunil went first on all fours. Kunsam clung to Jooseong's spiny back; his slippers dangled in the air and his trousers slipped down below the crack of his butt. I worried he might catch a cold.

Next, it was my dreaded turn. I stepped forward, made sure the lifeless child on my back was secured, then dropped down on my knees. At once a man leaped over me, nearly knocking me to my death. The struggle was short; a stick clobbered him on the head and he flew over the side. Ruthless penalties were the only way to maintain any kind of order among all this madness.

Gathering my courage, I crawled forward, clamping my fingers around the icy steel beam. Slowly I scooted forward, shifting my weight from side to side. My body felt as though it weighed a thousand pounds. Sweat beaded my forehead and ran down my face, stinging my eyes, but I kept inching on. Halfway across, I had the insane desire to peer down. Big mistake! When I saw how high above the ground I was, I became paralyzed. My limbs locked, my back stiffened, and my legs slipped underneath me. I was afraid even to take another breath, fearing if I filled my lungs with air the beam might snap. How I wished I could be transformed into a butterfly and soar over the river.

"Move on or let go!" the long line behind me yelled.

It would have been so easy to just let go and throw myself into the river and end this torment. Then I heard the boys call out to me, "Mother, hurry up! We are here."

I closed my eyes and salvaged my courage. Inch by inch I scratched myself along. "Ten more feet. Five more. Oh, please, God . . . please, God, give me strength," I mumbled over and over, concentrating only on my prayer.

Strong hands pulled me to solid ground. I was dazed, it was

as if I had been spun around a dozen times. I had no sense of what was up or down, but I kept moving. We had to find Dukwah. I grabbed the boys' hands and guided them back down the bank of the river. The farther away from the bridge, the less numb I felt.

We found Dukwah on her knees swaying between prayer and drowsiness.

"Dukwah-yah!" I called out.

She jumped up and wrapped her arms around my waist, clinging with all her might, afraid to lose me again.

"Oh, Mother, I was so worried."

"You are the smart one. We did it the hard way."

The boys broke out in laughter. Their sparkling smiles were contagious. Together we shared a rare moment of light-heartedness.

"All you had to do was ride a boat, Older Sister, but we hung from the clouds," Kunil giggled.

The laughter fizzled as we were reminded of our smallest member. *Ahghee* had the look of death on her face.

"We must bury her," I told the other children. But as I lifted her tiny body to my ear, to my amazement her breath continued to flutter in and out. I could not bury her alive. I would carry her until it was time to put her in the ground.

Tearing a shred from my inner hem, I wiped her blackened face, gently using spit to loosen the grime. It was a mother's secret healing potion to make all the hurt go away. Sadly, this time it did little good.

The night was approaching quickly and soon it would become pitch-dark. It seemed tomorrow would be a better day for walking and we set up camp under the naked sky. Again, the stout lady with the cowlike eyes found us clustered together near the river.

"Yongwoon's mother, it is dangerous to sleep here."

"Our legs are useless." I shooed her away.

"You have to go and go fast." Her eyes bulged with urgency. "The B-29s are coming."

She tugged at my jacket, until we went on our way again. Our feet were frozen, our bellies empty, and our energy spent. We were only a few miles away when we heard planes descend on the river. Bomb after bomb after bomb after bomb exploded, producing massive quakes. Gigantic roaring flames lit the sky, their heat so powerful it nearly singed our eyebrows.

"Let us go, children," I said, not wanting to witness any more slaughter. Years later I learned that everyone who stayed behind perished at the bridge, giving a new name to the Taedong River—Blood River.

We picked our way through the blinding darkness, the far-off moon our only guide. Time stretched out. We walked for what seemed like eternity, oblivious to everything except the need to find shelter. Eventually, we turned off one of the numerous winding roads onto a rutted path that led to more darkness. The thought of another step gave me a headache. Perhaps a family would take us in, and if they refused I would offer them my golden earrings.

We came to a large shed. The windows were blown out and the door removed. Inside sleeping bodies pressed up all the way to the walls.

"Find another place. Can you not see there is no more room?!" A man hid his head to escape the chilly breeze.

"Move on! Move on!" A shoe flew inches above *ahghee*'s droopy head.

I was not about to get mauled by an angry mob when we just escaped death by bombs, so we trudged forward again into the frozen night. Finally, at our fifth abandoned building, we were semi-tolerated. When we stepped inside I could see it was once a pleasant house. Someone's home, someone long vanished. Throwing ourselves on the ground, we settled in near the kitchen.

The smell of burnt rice from their scavenged meals lingered in our nostrils, teasing our starved stomachs. Nevertheless, sleep outweighed hunger pangs, so we lay down without food. The children fell fast asleep as soon as their heads hit the cold *ondul* floor. All I could offer were the three wool coats to cover them. That night I dozed in and out of sleep. I kept one eye on the wool coats to guard against thieves and the other on the children. Thoughts buzzed in my mind, for so much had happened. We left our home, we lost Grandfather and Meenah, and we saw lives burn up in flames. It was unimaginable that all this occurred in a single night.

The sun rose early and everyone was up and out the door, tasting their morning breath. On this new day ahead of us anything could happen—missing limbs, loss of a family member, death. The house emptied in a matter of seconds. I was not as quick; I stood up and stretched. My body ached as if I had been beaten. I was about to wake the children, but they looked so sweet with their arms tangled together. I decided to let them dream just a little longer, though I knew each minute we lingered was dangerous.

I stole outside to the well. The bucket and rope were lying at the bottom. In their place was a man's rubber shoe dangling from strips of rags knotted together. Carefully I lowered it and after several attempts I pulled up a shoeful of cloudy water. In the kitchen hardly any of the dishes were unbroken. I used a dented pot to cook the rice I brought along, happy to lighten the load. The portions were stingy, for this tiny supply of rice was all the food we had for however long.

The warm aroma wafted upward and it was time to wake the children. I bent down to where they slept and touched their brows. They dragged themselves off the floor and went to their bowls, which were served on a makeshift table. It was more water than rice, but it would warm their hands and soothe their stomachs. I watched as they lifted the chipped bowls to their blue lips, blew on them, and slowly sipped. They swallowed the food without a word. Then I crawled over to the baby; she was still alive. I thought I saw a slight smile when she felt my nipple brush against her lip. Together *ahghee* and I sipped our morning meals. The hot broth seemed to travel through my chilled body and directly into the babe's mouth. I should have eaten more, but I ate only enough to keep producing milk.

"Let us go," I said after every drop of rice was licked up.

We clutched our garments about us and, shivering, began walking, joined together by hand and skirt. Outside, the morning sun was radiantly bright. It peeped over the mountaintops, etching their sharp features, but fear and cold dimmed even the most radiant horizon. The wind howled and hissed at us, blasting through our bones. We walked against the winter wind, teeth clenched.

I discovered we had wandered quite a distance off the main road; fortunately, it was easy to find our way back. As far as the eye could see, a large column of people stretched across the land. It was an amazing sight, so unreal this scene before me. It was as though all of North Korea was fleeing in a mass exodus on this one road—the Imperial Highway, Shimjannoh, the only major road in the whole peninsula. The Japanese had built this graveled road to run from the Yalu River to Uiju through Pyongyang on down to Seoul.

The highway was cluttered with people, sleds, and oxcarts. Men with *chiges*, A-frames, were bent over at the waist from hauling massive loads on their backs. Mothers, like myself, carried children on their backs and packages on their heads, oftentimes performing incredible balancing acts. Only the very young and very elderly traveled light.

The snow beneath us was muddy and slushy. Poor misguided animals slipped off the treacherous road, pitted with large and small craters. It was crucial to watch every step to avoid the same mishap. Each mile we passed rubble and ashes. Why the bombers wasted their destruction on us fleeing refugees, I did not understand. What threat could we possibly be? I learned later why the UN air forces bombed us. The Reds, disguised as refugees, were hauling artillery and food supplies on horse-drawn carts and *chiges*. It seemed impossible the planes miles above could detect a Red when I could not see them walking among us.

By nine o'clock in the morning, a weariness began to settle in my muscles. The journey had just begun and already I felt so weak. The bag of rice bruised my head and sweat glistened on my face from the load. Behind me, two women talked quietly about something or other. I had no energy to eavesdrop on their conversation, much less ask their names. Here, what difference did it make?

"I must keep going. Feet, walk." I urged myself on . . . and on . . . and on.

Without warning the earsplitting sound of bombs crashing up ahead of us sent screams of terror rippling though the long columns.

"B-29! B-29!" Hysterical men, women, and children dashed

here, there, trying to avoid death. Some collapsed to their knees and hid their faces. Others just dropped dead. WHACK! WHACK! It was the sound of bullets slapping into flesh.

"Mother! Mother!" I heard my children wail. Their cries shook me more than the earthshaking bombs. "Mother, where are you?!"

"Stay down, children!" I screamed.

I could not find them through the smoke but I knew they were near. "Stay down!" I shouted again. Crawling on my belly, I scooted along using the sound of their voices to guide me. *PONG!* The woman just a few feet ahead flew through the air, killed instantly. I felt so desperately vulnerable, exposed—a duck in an open pond during hunting season. Quickly I untied *ahghee* and shielded her with my body. I crouched there rather than run toward smoke and flames that were so thick they choked my throat and teared my eyes.

The planes flew down the line, toggling a bomb every few hundred yards, then swung back to machine-gun the blazing ruins. Bullets hammered the ground, forever stitching bodies to the earth. I was surrounded. In front, to the right, to the left, behind me, shells flashed and danced madly. With each shot, I jerked as if struck. I was certain one mortally wounded me.

I stayed huddled until the throbbing sounds of engines receded and the last low-flying aircraft made its sweep overhead to inspect the wreckage. Then out of the chaos came silence. Silence all around, broken only by moans and groans. Slowly the dust and smoke lifted, unveiling a museum of slaughter. Corpses twisted in a multitude of poses like the armless, headless Greek statues. Blood squirted from ripped limbs and punctured wounds, signing their final bloody signatures on the snow. Crying babies lay pinned underneath their wasted mothers. No one stopped to rescue them. War forced people to close their hearts, to shut out the cries of other people's children. War forced us to worry only about our own burdens, and even that was a great responsibility to bear.

"Children, where are you?"

Other mothers began to dig through the stained snow for their missing children. I witnessed layer after layer of hope melt away. Such anguish.

"Dukwah-yah, Kunil-yah, Kunsam-yah!" I desperately yelled out each of their names. To my disbelief, all four of my children were still alive. The boys were crouched next to their older sister with their thumbs shoved in their ears, second and third fingers pressing down on their eyelids, and fourth fingers plugging their nostrils—a drill taught to them in school.

I gathered them up in my arms and checked each child for any severed parts, gashes, bullet holes. No blood! So we scrambled to our feet with the other survivors and moved on, maneuvering through a harvest of unplanted corpses, tilted carts, and potholes as wide as houses. All those years spent in China, I had never seen explosions hurl people and enormous animals through the air.

"Come on, children, we must go before they reload." I hurried them forward.

"Shall we find Father today?" Kunsam asked.

"Are we going to die?" Kunil inquired.

"Possibly," I replied. I did not want to deceive them; I wanted them to be prepared in case death came for them during the next raid. "Listen carefully. When the planes swarm again, do not yell out my name. I cannot protect you from the bullets. Call out Jesus' name. He is the only one who can save you. Do you understand?"

"Yes, Mother. We call Jesus." Dukwah nodded.

And the planes did come again and again, swooping down for the kill. Each time the children dropped into their drill positions and summoned, "Jesus! Jesus! Jesus!"

Each time the air cleared, more victims and more animals were tossed dead, lying in their own red juices. One by one I threw out my children's names into the smoke to see which, if any, of them survived. One, two, three, plus *ahghee* miraculously escaped death.

So petrified that I might lose the boys, I found myself squeezing their hands tighter, cutting off the circulation. They complained and whined but I ignored their tears because we all hurt.

We walked and walked. No time to stop, no time to rest. Whips constantly cracked in our ears as men urgently shouted at their beasts to hurry on through blockades of warm bodies and abandoned possessions. It was a scavenger's dream come true. The open road was a gigantic marketplace. Anything could be found there, suitcases, knives, plates, books, faded portraits, tables, porcelain tubs. They were for the taking, but only fools dared to lug the extra weight.

Walk, walk, walk . . . It was all we did. Walk . . . walk . . . walk . . . for days and days we walked. Walk . . . trip . . . drag . . . for weeks we walked. In every corpse I passed I searched for Husband's or son's face, afraid if not this one, then the next would be one of them. But it was always someone else's husband or child. Still, their senseless deaths affected me as if they were my own flesh and blood. Soon, I stopped searching the blue frozen faces. I needed to keep my wits and courage up, especially when the nights descended upon us and the temperature dropped. Finding shelter was on every mind. Thousands of frenzied refugees fought for the same few homes, barns, and outhouses along the highway. Anything that provided some bit of insulation was far better than complete exposure. It was a battle well worth fighting even after a long exhausting day of dodging air strikes. Unfortunately, the children and I rarely got a chance to stake our claim. Our tiny footsteps were always miles behind the slowest refugees. We spent many nights walking. To sleep in the cold was to surrender life.

At first I thought it was better to travel under the safe cloak of darkness. But I was naive to think war slept. Nights, too, became dangerous, as the planes flew lower over our heads. They targeted anything that moved. Red tracer bullets blazed across the sky, so the pilots could see where the shots went. When the planes all fired at once, it looked like a swarm of killer fireflies.

I pushed the children hard. I had to. Only when they were past exhaustion did I let them rest a bit. I would find a dull spot that hid our reflections. A fire was a luxury we could not afford. Together we would press against one another in an effort to keep out the blasting chill. Always we wore our shoes, ready to run at the sound of a whisper or whir of an engine. Often I wanted to sink down next to them and steal a few precious blinks of sleep. No. I forced myself to stay alert.

One night as the children and I were about to settle under the infinite ceiling of stars, the crackling sound of a warm fire caught our attention. I could not believe my nose—beef. In the near distance, a group of men lounged around a low flickering campfire, fueled with abandoned items found on the trail. I tried not to surrender myself to the mouthwatering fragrance, but when you have not eaten meat, much less something remotely solid, for weeks, it was all you thought of. They must have butchered one of the dead animals lying on the road freshly refrigerated in the ice.

The children said nothing. They only licked their chapped lips, then fell into a deep sleep. My failure to feed them was agonizing. So when I saw the men's silhouettes retire for the night, I cautiously tiptoed over to their dying campfire. With each crunching step, the sound shot electricity through my toes, up the length of my body. I raised my foot just where I placed it, being careful not to chip any more of the icy snow than I had to. As I went nearer, the wonderful aroma got stronger and the growling in my stomach louder. I was sure the noise would be the death of me. And then there it was, roasting over the flames, the cadaver of a baby ox. It cast a shadow on the faces of the sleeping men, who lay like a chain-link fence around the kill. My heart sank as I stood outside the circle of bodies, unable to snatch the meat just inches away. In despair, I lowered my head and that was when I saw a half-opened hand cupping a rib with chunks of flesh still clinging to the bone. Possessed by hunger, I found myself reaching down. My hand shook so wildly I had to quickly pull it back. I waited a perilous moment, then tried again. I had it! Suddenly something clamped onto my hair and jerked it hard. A man's snow-covered eyebrows darted down at me. His hollow dark eyes were as young as my Yongwoon's. They must have been the same age. Then, without explanation, he released his grip and rolled back to sleep. I was set free, my fingers still latched around the rib.

The children were lost in slumber when I returned, so I let them dream on. Knowing they had meat to sustain them for the new day, I allowed myself to relax. For some reason, that night seemed endlessly longer than all the others. Perhaps because I was searching for an answer to all this meaningless destruction. Then the answer dawned on me as I watched an unknown pilot drop a bomb from high in the sky. If only all these pilots could see our faces and hear our cries, they would surely stop the killing. It seemed so simple, but they never did. They stayed miles above in their safe cocoons.

Finally the moon slowly ducked over the horizon and the sun rose to take its place. The snow continued to fall in thick flakes, but the sun's rays thawed my blood a little, making it easier to move around. I almost felt revived, almost. Stretching out an arm, I touched my children. "Wake up, it is time." They half opened their eyes, but when they saw the rib they sprang up right away. Each child received a good round chunk of meat, which he gobbled immediately. I spared nothing for myself, I was content sucking on the marrow. It was delicious.

Near us there were two young boys. The little one tried unsuccessfully to shake his older brother awake. Death had seized him silently, peacefully during the night. His brother's frozen weight was too much for him to carry, so he curled up next to him and closed his eyes. Again the toll of innocence rose, and again my heart was slashed with the cruelty of war.

"Move on," I told myself. "I can only worry about my own." Such selfish words, not the Christian thing to do, and yet I think God understood the terrible decisions I often had to make.

So we stumbled forward, hand in hand, amid an icy maze of peaks and turns. My feet throbbed constantly. Ice speared through the bottoms of my slippers and tore at the rubber soles. Soon there was hardly any protection. I hobbled along using a broken branch to lean on. I badly needed another pair of shoes more suitable for walking, and not two sizes smaller for appearance' sake. Determined, I eyed each stiffened corpse along the road, examining the quality and size of shoes. I came across an ROK soldier whose face was blown away. I felt no remorse as I tugged his leather boots off his feet. They were several sizes too big, but at least they were wide at the toes. Easing the tattered rubber slippers off my feet was sheer pain. The cold had glued them to my raw skin. I had to use a knife to cut them off, slicing flesh with it. I was stunned beyond sickness by the sight. They were bloated with pus, gnarled beyond recognition. I tried to alleviate the pressure by puncturing the skin and letting the clear yellow fluid ooze out, then buried them in the ice to deaden the nerves before squeezing into the boots. My feet felt detached from the rest of my body and that was enough to get me back on them.

"Faster." They pushed from behind. Stranger after stranger passed us. We were constantly haunted by new worn faces, never the same unknown ones. Refugees staggered, fell, dragged their lives in packs. They passed without even a glance in our direction. I envied them for their speed. The children and I struggled with all our might to keep up with the moving mass but it was impossible. Discouraged, we fell farther behind. Each moment my mood shifted. The strain showed in my face, drawn and sour from weariness. Sweat soaked my clothes although it was very cold. My breath came and went quickly.

The planes, the cold, this damn country, the stench of my own filth pricked at my sanity. Now my worst enemy was not the bombs but my own weakness. I was fearful I would snap like so many others and collapse sobbing. I wanted my home and family back. Those longing images poisoned my will to place one foot ahead of the other.

Red spies, dressed in farmers' garbs, crept up on us and tried to lure us back to the North.

"Are you tired, *Ahjoomah?* I miss my home. Shame, I should have not abandoned my elderly parents. They need me. It is still not too late to turn back."

They knew my weakness, they knew exactly what emotion tremored inside. "Maybe we should go home." I broke down in front of the children.

"No! We must go where Father is," Dukwah exclaimed.

"He is probably waiting for us at home right now."

"No, we must go find him across the border," she said with conviction.

If it were not for the children's desire to find their father, I would have turned around miles ago, because I was certain we had used up all our miracles. So against my better judgment we forged on among the flames, rockets, screams, and eruptions. "We are almost there," I would mumble blandly, giving neither them nor me any kind of reassurance. I said it anyway just so I could hear the words.

The bag of rice was now gone. We had exhausted our food supply. We were living on yesterday's rice and snow. *Ahghee,* who was at death's door, was unwilling to let go of life. Carrying her made my journey more laborious. All the muscles in my body were one drawn-out wail, even my lashes ached. I had to make an unthinkable decision. I had to choose between *ahghee*'s life and ours, and I picked ours. The choice was justified and inhumane at the same time. It was the best I could do. The three older children had a greater chance of surviving than this frail little one. I freed her from my back and propped her behind a small boulder so she would not be trampled. Immediately my body felt lighter, though my heart weighed a thousand times heavier with grief.

"Mother, how can you just leave her here to die?" Dukwah cried.

"Leave her!" I barked. The horror in all three of their faces was more than I could stand.

"We have to take *ahghee*."

"She is practically dead anyway."

"If one of us dies, then we must all die. If we go, we must all go together!"

"Do not question what I do. I do this for you and your brothers."

"Then I will carry her." Dukwah swooped *ahghee* into her arms.

"I said we are leaving her behind."

"How can you be so cruel. Will you discard us, too, on the side of the road if we become a burden?"

I smacked her hard across the face. I could not stop hitting her. Dukwah stood there and took my abuse. She let me vent all my sorrow and frustrations out on her.

"I make this ultimate sacrifice so you may survive. This war is not my fault. If only *ahghee* was born a few years later or if your father was here to carry her, if . . . if . . ." I could not speak any more.

I grabbed the boys' hands and started walking, staring straight ahead at the road. I refused to allow Dukwah's naive righteousness sway my decision.

Out of the corner of my eye, I saw her struggle beside us carrying *ahghee*. With each step, Dukwah began to lag behind. Her arms and legs betrayed her, but she was unwilling to give up. Every mile or so she crouched down and rested. She repeated this insanity for several miles before she finally collapsed. I rushed to them, peering down at their young faces.

"Give her to me." I held out my arms.

"No, I will carry her."

"Give her to me," I repeated, prying the babe from her arms and tying *ahghee* on my back. Half a mile later, my legs wobbled terribly again. Dukwah came to my rescue. But first she reached under her sweater and unraveled the cloth bandage she had wrapped around her chest. Out fell a schoolbook and a Bible. She had hidden them all this time without my knowledge, and now she was willing to forgo her dreams.

Three weeks after we left our home we arrived at an intersection. The road on the right curved toward Haeju, the capital of Hwanghae province, just north of the 38th parallel. The road on the left led to Sinmak, a small town east of Haeju. Haeju was nearer but people had to rely on boats to carry them down to Inchon, to freedom. My heart jolted at the thought of another body of water to cross. Sinmak, on the other hand, was a longer distance. Which road?

Standing on a tilted rock platform, a pleasant-faced old farmer, wearing baggy trousers, a long gray *chogori*, a worn-out wide-brimmed wicker hat, and a *chige* on his back, directed the confused refugees.

"Tonight you must go to Haeju and take the boat to Inchon. Your chances are better. If you go to Sinmak you will be captured by the Reds. Go to Haeju." He said all this in Pyongyang accent.

Everyone took his advice and started down the path toward Haeju.

"We will also go there," I decided.

"Look, Mother, Older Brother's classmate." Dukwah pointed to a face in the crowd. It truly was the face of Yongwoon's friend Daekun. I ran to him, singing his name. He recognized me at once even under all the dirt and grime.

"Where is he, where is my son?" I exclaimed joyfully.

"I do not know. I was separated from them just an hour ago right where we stand now."

The unbelievable news stung my ears. My son stood at the exact spot an hour earlier. What if he was alone? No friends, no family to comfort him if he was afraid or, worse, injured.

"Which road did he take?" My voice choked with anxiety.

"I am not certain."

I berated myself for not arriving an hour sooner. I went quickly to the farmer standing on the rock. "Excuse me, Grandfather, how long have you been standing there?" I asked.

"All day," he replied.

"The group that was here an hour ago, which road did they take?"

"If you hurry, you can catch them at Haeju. Freedom is there."

I thanked him and informed the children we were going to Haeju. At the mere mention of Haeju, Kunil broke out in a feverish rage. Without any warning, he became deathly ill. His forehead scorched my palm. His eyeballs became bloodshot and rolled back in his head. Too weak to stand, he slithered to the ground. I frantically began to massage his arms and legs.

"What is causing you so much pain?" I cried.

"Sinmak, Sinmak, Sinmak," he slobbered loudly.

"Nonsense, we are going to Haeju," I scolded.

"I do not want to go to Haeju. I want to go to Sinmak."

"But your older brother waits for us in Haeju."

"No! No! No! I want to go to Sinmak," he screamed, gasping in between each word.

"We must go to Haeju or we will be caught."

"Sinmak! I want to go to Sinmak. Please take me to Sinmak, Mother."

"You are only a child," I chided. "What do you know?!"

". . . Sssinmaaak," he whispered, and then passed out in my arms.

I looked at Daekun and my other children. "It is for the best. We will go to Sinmak and let the Reds take us back to Pyongyang."

"I will carry him to Haeju on my back," Daekun volunteered.

"You go ahead and find my son. Tell him to return to us when it is safe. I am tired of running."

We watched as Daekun followed the others to Haeju. Once again we were left behind. It was impossible to carry Kunil, so I ripped out one of the golden rings sewn into the hem of Husband's coat and bought a crude sled made from a door. Even for gold no one was willing to accompany us down the wrong trail. We had to drag him ourselves. The closer we got to Sin-mak, the more I felt Yongwoon's spirit pull away from mine.

The village was completely deserted except for a few dogs. To our delight the homes were left for our picking. I greedily selected the finest and cleanest house. Inside, the rice bin was a quarter full and there was plenty of *kimchee* left undug in the icy ground. Without delay, I started a fire using a handful of splinters and dry grass I found in the corner of the kitchen. Delicately I arranged them in the mouth of the oven, making the most of every piece. Then from an old flint and iron I caught a flame and thrust it into the straw; soon it was ablaze. I cooked up a feast, adding whatever spices and ingredients I could scrape off the shelves.

Everyone received a full bowl of steaming rice, and I made some soft rice porridge for the baby. It was more than we had to eat at one time in many weeks. Our concave stomachs growled, but when the food was in our mouths we could not swallow it down. Our bellies were in shock. Even our fingers had forgotten how to use chopsticks. It was as if they had never held them before. I tried coaxing the children, and when that failed I threatened them with punishment if they did not eat.

"We must eat even though our bellies do not desire food. Begin slowly, roll a single grain of rice in your mouth," I instructed them. I took the advice myself and chewed a bit at a time, then when my stomach remembered the warmth of food and how it felt to be satisfied I shoved it all in. I ate until my belly swelled and then I ate another serving. Nothing I had ever eaten—New Year's cake, sweet candy, popped corn—tasted so fine.

When I was stuffed, sleep overcame me. I threw myself down on the bedding, smiling, though I knew the Reds were coming for us, tonight, in the middle of the night, tomorrow morning, whenever. It seemed less earth-shattering now that my children had been fed well.

The sun was hiding when we awoke. We waited all morning for the Reds to cart us away, but they forgot about us. The street was empty of trucks and soldiers.

As we waited some more, we ate our morning meal undisturbed. Even Kunil, who showed no signs of fever, ate heartily. He recovered completely. When I questioned him about his

outburst and insistence on coming to Sinmak, he could not recall any of it.

Annoyed with waiting, I reluctantly bundled the children
and we were off again. We followed the desolate icy path, the
Taebeck mountain range our guiding landmark. Its high snowcapped peak looked as though it kissed the heavens.

Piles of wreckage from retreating UN and ROK forces were our
unwelcoming mat once we neared the Imjin River. The river was
located thirty miles north of Seoul. Not a single gunshot or engine
was heard. The momentary silence jangled my nerves. Pale-
faced refugees squatted at the riverbed, their heads sunk upon
their shoulders. They were waiting and wasting away. They had
been there for a while, for their scalps were dusted with snow. Not
again, I thought, inspecting the water, but this time the river was
frozen solid except for footprints that ended abruptly where
the ice was broken and bullet holes knitted tombstone patterns
around their watery graves.

"What are you all waiting for?" I shouted.

"They think we are Red Chinese," someone answered.

A loud megaphone voice boomed into our ears from across
the river. "Retreat! Do not attempt to cross the river or we will
be forced to shoot. Retreat!"

Was he serious? Go back where?! I was boiling with anger,
unwilling to accept this end after we had journeyed so far. No
invisible barrier was going to prevent me from crossing. I had
suffered too much, risked too much.

Turning to the others, I announced, "You can sit here if you
wish, but my children and I are going across that river because
there is too much death behind us. I would rather die with a
bullet in my front than in my back."

To make certain I would not lose my courage and back
down, I reached into Husband's wool coat and pulled out the
two property deeds I had kept for so many years, in hopes of
returning and claiming our land someday. It was my last tie
to the North. I scanned the documents one final time, finger-
ing the red family stamp that had sealed the deal, then without
delay I shoved them into a bullet hole in the ice. I watched
them disappear forever. And with it, any fantasies of going
back.

My eyes searched the horizon for some bit of strength, then

I saw a glimmer of light on the hill. To my dismay, the sun reflected off a barrel of a rifle pointed directly at us.

Hand in hand, we stood stiffly before the river edge. Guns ready to strike us down. Slowly, I slid my right foot forward on the smooth surface. Wild shell fire fractured the ice.

"Halt!" the same emotionless voice shouted.

I stopped in mid-step, legs locked. I was not a martyr; I did not want to die, I was willing to wait to hear what the gunman had to say.

"Come across!"

Hallelujah! Frantic refugees leaped to their feet and scurried past us. A man even tried coaxing his ox across; unfortunately the ox plunged to its death. One second it was skittering along the surface, the next there was only a large hole in the ice where it once stood with all its mighty weight.

Many abandoned the last of their carts and possessions after that. For the first time, I was grateful for our starvation diet, which had shrunk us way under our normal weight. My arms and legs were like four sticks wrapped with a wet sheet of paper. Underfoot, I could hear the water splashing against the ice with each tiny scooting step. Step, step, slide, step, step, slide. I filled my head with only light thoughts, hoping it would take off a few more pounds. Step, step, slide, step, step, slide . . . We made it!

I dropped to my knees and embraced the ground for all it was worth and it was worth a lot. It was more than freedom to me: it meant the reunification of our torn family. "We made it, Husband. Mother is here, son," I wanted to shout at the top of my lungs, as we had done on the day the Japanese left our country.

Less than two weeks after we crossed the Imjin, on January 4, 1951, the UN and ROK forces retreated south of the 38th parallel, where eventually the battle lines settled. This famous but tragic period was known by all Koreans as *Ilsahhootae*, 1-4 retreat. The last of the refugees were allowed entrance to the South. After January 4, people were forced to turn back. I grieved for those who missed the final cutoff. They had to return to a place where spirits were caged and hope aborted.

We traveled several more days to reach Seoul city. It was Christmas Eve 1950, almost four weeks after we began our trek. The great city of Seoul was like nothing I had expected—

shattered, ruined, and most of the population gone. The people who were still around, the South Korean police were turning their gunfire on them.

Somehow I found my way to Sister-in-Law's house in Young-dungpo province, at the far south end of the city. Her family had moved here after leaving us in Pyongyang. I was certain son and Husband would be waiting for us there.

No one greeted us. The house was left unguarded. In the middle of the floor a pile of worn socks were ready to be mended; in the bedrooms blankets were neatly rolled out. If it had not been for the thick coat of dust, I would have thought they were returning shortly. They must have left unexpectedly to a safer location, for the Red Chinese were heading directly for Seoul. That meant we, too, must flee as soon as possible.

Suppressing my disappointment, I lit a kerosene lamp. Its soft glow warmed the room. I rummaged through the storage shack hunting for food, despite my weariness. I bulldozed through every door and cabinet. I hunted for secret panels. All I found were a moldy garlic clove, a shriveled red pepper, and a few orphaned anchovies.

"I am hungry," Kunil whined.

"Me, too," Kunsam joined in.

"I know," I said abruptly, nearly biting off their heads. I was not angry at them, just weary.

Feeling sorry for myself, I went outside to cool my smoldering temper. How miserably beautiful everything appeared. The way the snow laced the tiled rooftop; the way flakes trickled off the leaves of the tree; and the way it capped the ten-foot pyramid of overturned earthenware *kimchee* jars. Those large ceramic jars . . . that was it! Sister-in-Law's favorite hiding place. I heaved my entire body weight against it. The stacked pyramid tilted, then thumped to the ground. There it was, concealed under the bottom center jar—a sack of wrinkled potatoes and a bag of rice.

"Potatoes! And rice!" I hollered. The children skipped up and down, as if I had discovered a barn full of candy and toys.

"We shall have a banquet tonight," I said merrily.

The blood grew warm in my veins as I bent over the cauldron to ladle out the steaming potatoes into Crock-Pots. I had decided to save the rice for another day. The potatoes were the perfect food to honor Christ's birthday, but the celebration lacked the giving of gifts. Remembering the gold jewelry, I ripped out another child's one-hundredth-day ring, never bothering to read the engraving. I did not care to know whose I was selling this time.

I sneaked out to the main street with the ring hidden in the crack of my breasts. Beggars, crouched here and there on the frozen ground, reached out with their grimy claws for scraps and coins. Beggers of all kinds—men with stumps instead of legs, children without mothers, and mothers with their half-starved babes clinging to their backs.

"Cigarettes, *Ahjoomah*? A piece of cloth? How about some string?" a woman offered. She spoke the same language, but there was something queer about her accent. It sounded lazy.

"I know what you desire—rice cakes. They are only a few days old, I swear." She flicked her black cracked nails.

"How much?" I asked, pointing at them.

"These are my very special rice cakes. Inside they are filled with sweet red beans," she boasted as she fumbled within her rags for a yellowed newspaper to wrap the cakes in.

"How much?" I repeated.

"For you a special price. A bit of silver or gold for three." She winked.

"That is outrageous. Have you forgotten there is a war being fought?"

"Check anywhere. Everyone charges the same." She swiftly pulled back the package.

It was true, the war brought with it inflationary chaos. Crooks were charging the price of ten rice bags for three stale rice cakes.

"Older Sister, can you spare a bit of change so I may feed my baby?" a young mother cried, her three weary boys kneeling beside her. Their heads were lowered to the ground. They were not bowing, they were covering their faces in shame while her daughter stepped forward with cupped hands.

"I do not ask for much, anything you can spare." The young mother looked up at me with empty eyes and empty hands.

I kept walking. When I reached the end of the street a

woman and her babe held my attention. Over half her face was burned red by a napalm flame thrower. Only her lips and nose were distinguishable. As I drew closer to examine her peddler's cart, I noticed the infant's eyes were permanently glazed open.

"Your babe . . ." I started to say, then I caught myself. She sat there rocking her child, softly humming a familiar lullaby. How I hated this war! I was powerless to help this poor young woman, I was powerless to help myself.

I wrapped four of the tiny hard cakes in my skirt, and in their place I dropped the ring. I ran back all the way to the house; I wanted to escape this outside world. When I arrived, Dukwah was tucking the children in bed.

"Tomorrow is Jesus' birthday," I announced. "And these treats are special gifts to celebrate this important occasion."

The children devoured them. Kunsam drooled all over himself, the red-bean filling oozing down his chin. I caught the dark syrup with my finger and put it in my mouth, savoring the sugary taste.

I saved the smallest piece for *ahghee*. I chewed it into soft pulp and then, putting my lips to hers, I pushed the food into her mouth. Her upper toothless gum moved over her lower gum. She of all the children deserved the cake. So many times when I thought she was not going to survive, she clung on.

THE LONG TRAIN RIDE

Early the following morning I went scavenging for news. I discovered there was a great concentration of refugees from the North as well as the South in the port city of Pusan, the only southern city that had not been taken by the Reds. I was convinced Yongwoon and Husband were there among the thousands and millions. Even if there were ten billion people I would find them. But how would we get there? I agonized. We had a better chance of flapping our arms and trying to fly than walk two hundred and fifty more miles. Then I heard the train was still in operation.

Linking hands, the children and I dragged ourselves to the Youngdongpo train station with a newly replenished sack of rice on my head. Gutsy men and young boys gathered all along the double railroad track, waiting to hop on as the train roared by. It would have been suicidal for us to try to catch a moving train. I decided it was wiser to wait on the designated platform farther down.

People squatted everywhere, stiff and brittle, waiting for the train to pull in. After a few hours had passed, we heard the sound of an approaching train in the near distance. The sight of the engine spurting out smoke and steam sparked hot life back into the crowd. All around, people struggled to their feet. As the sound grew deafeningly louder and the train churned closer, the throng of determined refugees moved dangerously near the track. Those from remote farm areas turned their backs and hid their faces as the black iron beast screeched to a stop. Sparks flew and a large white plume of smoke descended on us. Having climbed into its hollow belly many times before, I stared straight ahead, searching for an opening. Not a single metal spot was left uncovered. Bodies lined the entire train like an outer coat of human paint. People clung to the sides, front, back, and roofs. How vulnerable they were. They could be tossed off at any sudden lurch.

In the confusion we pushed our way forward. Using my arms, shoulders, and hips, I tunneled a path through the frenzied mob. One by one I hoisted the children into an open door while refugees used my head as a stepping block to scale up the sides of the car to the roof. I pulled myself in last, smashing several fingers and toes under my boot.

"Get off!"

"*Ay-yah!*" they screamed.

Inside, I found myself in a cattle wagon held together by warped wood. A mist seeped through the cracks between the loosened panels. The walls and floor reeked of livestock and manure.

"There is no more room for you here. Get off!" The people within glared at us as if we were a pack of rabid dogs.

"I am scared, Mother." Third Son burrowed his head into my skirt.

"Silence," I ordered sharply. Although my legs trembled, I wore a fierce mask on my face.

"I know it is crowded in here and there is not enough air for us all. My children and I will leave, but first one of you must surrender your chance at life and lead the way off this train."

I waited but no one was insane enough to give up their spot, just as I expected. I scanned the car for a place to sit the children. Those straight-backed hard benches would have been a welcomed luxury now. So without any polite or excusing words, I squatted down right where I stood, forcing the people around me to curse and moan. My arms and legs were pinned tightly to my body. At least, I told myself, we were safe from falling off the train.

With the whistle's long wail, the train started coughing up smoke again, its rubberless wheels straining. The train panted and wheezed like an old man. Since the Japanese left our country, the railroads deteriorated to an appalling degree; however, I would never have mentioned it to the others. I kept that secret to myself.

We all held our breath, hypnotically urging the train forward.

"Gooo, gooo, you old piece of crap," someone cried.

"Do not make it angry," a woman reprimanded.

"Gooo," I echoed, and finally it did. The train rolled forward. The wind and the dust flew up through the floor as it put-putted along, taking its leisurely time—the speed perfect for the scenic traveler, which none of us was.

The first day we managed to travel only five or six miles at the most. The rest breaks were erratic; at times they were long enough to build a fire, other times they barely gave us a chance to stretch our legs. We never knew when the train was going to take off again. People anxiously ran to the bushes and back to relieve themselves. Young women always returned with a mixed look of relief and self-consciousness; embarrassed because everyone knew what act of nature they had just committed. Men and children had it much easier. They merely climbed to the rear of the train and urinated. Thin miniature yellow rivers flowed from between their legs.

Cooking required more time. First dry twigs had to be dredged up from beneath the snow to light a small fire. For us our uncooked bag of rice was our only food and each stop was crucial. Others came better supplied with dried fish, pickled vegetables, bundles of seaweed rolls, and other mouthwatering fantasies.

By the following midday, I was hungry enough to risk it. I waited and waited for the train to make another stop but it kept inching forward. Toward evening, it slowed down. I jumped off with the bag of rice before it came to a complete halt. Quickly I dug a hole in the snow and lit the moist brush underneath it, using a torn portion of my skirt to catch the fire. I watched the snow melt into water in the small tin pot I brought along. Just when I was about to pour in the rice, the whistle blew its warning. The shriek was so startling, I spilled most of the rice. To my disappointment, the whole thing had to be aborted. I clambered back with the nearly empty bag and empty pot.

"Wait! Stop!" an elderly man shouted. Out of the bushes he came hobbling after the train, one hand pulling up his trousers and the other waving his cane in the air. "Stop! Oh, please stop!" he begged, but the train had no ears. He attempted a daring leap, far too physical for a man in his late years; however, when all was at stake an astonishing amount of courage and madness overcame age. He dangled from our car, half of him in and the other half trailing on the ground. His trousers ballooned around his ankles, exposing his flapping genitals.

"Go back to your own car, Grandfather!" a student near the door yelled.

Passively I sat by as he pried loose the old man's fingers and pushed him to his death. From that moment on, the children were forbidden to leave the train for any reason. One cannot imagine how difficult it was to keep six- and nine-year-old boys in one place when they wanted to run around and play. They complained endlessly about the hundreds of tiny needles pricking their legs.

It was hard for me as well. My buttocks felt as if they were melting on the floor. Standing up was no longer an option after continuous hours of sitting with my knees pressed against my chest. Attempting to balance on my weakened legs against the jolts and sways required too much coordination. Thus, we did everything right where we sat. The tin rice pot became our chamber pot. We had to be very careful and hit our target or it put everyone in a fouler mood. Then the pot was passed to the person nearest the window and emptied over the side, fertilizing the vegetation along the track.

The boys had no objections to urinating in the open, but for Dukwah, myself, and all the other women and young girls, we despised it. A blanket screen was propped around our waist as we squatted before a carful of men. When a blanket was unavailable, a stretched skirt, a piece of cloth, a wide body was used. We had Husband's wool coats, but they were our future and I refused to risk soiling them.

Dukwah held her water for three days. She was internally poisoning herself, but still she avoided the pot.

"Dukwah-yah, forget about the people. They have all done it," I assured her.

"Mother, you do not understand."

"I understand that you will become very ill if you hold it all in."

"I cannot, it is too embarrassing."

"I will hide you behind my skirt. No one will see."

"They will hear it splashing against the metal."

"Nonsense," I said sternly, and sat Dukwah down on the pot. Tears trickled down her cheeks. "The longer you refuse to relieve yourself, the longer you will sit right there in front of everyone."

I refused to let her kill herself. Stubbornly she tried to escape my grip, but I held on to her firmly. Finally her constricting muscles tired enough to release her waste. Relief overcame me, though I worried I could not replenish the nutrients and fluids a growing girl needed.

On the fifth day the children's bodies had nothing more left to discard. The uncooked sack of rice was my constant reminder of my failure to feed my children. It was good for only one thing: cushioning our bottoms. I loathed the sight of it; I would have stabbed it to pieces if I had the strength. The hunger worsened so I forced the children to chew on the chalky uncooked raw grain, three or four pieces at a time. It tasted like dried paste and it settled like cement in our stomachs. All day long we chewed while others talked forever of food. Listening to their wishful jabbering was worse than being deprived of it. Daily I grew weaker, teetering on the brink of semi-consciousness. I tried to conserve my energy, but *ahghee*'s mouth clung to my nipple like a leech, trying to milk whatever she could.

On the fifth day I scarcely lifted my head. I saw only flares of bright light. I needed food, but I had reached a point where I was no longer hungry. There was no doubt in my mind that I was near death. I began to moan, I could not stop myself. I knew it was a matter of time before I blacked out. "Mother! Mother, are you sick?" Dukwah loomed over me, rubbing my cheeks with her palms.

"I am dying," I managed to mutter.

"No. You are fine. You will feel better if you rest a little." She was panicking.

"Listen to me carefully, Dukwah-yah. Promise me you will take your brothers and sister to Pusan. Never leave them." I made her swear before I slumped sideways and lost consciousness.

In a panic, Dukwah disobeyed my strict orders and sneaked off the train in search of food. Kimchon station, which was located about fifty miles north of Pusan, was crowded with vendors, peddlers, and thieves looking for easy marks. Dukwah had nothing worth stealing.

"Seaweed rolls! Seaweed rolls!"

Like a hawk, Dukwah homed in on the aroma. Her eyes lit up at the sight of the six long, thin rolls in the woman's basket.

"Please, *Ahjoomah*, can I have just one?" She tugged at the woman's sleeve.

"You are ripping my jacket, you little pest!" the woman blared, and disappeared into the mass. Dukwah ran after her.

"Please! Our mother is dying." She grabbed the woman's sleeve once again.

"Run along, you are chasing away my customers!" she hissed.

"Just one small roll, your smallest roll."

"Brat." The woman raised her hand in frustration and whacked Dukwah across the face.

Dukwah's fingers still clamped on tightly to the woman's sleeve. "Just one, please, I beg you. If our mother dies so will my two younger brothers and baby sister."

Whether it was out of kindness or sheer annoyance, the woman handed her a roll and pulled away. When I awoke sometime later, I thought I was still delirious. I thought my eyes were playing a nasty trick on me. But it was no illusion, I held the roll in my own palm. It felt real . . . it was real!

"Now you will get better," Dukwah assured me.

"We are hungry, too." The boys' little blue lips quivered.

My natural reaction was to offer it to them, but Dukwah slapped back their reaching hands. "Take one bite and I will hit you again. The seaweed roll is for Mother so she will not die. You take her food and we will all die," she scolded, and then made them turn their backs.

I remained slouched for I was unable to sit up. Clutching the roll greedily, I admired it for a moment. It was no thicker than two of my fingers and about the length of my hand. Dukwah's imprints still dented the soft black seaweed skin. I shoved it all in my mouth, mentally forcing my teeth to break down the rice. With each swallow, I kept assuring myself, "They will understand because I eat for them."

That was one of the most selfish things I had to do in the presence of my undernourished children. The image of their hollowed eyes glaring at the roll is still vivid in my mind.

PUSAN

Dukwah became our little scavenger, begging from station to station. I was incapable of doing anything except watch the passing scenery. It seemed the farther south we traveled, the more tolerable the winter chill. I thought this port city by the sea, Pusan, would have been a nice place to visit if the war had not forced me here.

Amazingly, Pusan escaped the devastation the rest of the country suffered. It was now the home of refugees and military convoys. Northerners, Southerners, refugees, beggars, prostitutes, orphans from all over Korea flooded the area, overcrowding the streets. They crammed into every house, every shack, every possible shelter. Cratelike structures arose from out of the debris to become the trendiest type of architecture around. They were held together with plastic, splintered wood, bits of cardboard, and other junk.

We arrived sometime in early January 1951, looking like the victims of a violent crime. The train discarded us at Nampodong station. Passengers grabbed their bundles and dashed for the door, stumbling over themselves.

"Come on, children, at last we are here," I declared feebly.

I felt my legs sink beneath me as I attempted to rise. Dukwah and the boys grabbed my arms, heaved their combined weight against mine, and lifted me to my feet. I stood there weakly as Dukwah tied *ahghee* onto my back, securing the blanket around my chest. All I could manage was a look of gratitude.

"Let us go, Mother. Father must be worried about us," she said.

"Yes, Father," I breathed. The words dry in my throat. My husband. It had been so long since I had seen him. So much had happened that I had almost forgotten what he looked like. "Yes, we must find him. Both of them. They will take care of everything."

As soon as we stepped off the train, we were swept up by a stampede of rushing people. We had no choice but to run along with them, pressed so tightly my bones were being squashed. I ran and ran, my feet barely touching the ground. I was not sure if we were heading in the right direction, but this seemed as good as any. Block after block, packed together, we were carried forward until we came to a large city of camouflaged tents. Tents as big as houses, even bigger, inflated like hot-air balloons with each gust of wind. There we were suddenly released.

Off in the distance, a church steeple caught my attention. It rose out of the skyline of poverty, implanting a fresh bud of hope. I felt myself drawn to it. It was the house of God and I needed to be close to Him, surrounded by His healing walls.

The children and I followed the point of the cross down a long stretch of cardboard shacks. A group of people, mostly men, were climbing on top of one another trying to read the countless scribbled messages. Signs and flyers cluttered the church's exterior like a mural of a country torn apart. Name after name, flyer after flyer, the men searched, hoping they would find lost family members who might have survived. Here at Changjin church, believers and nonbelievers gathered to offer one prayer, a thousand prayers, for the dead, the living, and the missing.

Before I could mutter a single word, every male scrutinized us, tracing our figures with their hungry eyes. The children hid their faces deep inside my soiled skirt. I, too, wanted to hide from those many drawn and shallow faces.

"Yongwoon's mother! Yongwoon's mother!" a distant voice called. It sounded as though it came from another world.

A short woman, arms outstretched, rushed toward us. It was *Kwonsaneem,* the woman who led me to church, the woman in my dream. Her appearance was no longer neat. Her hair fell loosely about her neck.

"*Kwonsaneem . . . Kwonsaneem . . .* is it really you?" I asked faintly.

"How did you get here?" she gasped, clucking her tongue as she took in our sight.

"I am not sure," I replied dumbly.

"Thank God, you are safe."

"Yes, thank God," I echoed. But my focus was not on her, or the joy of a familiar face; it was still on those many desperate unshaven ones.

"Do not let them trouble you. You remind them of their missing wives and children."

"But why do they keep on staring?"

"They think if they stare and wish hard enough, you might magically be theirs. Nearly all of these men and boys journeyed alone after giving promises to their mothers, wives, and children that they would return. But those promises were destroyed with the sprouting of the imaginary wall that now divides our two bickering sides."

"Which route did you take?" A man lifted his black eyebrows.

"Did you meet a woman from Songjin with three young daughters?"

Another pushed his way to the front to ask, "A woman from Unggi with two boys?"

"Pohanh?" "Ulsan?" "Hungname?" they all hollered at once.

I was just as eager to throw out Husband and son's names. "Has anyone seen my husband, Lee, Dukpil?" My voice sounded hoarse. It was not my usual soft controlled voice, but someone else's, low and masculine, limned with adrenaline.

And like the Red Sea, the throng of bodies parted and he appeared. I recognized him the moment I laid eyes on him. No, I had not forgotten. His gaze was hypnotic; I dared not blink even once, petrified I would wake and find myself on that hell train again. Finally, he glided toward me. I could have sworn he floated. My heart pounded violently inside my chest and my head swam in circles. So much feeling. We embraced each other tightly. The children were caught in the middle, but they did not mind, because their father sprinkled salty kisses all over them. For the first time in our married life, I did not care who was watching. I just wanted to be held and touched and comforted.

"*Yobo, Yobo, Yobo!*" I cried out uncontrollably.

"Darling, you are real and I can feel you." He was weeping, running his hands all over my back and head, making sure I was not a dream.

"Yes, I am real."

"I thought I had lost you and the little ones forever."

"Shhh, I told you I would never allow that to happen." I clasped his face in my palms to wipe the tears, then the moment exploded and time sped forward as if one, two, three, ten years had elapsed. It was no longer the face of my young beautiful husband. How old he had grown! His lips were withered, his eyes sunken deep into their sockets. And the skin on his face clung to his skull. Everything about him bore witness to extreme fatigue. He wore the same farmer's rag that he left in. It was unrecognizable to the untrained eye, but I had memorized every single detail of the day he fled so that no amount of dirt could have fooled me.

Then I remembered my own face. I wondered if I was his mirror image. I checked my own hands. Every particle of flesh was gone, the bones pierced forth under the sandpaper skin. I bowed my head forward in a desperate attempt to hide the ugliness; I did not want him to see me this way.

Husband brushed his lips against my forehead and whispered so only my ears could hear. "Once when I was a naive boy I valued physical beauty. I sought it out, as you know, but it brought me nothing but emptiness inside. Now as a man I realize my life is full because I have you and the children to fill it."

Indeed my baby-faced husband had become a man. The war had matured him in ways I never could. I loved him more now than ever before. "I want to grow old and fat with my beloved wife and all my children around me." Husband's face beamed and the children giggled. Their high-pitched laughter was music to my gun-shocked ears.

"Where is our eldest son, *Yobo?*" Husband stretched his head around me as if I was a large boulder.

My tongue suddenly dried in my mouth as I repeated his question, "Where is he?"

"I do not see his face."

"I . . . I thought he was with you," I stammered.

Frantically, I searched among the mob of men, hoping the sea would part for me once more. I willed it and willed it, but my Yongwoon never appeared.

SHATTERED

FAITH

All we could do was pray and wait for Yongwoon to find us. In the meantime we were assigned temporary housing in one of those large green military tents, contributions from the United Nations' relief organization. It was better than roaming aimlessly in the snow even if it meant being sprayed with white powdery stuff called DDT—the all-purpose bug killer. It destroyed lice, fleas, and any other parasites that crawled in our hair and on our skin. An American soldier shoved a long, thin metal spout up each sleeve, down our pants, under our collars, and on top of our heads. We looked like living snow people as we searched for tent number eighty-five.

Yes, they were definitely green. In fact, almost everything was of that same deep earthy green shade. Still to this day, when someone mentions the color green for a wedding, a car, a room, the image that comes to mind is not one of majestic pastures and picturesque meadows, but of tents and war.

Our U.S.-made tent was the closest I had ever come to actually being in America, but living conditions were no American dream. Rats camped in our blankets. Showers were nothing more than sawn-off pipes leaking cold water. And for lighting, naked lightbulbs swung dangerously from above. The worst hardship, however, was the lack of privacy. In many cases five to ten families were packed together in one tent. Blankets were strung up as room dividers but the ocean winds blew so furiously they were more useful as flyswatters. I was never quite sure when it was safe to wash or to change. Often I would have Dukwah stand guard, acting as a weight to hold down the blankets.

Each family received small weekly rations of rice and some stale vegetables, barely enough to sustain us. There was a chronic shortage of food and supplies. As a result, the menu rarely varied. It usually consisted of a bowlful of milky paste made from rice or the peeled skins of yellow soybeans. Sometimes I would dice weeds into our broth. For seven days a week, twice a day, that was our diet. The food would pass right through our systems. Watery it went in and watery it gushed out just a few hours later.

Once Husband brought home a single sweet potato. It felt heavy in my hand. The children salivated as they licked the bruised potato with their eyes.

"It is so big! Is it someone's birthday today?" the boys asked eagerly.

Yes, it was someone's birthday in some pathetic sort of way. Any small treat, no matter how bruised, was an occasion for celebration.

For months we lingered, just waiting for Yongwoon to arrive. Every hour, I watched the road for his figure. I prayed endlessly, morning, noon, night, late night, through January, February, March, April. Spring had finally arrived. Husband wanted to sell the three wool coats and use the money to move the family north to Yeachun, where Mother was. It was safe now since in mid-February the UN forces had driven the Red Chinese and the North Korean People's Army out and up to near the 38th parallel. The fighting had presently reached a temporary stalemate.

"How is our son going to find us if we keep moving?" I pleaded.

"We will paint a big sign for him and post it at the church."

"No! I will not abandon him twice. Please, Yongwoon's father, do not command me to leave."

"You know I would never force you to do anything against your will. You are too stubborn a woman."

"It is because I gave birth to him. If his own parents give up on him, what chance does he have?"

To keep active, I walked to the church each day to search the new faces and graffiti of names. I went so often that I instantly recognized when a flier was added or taken away; heartbreakingly, it was always another person's name.

Slowly the warm breezy days of April gave way to summer's excruciating heat. The humidity lay heavy on our bodies. Unfortunately, the heat was only one of our torments. Oversized fleas and mosquitoes, attracted by the dripping showers and pools of urine, bit our exposed skin and sucked our blood constantly. We nearly went mad with irritating red rashes. Still I refused to give up my vigil.

Unable to rest, I spent my nights sitting outside the tent under the moonlit sky, drenched to the skin. Then out of the darkness one miserable sticky night, I saw a silhouette approach. His tall outline was hunched over, the tips of his boots dragged on the ground. My mouth opened but no sound came out. It took a moment for the words to first resonate in my head before they finally welled to the surface.

"Yongwoon-yah? . . . Yongwoon-yah!" I fell to my knees, throwing my arms around his legs. My sobs were so loud it stirred the entire tent. Husband stumbled out. "Our son has found his way," I cried joyfully.

"Yongwoon-yah, my Yongwoon-yah. It is our eldest son, *Yobo*. God has brought him back to us." I sobbed deeply.

A strangely sad expression flashed across Husband's face; he dropped his head, burying his chin in his chest. I was suddenly furious at him.

"It is, it is our Yongwoon!" I insisted. "Step into the moonlight so I may see that you are unharmed," I blubbered.

I squinted my eyes so tightly stars appeared and once they cleared I saw that the large figure hovering above me was not my son but his friend Daekun.

"Where is my son?" I tugged at his hem, almost ripping off his shabby coat.

"First let me help you up." He offered a supporting arm, then gently sat me on an overturned crate.

Those words so alarmed me it required every bit of self-control to hold back months of pent-up emotion. I had already endured so much, I felt, nothing could shatter my starved spirit anymore, but the thought of what I was about to hear made me tremble.

"After we left your house . . ." His voice was high and tight and his speech was clipped at first, but then the agony of his journey poured steadily forth and drowned my soul until I could bear no more, but I did. I had to know every last grim detail.

"Yongwoon, Bonghwen, and I safely crossed the Taedong River that first night. We hid for a few days near the woody banks like three frightened escapees, struggling with the idea of heading farther south, for each one of us had promised our mothers we would return. But how? The shots never ceased and the fires grew brighter. Our only hope was to continue on.

"Three young men: we were as conspicuous as pregnant women. But not once did we leave each other's side. During the days, we kept close to the ground, crawling through fields and rice paddies, trying at all costs to avoid the crowded main road. We traveled swiftly in the dark along deserted trails, always listening with a sharp ear for any sounds of movement.

"We arrived at the Haeju-Sinmak crossroads in December. There I got separated from them and saw you and your children. Like many others, I listened to the old farmer who stood on the rock waving his hand toward Haeju. 'There will be a boat to take you safely down to Inchon, to freedom,' he lied.

"In Haeju I was reunited with your son and Bonghwen, who had already arrived. Hoping you had changed your mind and followed the road to Haeju, Yongwoon insisted we wait overnight. As we all slept confidently in the abandoned homes, an explosion of gongs and blowing bugles woke us to a living nightmare. Rows of military trucks surrounded the tiny village. There was no escape. Ruthlessly, every last person was tossed into the backs of the trucks and carted north.

"Immediately upon arrival we were taken to a massive pile of decomposed and mangled bodies. 'Here lie your families, who were made to suffer your punishments,' we were told.

"Women, children, and your Yongwoon were handed shovels instead of rifles and forced to dig graves. Bonghwen and I, being of military age, were involuntarily drafted into the Red Army and sent directly to opposite ends of the front line to fight for the side we were trying to escape from.

"When I found myself there, fighting was the last thing on my mind. With the rifle flung over my shoulder, I marched into battle and right through it. I kept running south, faster and faster in a panic. Then suddenly my boot tripped on a land mine, which blew me into the air, knocking me out. When I gained consciousness, it was dusk. I thought I had died until I saw the pool of blood underneath my face, my own blood. I realized then I was not in hell but in war. I lay there for a moment, testing my arms and legs for missing parts. Everything was still intact and working. I peeled myself off the ground; to my shock my jaw dangled at my chest. The explosion snapped the lower jaw off its hinges; it was suspended only by the elastic skin. I staggered to my feet. With one hand under my chin and the other supporting my weight on the rifle, I skittered slowly on, leaving a bloody trail. Waves of pain shot all across my face, but I kept moving, often with my eyes closed.

"Somehow I came to a house along the path. Not knowing if the inhabitants were friendly or hostile, I dragged myself in. The room was crawling with ROK troops. Their trained guns cocked in a melody of ripples. All aimed to take me down, but before they could fire I fell unconscious.

"They evacuated me to a military hospital behind the lines and reattached my jaw. From there I was shipped to Cheju Island, sixty miles off the southern coast, with the rest of the prisoners of war. I escaped with the help of a fisherman . . ."

I could scarcely hear him any longer, for blood thundered in my ears. Confused, I stared at his grotesquely protruding lower jaw for a very long moment. It was all so incomprehensible, unbelievable. Did that mean Yongwoon was alive . . . or dead? I wanted a definite answer.

Down Husband's ashen cheeks ran two large tears. I was too angry to cry. At first I blamed myself; it seemed the right thing to do. "Damn me! Why did I let him go? Damn me!" I cursed.

Then I heard a voice within, my voice: "God has forsaken you, fool," it hissed. "Why?" I moaned, throwing up the question to heaven. "Why him, God? Why Yongwoon? I hold You responsible for all this . . . I loathe You!" I screamed even louder.

At that moment my spirit was raped. I felt a chill creep over my heart. I had no more tears to sacrifice; they had all dried up in a blaze of hatred.

That was the last I heard of my Yongwoon. Alive? Dead? Suffering? So much uncertainty, it caused my face to harden into an expressionless mask. I tried to think about other things, but it was fruitless. I tormented myself wondering if he had thought I had deserted him. Was he frightened? Was his last cry my name? Perhaps . . . perhaps . . . Shall I ever know?

Eventually I shut off all emotions, even hate. It was the only way I could tolerate another empty hour. My body was just a false shell that looked like me. The wife of Lee, Dukpil, the mother of five, the God-loving woman, was gone. All I desired was to be left alone. I spent most nights and days sitting on that same crate, a moist cloth pressed to my forehead, legs parted and exposed to mid-thigh. I was the focus of gossipy tongues.

"Has she no modesty?"

"That is indecent!"

What did I care about modesty and decency? Would it better my miserable life? Would it bring back my son?

Rarely did I remove or change my crusty clothes. I smelled like a rotten dishrag left out in the damp too long. My daily ritual of wiping and shaking out the dust from our bedding became a bearable nuisance. I watched with great interest as a thin carpet of mold slowly sprouted into a garden of mushrooms. Not even *ahghee*'s cries brought me back to my old self. It was a terribly lonely time without spirit.

The children ran around like renegades, unsupervised and filthy. They had no games to play or school to attend, so they would sneak away to the port and watch the ships plying the sea. Other times they rummaged through the UN supply dumps for salvageable trinkets they could hock.

"Do you see what your children are doing?" Husband asked, outraged.

"They are doing what children of war should do," I replied.

"They are becoming savages. Second Son prowls around with a pack of orphan beggars. You are their mother. Do you not care about their futures?"

I thought hard. No, I really did not. And somehow he read what was in my heart and for the first time in our marriage Husband took charge of all the burdens. He disciplined the children and turned them into little workers. He sold the wool jackets on the black market and started a small peddling business. He bought packs of American chewing gum and cigarettes from the seedier American GIs, and he and the children resold the merchandise to other refugees one stick, one cigarette at a time. He even coached the children on how to hustle the gum from tent to tent.

"It is in the attitude. Convince them they are buying something more wonderful than a simple chew or smoke. It will take their minds off their hardships." He made it sound so ridiculously poetic. "Sell the gum for a higher price. It lasts longer," Husband instructed. He was right, it did last longer, but only if the buyer did not swallow it from inexperience.

Dukwah sold the most. This was not due to her friendly attitude; in fact, she had the opposite.

"You will act exactly as I tell you." Husband raised his voice, which hurt him terribly.

As her mother, I knew I should have kept my young unmarried daughter off the streets. Under normal circumstances I would have tucked her safely in the house and made her sweep, clean, cook, and mend, as my mother had done for me, but these were uncertain times. Who knew if she would live to see her wedding day? And what good was it to hide her in a dust-filled tent? Besides, we needed the money, and the boys and young men who came back often to buy a stick of gum or a cigarette did not seem to notice the scrawl on Duk-wah's face. They only saw the pretty, shapely girl, who held their attention.

The months passed, and the monsoon rains were at their height. They came suddenly, falling in sheets. The rains played havoc with the fabric tents and dirt roads. One day all was calm and clear. Then the next day violent storms drenched and shredded everything in sight. Pots and pails clanked inces-santly, catching water. We played an ever-losing game of trying to stay dry. We lived in a canvas fishbowl, but there were no fish, only rats seeking shelter.

The weather hardly bothered me. Wet or dry, I spent the hours sitting on the crate, now worn and dented under my weight. Fanning away the heat and flies was my only exercise. My body was so heavy from lack of use, I had to examine my limbs to be sure I had not turned to stone. Every once in a while, if I had the strength, I would drag myself to the bug-infested water barrel and scoop up a basinful and pour its cold-ness all over my head, letting it trickle down the length of my neck, rousing me from the paralysis of sleeplessness.

One morning while I was doing this a hand squeezed my shoulder. To my surprise, the hand belonged to Baby Sister. I grabbed it, feeling for the truth. She was real. Her glance met mine and she read all the sorrow. "Older Sister, thank good-ness you are alive," she cried.

"Barely," I sighed under my breath.

A teenage girl stood beside her. I pondered who she could be. She looked so familiar.

"Hello, Aunt."

"Who are you?"

"She is Crippled Sister's daughter," Baby Sister answered.

"*Uh-moh-nah*," I mumbled. "Of course, you are the identical image of your mother without the pockmarks. No wonder you look familiar."

"Come, Older Sister, we must pack your things; we have quite a distance to travel."

"I wish to stay."

"You cannot live like this. Your home is with us in Yeachun. It is safe there. We are surrounded by mountains."

"I have no home. It was stolen from me."

"Say no more. You will come with us. In Yeachun, you do not have to sleep in a tent. We can all live together in a house with sturdy walls that do not blow with the wind. Think of your children."

"My children?" I repeated. I had neglected the four I still had left for so long, I decided it was the least I could do. "I suppose you are right," I agreed.

When I look back on those eight eternal months, it all returns in a blur. I had become one of those living ghosts I feared so much as a child.

YEACHUN

Aparade of us arrived in Yeachun, located about halfway between Pusan and Seoul, cradled deep in a buttonhook mountain which nearly ringed it. Baby Sister led us through a labyrinth of aged roads and narrow streets. We turned several dark back corners, slippery with slop water tossed out carelessly. Soon we halted in front of a small house. Baby Sister stepped forward and rapped on the door, clunk, clunk, clunk. After a while the gate opened a crack, shining a slice of light on our feet.

"Who is out there so late?" a witchy voice screeched.

"It is your family, Older Sister." Baby Sister identified us.

"How do I know you are not a Red spy?"

"If that was true, we would have kicked down the door instead of knocking politely."

The door inched open and there Crippled Sister was on the ground; I recognized the twisted legs, but I was stunned by the dramatic change in her face. It was now just as twisted and contorted as the rest of her body. No longer did she look intoxicated with love. She had the face of a bitter old woman. The three deep wrinkles that cut above her eyebrows deepened at the sight of us. By the way she curled her upper lip to plug her nostrils, we must have smelled just as bad. I lived so long in scum, I was desensitized to myself.

"Well, are you all going to just stand there and look retarded?" she snapped.

There was so much fury in her I was truly dumbfounded. Growing up, she had never let her legs defeat her, but war had beaten her down. I wondered which was worse, her venom or my lethargy?

It was a drab wooden shanty. The entire place was scarcely bigger than our largest blanket. Its chipped walls had never known a clean rag. A broken panel near a corner provided the only ventilation in this windowless structure. I wanted to get out of there, but I realized this was all I had, we had, in the whole world.

Suddenly I knew what had to be done. I made my way along the dim house to the detached kitchen. There on the floor I saw what I needed—a kettle. I filled it with water and heated it to a boil. I dumped the water into a basin in the middle of the room. Husband bathed first. While he stripped down to his bare skin, the others minded their own business. I also turned my back because I was filled with guilt. For many months, I had neglected my wifely duties and withdrew from Husband when he begged me to comfort him. And I still stayed away. Only when he was done and clothed again did I move toward him, handing him some warm water to drink. It was all I was capable of offering him.

Armed with soap and scrubbers, sisters and I formed a human chain. The children passed through one at a time. We rid them of their lice-infested rags and dunked them into the same scorching water, head and all, scouring them vigorously from top to bottom, from outer skin to inner ear. Three pairs of hands rotated systematically. Skin forgotten beneath layers of neglect was once more raw pink. No child was set loose until he or she passed Crippled Sister's sniffing inspection. She checked them behind their ears, under their arms, and underneath their nails. The freshness of soap mingled with slop and urine from outside created an eerie fragrance.

Baby Sister went next. As she was scrubbing herself, I tucked the children and Husband in bed. Finally, at last, it was my turn. I slipped out of my dress and sat alone, naked, near the feeble candlelight, and picked up a small cracked hand mirror. I had not seen my image in over a year. I was overcome with revulsion when I saw the hideous creature who gazed back. My hair had knotted into a thick ball of dirt and oil; my face, with continued exposure to sunlight and ground-in stains, was dark and leathery. The war had etched severe lines around my eyes and mouth.

I refused to feel sorry for myself. Instead, I plunged into the used water. Its lukewarm comfort was pure ecstasy. For a momentary flash, an endless year of strain and exhaustion evaporated. A great heaviness lifted from my body as I soaked. I could feel the scum loosening from between my toes. I was obsessed with removing every last bit of dead skin, and I did before rising.

Not a strand of hair stayed in its proper place. I tried to run a comb through the tangled mess. To my sisters' despair, I cut it off, all two feet of it.

Crippled sister handed me a pair of men's pants and a top. From the newness of the fabric, I could tell they had been lovingly preserved since the death of her husband. They felt good against my clean skin as I put them on.

Carefully I stepped over the sleeping children and Husband to the place nearest the door where my sisters lay awake, waiting for me. We ended up staying up most of the night, whispering in the darkness. The time was too short for all we needed to say. For hours, we wept, talked, and wept some more about our losses and heartbreaks. That night I learned what had happened to the rest of the family. After Older Brother and Father's deaths, Nephew brought his family and Mother safely to Yeachun.

Before dawn I sank into a deep sleep, shoulder to shoulder, with my family, under one big blanket. One roof. Our roof.

BROKEN

HEART

——————————

That night, I heard Crippled Sister's tragic tale. Her story-book marriage ended abruptly after only four short years. An unknown sickness claimed that meek husband of hers when she was pregnant with their second child.

Father had summoned Crippled Sister home, strongly be-lieving her husband's sick presence would tempt the demons to harm the unborn child, cursing it to be born deformed or still. Against her wishes to stay by his side, she was carried away to live in Father's house while Father went to care for her hus-band. She was forbidden to see him, although she pleaded un-til she was hoarse. Even her attempts to escape were useless; she was trapped in her body. She could only wait as Father sent further word on her husband's deterioration. The doctors and herbal specialists could not explain what caused him to lie like a vegetable, unable to recognize his own name. Two weeks before the birth of his son he passed away, never knowing that his legacy would live on. Still, Crippled Sister was forbidden to bid him farewell, not until the boy celebrated his one-hundredth-day birthday and the dead was deep in the ground with a mound of dirt on top of him.

The bottomless grief left by his death she shared with no one. She kept it locked in her heart, letting the salty tears singe her soul. She had a tongue sharper than any knife. It challenged anyone and defied everyone. Whether she said "crap" or "roses," it all sounded and smelled the same. And gradually, her inner grief began to disfigure her face. She wore a permanent frown.

Mother pleaded with Crippled Sister to remain in her childhood home, for Mother feared the dark omens in Crippled Sister's house might snatch their grandson's life. Father had other fears. He worried she might be "sacked." Every now and then we heard dreadful stories of widows being snatched away on a peasant's back. Widows were easy targets for those men who could not afford to buy a wife. Once violated, the widow either accepted her fate or took her own life because she was too dishonored to return to her family.

Crippled Sister ignored both their warnings and moved back to her empty home. Alone, she continued on, knowing she could never again see the world on their rusty old bike. Alone, she decided to reopen her husband's glass shop, vowing to fulfill his dream of sending both their children to school. He wanted them to become educated, something he never had a chance to be.

For some time she managed to run the store and raise her two children on her own. When Mother urged her to take her son and daughter and join the rest of the family in Yeachun, she stubbornly refused to give up the business even though the Russians, our liberators, were pillaging homes, stealing watches off people's wrists, and forcing themselves on women.

Her glass store, shortly thereafter, came to a smashing end with the outbreak of war. An explosion sent everything crashing to the floor. Unwilling to accept defeat, she started another business. She became a loan shark, lending out money at high interest rates, but she was a shark without fins. Her customers fled south, confident she would be unable to chase after them or her money. She quickly went out of business again. Still she would not give in to defeat, and began a *yut* business. They were supposed to be long, twisted breadsticks fried in lard and rolled in sugar. Instead, Crippled Sister made the first-ever Korean doughnut hole. Being born a cripple, she escaped the rigors of cooking lessons. A pound of flour was as foreign as the B-29s that flew over her head. Soon she abandoned her efforts to make *yut*, because daily the war brought more men with guns. For her teenage daughter's sake, she decided to flee south. But before they began their long trek, Cripple Sister did as our father had done for her—she bought her fifteen-year-old daughter a husband. She offered the potential groom all her savings to marry her daughter. The young man fell for the girl instantly, agreeing to the marriage. Little did he know the deal included taking his lovely bride, her younger brother, and his mother-in-law to Yeachun. And the money he had just inherited he had to spend on a *chige* to carry his in-law on his back. Crippled Sister, though, continued to worry about her daughter's safety. Thus, she asked her son-in-law to escort his wife to Pusan. Being a good husband, he did his duty.

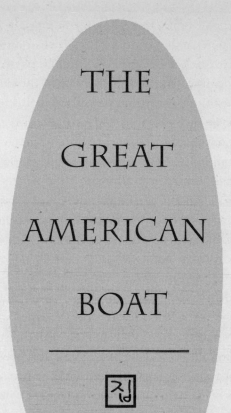

THE
GREAT
AMERICAN
BOAT

I tried to keep in contact with Baby Sister after she refused to leave China, but the civil war raged on, back and forth, like a loaded Ping-Pong ball. Communication stopped altogether as everything was coming to a solid freeze at the 38th parallel. Baby Sister and her three children finally joined the mad scramble of Koreans living in China to return home before the doors were forever closed.

They managed to get only as far as Manchuria by train before they were stranded. Luckily, though, Baby Sister heard that a big American boat was escorting refugees down to Pusan, free of charge. It was too unbelievable to be true, yet she went to investigate the boat for herself. It was a large military vessel containing a couple of hundred refugees and their possessions. Seeing other women with their children get on board, Baby Sister followed on their heels.

The whole boat opened up, the lounges, the gangways, the portholes. The Americans tried their best to provide the refugees with every possible comfort, though it was difficult, for they were all crammed into one long sleeping compartment located on the lower deck. Many became violently ill. An American military doctor tended to them. His prescription was to let nature run its course over the side of the deck.

During mealtime, the crew served rice with *kimchee* and generous slivers of meat to those who could still tolerate food. They were fed well, better than anything we had during our exodus. And sometimes after the last meal of the day, the crew organized games and musicales for the children.

Their journey along the country's western coastline ended three days later at the port of Pusan. Before disembarking, the refugees were administered a vaccination, sprayed with DDT, given South Korean currency, and rationed a day's worth of food.

Baby Sister took her children directly to Yeachun. She had hardly arrived at Crippled Sister's house when she was on her way back down to Pusan in search of Crippled Sister's daughter and son-in-law. They had been missing for over ten months and still there was no word of their safe arrival. Like so many people, they just seemed to have walked off the face of the peninsula.

Leaving her children behind, Baby Sister walked as far as Ahndong. There, she came across a stalled jeep on the side of the road. An ROK soldier, wearing khaki fatigues, showed himself from behind the bushes. She knew the jeep was his, because the paint job matched his camouflaged outfit. She approached the soldier cautiously, the back of her hands pressed up to her forehead.

"Please, good soldier, I am going to Pusan to search for my five orphaned children. One is blind and the other four are crippled," she lied. "I will sit very quietly. You will not even notice I am here. Please, oh, please, have pity on this wretched mother, I beg you." She dropped to her knees.

Her performance won her her first ride in an automobile. Never in her wildest imagination would she have thought she would cross the ocean on a palace-sized cruiser, be entertained by Americans, and be chauffeured in an ROK army jeep. If she could, she would have erased all these experiences from her life just to have peace and security again. She sat back with her eyes closed, daydreaming of Cornish hens stuffed with ginseng and crisp cabbage freshly fermented. But her fantasized banquet was cut short by a group of bandits.

"Put your hands in the air and get out slowly!" the masked leader shouted as he flipped the point of his rifle in their faces.

Baby Sister raised her hands high above her head as ordered. The soldier did the same. "Do what they say and try not to provoke them," he whispered. As he turned to step out of the jeep, he was shot in the back. So close to the firing, Baby Sister was knocked off the side by an invisible bullet.

The bandits, singing their victory song, drove off in the jeep. She waited until they disappeared down the dirt road before crawling toward the fallen soldier. She put her ear to his lips to listen for breathing. She heard a heavy panting, but it was hers. The bullet had entered cleanly through his lower back and tore his stomach wide open, spilling out his guts. There was nothing she could do; she could not even recall a childhood chant for him. So she left him as he lay, facedown, and continued on her journey by foot.

Her search lasted a full month. By sheer luck she found herself squatting outside the U.S. military base in Pusan, where a young woman crossed her path as she was pondering. Instantly they both recognized each other without ever being introduced.

"So this is what Crippled Sister would have looked like if she had no pockmarks on her face and was able to stand tall on her own two feet," Baby Sister murmured to herself.

Reunited, they came searching for us. And in the city of leaking green tents they found us, soaked to the bones.

A
WIDOW'S
REBIRTH

Husband and I fought constantly those days. The fights always centered on my vendetta against God.

"Those are His mysterious ways. We are not His judge nor should we be His accuser. His ways are oftentimes too wise for us to understand, but we must have faith that it is all part of a greater plan. God is good." Husband preached His gospel.

"That almighty God you worship is a cruel mythology. I refuse to hear your blind foolish faith anymore; it gives me a headache!" I bellowed.

Husband kept pressing me relentlessly. I tried to change the subject, but he would not allow the subject to be dropped. The harder he attempted to drive his point through my heart, the more vicious I became.

"In this world when we have nothing left, God will always be there for us, even when you think He has forgotten you. Pray to Him. He will lighten your troubled soul, *Yobo*, if you will just allow Him in."

"*Yah!*" I snickered bitterly. "I have long ceased to pray to HE who butchered our neighbors and tore my child from my bosom. He remained silent while the Reds pounded on our gate and threw me in jail. Where was He when the B-29s dropped their murderous bombs on our heads?!"

"He was there—"

"You are absolutely right! Of course He was; He was the pilot! I risked everything for Him and still He ripped my child from me."

"Have you forgotten that God, too, gave up His only son for us?"

"I never asked Him to sacrifice mine. I am not the mother of Jesus. I am just an ordinary woman!"

Suddenly I wanted to hurt Husband for reopening a painful wound. My words became more abrasive and bitter. "Hallelujah! Hallelujah! Is that what you want to hear me say? Oh, my GOD, how good You are, my LORD. So MERCIFUL, so JUST, I praise Your holy name!" I laughed hysterically, almost crazed. "You are so naive," I snarled, inches away from Husband's face. "Ignorant. You are still the child I married. Go back to thinking with your penis, you were more of a man then."

The blood rushed into his yellow face and before I could protect myself he slapped both my cheeks. I was stunned. He had never hit me before. Other men beat their wives, but never Husband.

He jerked the hand that struck me behind his back. I think he was more shocked than I, for his whole body trembled and his face contorted. I dared him to slap me again, but he turned away silently. For the rest of that day we avoided the other; however, it was impossible in a shack bursting with family members. Every time I took a step I bumped into him. Finally he made an excuse to leave the house. That was the beginning of our separation as husband and wife. He began to devote all his efforts to serving his God, alone, and I lived a Godless existence. But never did I pressure him to stop his charity. Nor did I complain when he brought a very sick pregnant woman to our home for me to treat with *chiryo*. I did it secretly for Husband. It had been such a long time since he asked anything from me.

The pregnant woman suffered from a disabling fever that left her unable to care for herself and her unborn child. Without warning, the fever spread through the town in epidemic proportions. By the time we became aware of this deadly disease called diphtheria, it was too late for my children and me. We became its victims, but somehow Husband and the others were spared.

Promptly the children, the pregnant woman, and I were evacuated to a makeshift quarantine area in a local church. Being under the steeple brought back memories which I quickly suppressed. There we lay on donated cots, crammed side by side. Everyone sucked in everyone else's coughs. The only people who were permitted to pass through the roped-off barrier were brave volunteers and family members. Husband came daily and sat beside my cot like a devoted pet. As for my two sisters, he forbade them to enter the church. He encouraged them to stay well for their children. I wished he had not done that. I preferred their company to his, for this was not an attractive illness. The fever caused my body to shrivel with dehydration and my hair to thin out. My heart sank to think that after escaping death so many times I might die bald in my beloved's presence.

"Please, *Yobo*, protect yourself and go."

It was more of a selfish request than anything else, but he continued to care for us, wiping the sweat from our foreheads and fetching water. I struggled to stay conscious as long as I could to keep Husband company, but I fell in and out of delirium, all the while dreaming only of my lost Yongwoon. Each time I awoke, Husband was there. His bountiful love inspired in us the will to fight for our lives. We needed him because medication and competent doctors were not available.

Despite all the odds, the children, the pregnant woman, and I survived while our cot mates shriveled away, one after another, without their families to send them off.

"Thank God," Husband sighed relief. "Thank God."

Still I refused to praise God's name. I refused to give Him credit for our recovery. "It was not God who saved us, it was your care. See, we do not need Him," I corrected Husband.

Then God finally chose that moment to end His silence. As though hit by a bolt of lightning, Husband was struck down with diphtheria. The fever quickly traveled throughout his body, settling in his heart, weakening it with each beat. I watched helplessly as he tossed on the same cot I had lain on just a day before.

"Water, water . . ." he whimpered.

I brought him a cup of water, though I was still very weak, careful not to let my unsteady hands spill even one drop. As I held the cup to his blistered lips, his red sunken eyes smiled up at me while he struggled to gulp it down. It pleased me greatly that I could bring him some comfort.

For days I sat and listened silently as his breath wheezed in gasps. His breathing became mine, urging him to take another. I propped him up against my chest, hoping it would ease the flow of air. Cradling his limp, dehydrated body, I felt how much he had withered. Slowly his fingers crept to my hand and held it.

"Sleep a bit. I will be right here when you wake," I said, trying to sound light. An emptiness had dulled his deep brown eyes. But even at the gate of death, so pure was his faith, his spirit was not beaten. He pursed his lips into a brilliant smile, the same smile that stole my heart so many years before. We were both too weak and moved to speak, but we understood one another so clearly.

Hours passed and I fell asleep with him still propped against me. Some time later a cold stillness in his body startled me awake. It was dark and death had come. I held him, afraid that the moment I released him I would lose him forever.

Light. Light. I needed light to see his face, to engrave his picture on my mind. But all around me it was pitch-black. How desperately I wanted to reveal all the things I had withheld from him. Why Husband and not me? Why my son and not me? I wanted to beat on something, anything, with my two fists. When I forced them open at last, my hands had turned white from clenching them so hard.

"Enough . . . ENOUGH, ENOUGH, ENOUGH!" a voice cried from inside. I ran my hands all over my face, letting the tears sting my roughened skin, then up to my aged gray hair.

All this time I had lived in a world without love and God, I had not wept once, but now the tears were heavy as wax because they were loaded with so much grief. I wept violently, I wept for all my life that night. Then an image flashed before my clouded eyes. It was the face of Jesus, the same penciled face Husband drew for me. Suddenly the anger blew out and I stood shaking. In spite of myself a long-suppressed prayer escaped from the darkened depths of my heart to Him.

"Please, let there be a heaven. Keep him safe and warm," I asked humbly.

I wanted so badly to believe again, to believe in a place called heaven where Husband would be waiting for me. From here on, I vowed to mend the road back to God.

I remained with Husband until the sun rose and I was able to view him in the light. When I saw that familiar smile, I knew I could never forget what he meant to me. Happiness swelled in my heart. It was so profound, so calming, so quieting, I felt peace again.

I hugged his shell tenderly, rubbing my cheeks against his five-day-old beard, for it was time to go and tell the children the news.

"Good-bye, *Yobo*," I whispered into his ear, and left.

On my way home, I walked on legs that staggered as if I was drunk. In a strange way, Husband's death brought me comfort. At least his end was final. There was no wondering as with Yongwoon's. In my mind, I rehearsed what I was going to say. I desperately wanted to make up a tale to spare my children another loss. They had suffered so much already during their short tragic lives, especially *ahghee*. She would never know the father who gave her life and me so much joy. She would never be able to utter the word *ahpa*, father, and know the man whom it belonged.

"Children." I beckoned to them. "Your father is dead!" I delivered the news quickly and sternly, lest my words turn to sobs. The boys listened calmly; perhaps it was all the death they had witnessed that made it less tragic, less unique. Whatever it was, I was relieved. Dukwah, on the other hand, quivered with anger at my indifference.

"Mother, you are pleased Father is dead." She pointed an accusing finger at me.

"Dukwah-yah, I know you are saying that because you are hurting."

"You wanted him dead. Why did you always have to argue

with him? I want to go see Father." She began to sob, barely able to catch her next breath.

"Dukwah-yah, you are old enough to understand that tragedy is a part of life these days. But the living must go on. Now there are only five of us left. Let us not bicker among ourselves. I do the best I can."

"I want to go see Father."

"It is unsafe. You are still too weak. I will bring him home when I can," I said, and left it at that. I did not want to battle with her. There was too much to worry about. Their four dim futures weighed heavily on my shoulders.

That night, I lay on my back staring at the patched mud-and-straw ceiling. The solitude was depressing, worse than hunger. I wept silently, holding it in so it would not disrupt the soft snoring of the others. How I wished the snoring was louder, to drown out the ringing in my head. Dukwah was so wrong: I did ache inside. My pain was deeper and darker than any well. It was a false myth that a widow loses her yearning for her husband. The unwanted title does not erase the desire to be loved, to be caressed. I was only thirty-nine. Oh yes, I suffered. Memories of how he used to make my blood rise and my flesh tingle in rapture haunted me. My body ached for his so badly, it felt as though I had lost my balance, the balance of male and female, *yin* and *yang*.

Unable to lie still, I rose. Carefully I tiptoed over the carpet of bodies to the doorway, opened the door, then crept out, wearing only my slip. I sat down on a stump that was once a large shady tree. The cold breeze soothed me. The stars twinkled and danced for me.

In the morning, I returned to church. Husband's body was exactly as I had left him, tucked under the blanket and still smiling. Two kind volunteers helped carry him home where he belonged.

The house was completely empty. I was glad everyone was gone so I could wash and prepare Husband alone. I bathed him as best as I could, being as gentle as I could, as if he were still alive. Alas, I had to dress him again in the same tattered clothes. It was all he had. Once it had been a fine wool suit. Now it was stained and worn patches held the wrinkled garment together.

"How shall I bury him?" I asked myself, looking for some kind of coffin or box.

The fever had sapped what remained of our measly savings. I would have sold my last pair of slippers for a proper burial, because the final send-off was as important as one's welcome into this world. For Husband, I was willing to beg from door to door, but tragically the entire country was made up of beggars. Many were in such straits they sold their daughters into prostitution. For me, that was not an option.

I searched about the neighborhood and all I managed to scavenge was an unraveling straw mat. "Forgive me, Husband," I said softly as I rolled him around in it. His darling head bounced against the hard earthen floor. The mat was about a foot too short; Husband's feet stuck out at the end, exposing a tear in his sock. I wept at the sight of his big left toe, naked for all to see. The more I tried to mend the hole, the wider the rip.

The day of the funeral I found a place to bury my beloved. It was far from what I had envisioned. I wanted to lay him in a beautiful spot, overlooking a picturesque plain, so his spirit would be pleased. Instead his final resting place was at the base of a hill, overlooking a sparse field of wilting corn.

A large procession of mourners followed behind us. I was greatly touched by the enormous turnout that afternoon. Husband had given so much charity since coming to the South that many people came to pay their respects. It was a glorious sight: everyone clothed in white garments—the colorless symbol of mourning as well as brightness and life. Appropriately fitting. One could not think of life without thinking about death. They were so closely intertwined.

I allowed myself to grieve loudly and unchecked. "*Ii-goo-yah. Ii-goo-yah,*" I cried as they lowered Husband's straw coffin down into the pit. The mourners respectfully stepped aside as I sprinkled the first layer of earth. The soft dirt sifted through my parted fingers evenly. Done, I stepped back and watched as men shoveled in the dirt. I imagined pebbles and tiny insects clogging his ears and filling his nostrils. I swore to myself, someday I would dig up Husband's grave and give him the oak coffin he deserved. And on that day, I would be dressed in a white hemp gown and my face would be powdered.

After everyone departed, I lingered behind. I stood there in front of my love's final home. Many times I had prepared myself for my own death, but never his. I felt completely disconnected. When I was a child I belonged to my parents. When I was a young woman I belonged to my husband. And over the years, as Lee, Dukpil's wife, I had given up my identity to please him. My existence was woven into his so closely that mine was no longer distinguishable. I was unsure of who I was now that my husband was dead.

For a quick moment I considered remarrying, but the penalties of remarrying were too heavy and would last for generations. A widow's disloyalty would jeopardize her children's chances of obtaining positions in life and thus would affect future generations. Once the family's name was blemished the stain could not be wiped away. Besides, the thought of another man taking Husband's place was repulsive. Husband was the first and only man who would ever possess my heart.

This was the first of many decisions I would have to make on my own and without anyone's approval. Frightened, I felt like running away from myself. Why me? What was my purpose for living? I was in a state of mourning. I mourned for the loss of my husband, the loss of my identity, and the burden of my responsibility. A white ribbon in my hair symbolized my status. I wore it always. I had it on when I heard voices cheer, "*Mansei!*" The war, after three long years, one month, and two days, after a million civilian casualties, a hundred thousand war orphans, three hundred thousand war widows, was over. An armistice agreement was reached on July 27, 1953, at Panmunjom, the Demilitarized Zone (DMZ). The cease-fire agreement sacrificed unification of our two Koreas.

The ending of the war did not inspire me to holler for joy as I had done when the Japanese were defeated. There was nothing to cheer about. I wanted the war to continue just a bit longer. The North Korean People's Army was nearly exhausted. I believed they could have been defeated if the war just held on. Now I would never know for certain if my Yongwoon was alive or dead.

I mourned, wondering why my life was worth sparing when so many were lost. What was my purpose for living? These words thundered in my head. Then I heard the same tiny masculine voice from deep inside speak to me once more . . .

. . . Yes, yes, I understood now. I had once made a vow to God to serve Him. He wanted me to fulfill my promise by serving the ill and the poor with the healing grace of *chiryo*. This was my purpose.

That night I felt I could never sleep again, but not because I was afraid or overwhelmed by the challenge. On the contrary, I was eager to get started. I was through with death.

Promptly after the morning meal I went searching for people to treat. My efforts met with jeers and frowns. My own sisters rejected the goodness of *chiryo*. They threatened to tie me up if I laid one hand on them. They scolded me for not properly acting like a grieving widow, expecting me to mourn for the correct length of three years. Three years! A night seemed like an eternity. I was unwilling to waste valuable time. So I tossed aside their criticisms and began to focus only on my mission.

Each morning, I set out filled with hope, and in the evening I returned deflated. Everyone I approached refused to unbutton their shirts or drop their pants. They frantically clutched their clothes and shoved me out of their homes.

"You must be mad if you think I will strip for you, much less pay you to beat me," a woman spat.

"My services are free," I informed her.

"I get enough free beatings from my husband after he comes home drunk every night."

"*Chiryo* helps the blood's circulation," I pressed. "The dark purple snakes you see on the surface of your legs are the result of clogged blood showing itself."

"It sounds like some sick torture to me. Get out of my house, you fraud!"

And so this was how it went, day after day. Discouraged, I treated the only person who understood the value of *chiryo*— me. Working my hands up and down my body, I pounded the flesh, covering every inch of skin with purple bruises and red tracks. I looked dreadful but I felt incredibly healthy. When I ran out of skin, I treated my children. They screamed and cried while I held them down with my legs. In China, the maid usually restrained the children while I worked on them. Here I received no cooperation at all.

The children and I became walking advertisements. The *chiryo* marks raised plenty of curious eyebrows among church members. Slowly, a few patients trickled in. I never asked for any payment. Those who had a little offered what they could spare—sometimes a handful of rice or splinters for the stove or a thankful prayer. That was plenty for me, but Crippled Sister complained ruthlessly.

"Your children barely have anything to eat, yet you refuse to work. You waste your time all day beating yourself and naked strangers from off the streets!"

"I know I have a good head for business and that I can make a lot more money doing something else, but money is not necessary. Just *chiryo*."

"Think clearly and give up your insane crusade. You are just a woman, not a professional healer. Leave that to the old men who study herbs all their lives. Think of your children."

It was unnecessary to remind me of them. To see *ahghee* still wrapped in one of Husband's old shirts tore at my heart. I was doing the best I could for them. Of course their welfare was continually on my mind. Every day when I walked out into the ruined streets, I thought of them. I was overwhelmed with the responsibility of salvaging their mutilated childhoods. I knew they had to go back to school, but it would take a year or two more for me to raise the tuition. I dreaded telling Dukwah. School was all she talked about in the refugee camp.

As before, the boys took the disappointing news quite well. In fact, too well. They grinned from cheek to cheek, anticipating another year of play. Dukwah, however, cast down her bold eyes to hide her boiling frustration.

"Just be a little patient."

"Mother!" Dukwah's eyes were wide open, staring at me as if I had struck her. "How can I miss another year? I will be behind my classmates!"

"One or two years will not matter. You are a very intelligent girl. It will give your classmates a chance to catch up to you." I tried to lighten her mood.

"I will go to school." She flashed a fiery look at me under her heavy brow.

"Now, be sensible. There are your brothers and baby sister to consider as well. Your father is dead and I do not have enough energy to feed you all and pay your tuition."

"Then I will raise the money myself."

"How will you do that?"

"I will go find Father's friends in Pusan. They will give me the money."

"Nonsense. They might have moved as we did, and your journey would be wasted. Besides, I cannot stop my work to accompany you on a scavenger hunt."

"Not you, Mother, I will go alone," she stated boldly, then stormed out of the house.

I stared after the defiant girl with the suffering young face. She was definitely my daughter, headstrong to the end. She returned much later, refusing to speak to me. I knew she meant what she threatened. I felt devastated when Dukwah defied me. So many times in the past I turned to her for support and she had comforted me. Always she was the first to make any necessary sacrifices, but school was one sacrifice she was no longer willing to accept.

That evening after dinner I slipped outside to find a solution before the national curfew siren sounded. Quickly I searched the roadside for a car or cart going to Pusan. By the time I returned home, I had secured a ride for Dukwah on a cabbage delivery truck. It was parked on the side of the road. The driver and his companion had just pulled over to consume their meal of rice and cooked pig's feet. The men seemed harmless enough.

Together, Dukwah and I walked to the designated pickup spot after the release siren blared at dawn.

"The driver will take you as far as he can, then you must walk the remainder of the way. Stay away from the roads at night and allow yourself plenty of time to find shelter before the curfew." I lavished motherly warnings on her.

She was frightened, but determined. I, too, was frightened, if not terrified. I had already lost one child because I let him part from me. I prayed I was not making the same costly mistake as I left her by the roadside. She looked like a beautiful wildflower standing there with the fiery sun rising behind her, lighting her silhouette.

A few minutes later, the cabbage truck came bouncing from the north. The door swung open and a puff of smoke descended on her. Once the smoke cleared, she saw the two men who would take her to Pusan.

"Jump in," the driver belched.

She hesitated for a second, contemplating whether to turn around or go. She decided to take her chances and climbed aboard. During the entire trip, she inhaled their cloudy fumes, and by the time they reached the city she was nearly green with motion sickness. She was never so thrilled to see that port city, which had been her prison without school for eight months. Ironically, she had returned to make that precise dream come true.

She located a small community of her father's friends. They could not believe their eyes when Dukwah walked out of their past and into their present. She recounted for them the story of her father's death and our hardships in Yeachun since his passing. They pitied the young brave girl who had traveled so far to seek their aid. Although they, too, lived a meager existence, they passed around a collection jar. Their generosity added up to a small fortune.

With the money, Dukwah paid for all three tuitions, uniforms, and supplies, and still had a bit left over to help her aunts start a noodle business. The profits from the business they ran from the shack rescued the entire family from starvation.

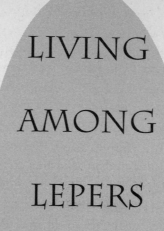

LIVING

AMONG

LEPERS

At thirty-nine, I became the master of my own destiny, but I did not have the freedom to choose freedom. It was thrust upon me. No one was around to command me. I belonged wholly to myself. In the old days, a widow was forced to obey her son or male in-law, but war changed even that. Gradually freedom transformed me into a totally daring woman.

That was how I arrived at the leper colony in Daego. It was exactly what I was searching for: hundreds of sick people confined in one place.

"Take me there," I asked a man whose brother was a leper.

"Why would you want to go?" His nostrils twitched.

"In a way I, too, am a leper."

"You do not look like one to me. You still have all of your fingers and both of your ears."

"But people avoid my *chiryo* like it is one."

"Are you not afraid you will catch the rotting disease?"

"No," I answered enthusiastically. The possibility of infection never entered my mind, because I knew I would be protected.

Summoning courage, I wrapped *ahghee* on my back and sneaked out while everyone was still fast asleep. The older children, I felt, would be better off staying in Yeachun, continuing their education. But the baby was so dependent on me. Although the time had passed for her to take her first steps, she was incapable of even crawling.

In a note I hastily scribbled, I made no mention of where I was actually going, saying only that I would be gone for some time, because if had I told them they would have dragged me back. I was sure of it. So *ahghee* and I slipped quietly into the new day.

The Daego Research Clinic was fenced off from the rest of the world. Bright, colorful flowering shrubs and trees along the fence camouflaged the decay inside the colony of outcasts. Here the staff and lepers lived together. Rarely did they receive visitors; that was why *ahghee* and I were welcomed with outstretched arms. I wasted little time and explained my reasons for being there. They were so understaffed and in need of a miracle, in any form, they were willing to try me.

I was given a tour of the facilities. I thought I had prepared myself for the disfigurement of the disease, but I was horrified at what I saw. They were regular people: women, men, college professors, farmers, students, musicians, and children. Miserable souls with inflamed and discolored skin, lumpy and thickened faces and limbs. Some had no hair, no eyeballs, no earlobes. Those with the most severe cases were the fortunate ones: their nerves were so damaged that they were spared from feeling pain. But that, too, caused misfortune. Once a leper's foot caught on fire. He had placed it too close to a burning log. If it had not been for a nurse, the flames would have consumed his entire leg before he noticed what had happened.

I went to work immediately, handing *ahghee* over to the lepers to watch. She did not cry at all as grotesque faces cooed at her. Seeing how well she was being cared for, I went into the adjoining room and called in the first patient. A woman my age was brought in on the back of a young man. At first I thought she was a child because of her slight frame, but when he laid her down on the mat before me, her face revealed her true age. She looked up at me pleadingly. Those eyes hinted at inner turmoil.

"My mother just stares and does not utter a word. She has been this way since she took a dull knife to her thighs and tried to cut the spoiled flesh herself." He dropped his chin in despair.

"I will try to help your mother," I said as I pulled up her skirt to examine her legs. Indeed she had butchered herself. The deep gash had not healed.

"Shall we get started?" I spoke as casually as I could to the son, who was rising to leave. "I may need your assistance in holding her down."

He turned pale at my request. "I cannot. She is my mother," he protested.

"You must, because she is," I reasoned, and he sat down reluctantly. He took a seat on the other side of his mother. "Let us pray." I bowed my head and shut my eyes. "Heavenly Father, I ask You to guide my hands to do Your bidding. Amen." It was a short but good prayer, a prayer I would use many times.

As the Chinese woman taught me, I began at the neck, pinching long red vertical marks from the base of her chin to the tips of her nipples. It gave the illusion that she was wearing some type of tribal neckpiece. I slapped the skin around her belly, making sure I did a thorough job. She squirmed very little. The sound of my hand bothered her more than the physical pain. When I finally managed to work my way down to her slashed thighs, a queasiness fell over me. The tips of my fingers tingled whenever one slipped into the open gash. I had to stop several times to peel off decayed flesh and clotted blood that had stuck to them.

By the end of my first day, I had seen the disease's gruesome effects and different stages of deterioration. It was no wonder the rest of society wanted the lepers tucked far away where their ugliness could not repulse others.

I was exhausted, but never too tired to reject food, so I followed the zombie crowd into the building for eating. There were large earthen stoves, and on them six enormous iron cauldrons as big as washtubs. The wooden lids danced as the water bubbled. When the lids were pried off, a mushroom of steam rose up. There was no fragrance as sweet as that of freshly steamed rice. We all pressed forward as the rice was ladled out in shovels. It was served with cabbage, squash, and green onions grown in the garden. Who would have thought that at a leper colony I would eat like royalty . . . who?

I could have slept anywhere that night with *ahghee*, but I was grateful when they assigned me to a room with ten other women, modeled after a Western-style apartment. It was the first time I had ever seen a walk-in closet, a boxed-off space in the wall where clothes were supposed to be stored. It seemed ridiculous that they would build private rooms for such trivial items when people were sleeping out on the streets because they had no place to live.

For a long while I lay awake with the blanket pulled over my ears, trying unsuccessfully to tune out the moans and screams. So much misery. The women's cries bounced from one wall to the other. I knew I had made the right decision to come here. These lepers needed my services.

I worked six days a week, often from dawn to dawn. The days seemed to bleed into longer weeks. Sundays were the only days I allowed myself a bit of rest. That day I attended chapel. A minister was brought in to give the weekly sermon. He stood in a barbed-wire cage to protect himself against infectious hands, but no leper ever reached for him. Like me, they sat and listened as he preached about faith, but he lacked the ability to inspire even a sigh from his flock of decomposing lambs. His unnatural gestures and uneasy voice made me feel uncomfortable. It seemed he was more concerned about a leper's reaching hands than about what he was saying. Shame. He was the only reverend we could lure. Everyone else stayed away.

I began to notice slight improvements in my patients. *Chiryo* seemed to stabilize the disease and improve blood circulation where there were still functioning limbs. That was all I could hope for. I was realistic, I knew *chiryo* could not regrow fingers or toes, and I never misled those who came to me.

The work was almost enough to make me happy. But the overwhelming feeling of guilt for sneaking out on my children began to affect my ability to remain focused. I berated myself for not at least saying good-bye, assuring them their mother was not abandoning them. I wondered if they knew I would be back. This tormented me. I had wanted to help these lepers so badly, I had forsaken my responsibilities as a mother. Finally, I decided to send a letter to the family.

"Please, children, try to understand. Mother has not abandoned you nor can I abandon my work. I shall spare you the details of all the horrible things I have seen, but trust me when I tell you my services are needed more here."

They wrote back immediately, one letter after another. They always started the same way. "Come back, your children are suffering without their mother," my sisters pleaded. When all their letters failed, Crippled Sister arrived at the clinic unannounced, her twisted body borne on the back of a strong young man. Using his legs, she snooped around the clinic, striking the lepers with her long spiral cane when they approached her out of curiosity. She caused such havoc, my work was disrupted.

"What is the meaning of this?" I barked at the old crusty gatekeeper who came to fetch me.

"Sorry to disturb you, but there is a madwoman yelling for you. She claims you are her older sister," he said, wiping his forehead.

"Is she crippled?"

"Why, yes. Shall I bring her to you?"

I thought for a moment, wondering what I should do with her, then it occurred to me she came to the right place. "Yes, take her into the next room." I smiled.

I heard her long before the door slid opened. She was hurling her usual curses at the old man who showed her the way.

"Aunt, you have come to visit me," I greeted her.

"I assure you this is no friendly visit. I am here to convince you to give up your nonsense. This place is full of diseased animals. The demons are inside everyone of them. They are possessed and it is making their flesh spoil. We must get out of here before they come after us," she warned.

"There are no such things as demons. Those are merely superstitious tales."

"Shhhhh, they will hear you and get angry." She looked around the room for one to show itself.

"Come, rest here on the mat."

"Well, maybe just for a moment." She yawned.

And when she did, three nurses came in and pinned her down. One grabbed an arm, another held both legs, and another restrained her head.

"*Ay-ya*, get these lepers off me!" Crippled Sister shrieked.

"Hold still or I will slap harder."

She jerked and thumped her head against the ground while I slapped her. The harder she hit her head, the harder I hit her. She struggled, scratched, and bit us all. Such raw power, it took two more additional hands to hold her still.

I knew her skin stung and burned, because my hand felt the same heat. As though my hands were on the warpath, I beat her toneless flesh. Her flesh quickly responded. Large black-and-blue patches bloomed from underneath, bleeding together on the surface to form one huge bruise.

Crippled Sister began to cough hard, spit squirting out of her mouth as she choked on her own saliva and tears. I ignored all her rants, except her plea for water. Throughout the long five-hour treatment, she begged for one cup of water after another. The water spilled streams down her chin and bare chest as she gulped it down slowly. When she sucked on the glass too long, I snatched it from her.

"I am not finished yet!" she protested.

"You want to get better, do you not?" I asked, but before she could curse a response, my hands silenced her.

When we finally released her, she gathered her clothes and slithered out of the clinic, screaming, "What have I done to you to make you hate me so, Older Sister?!"

I did not expect her to understand that I did it because I wanted her to live a long and fulfilling life. It was too soon and the pain still too fresh for her to see the benefits of *chiryo*.

ADVENTURES

OF

CHIRYO

―――――――――

After five months, I eventually returned home to my family. I left in good conscience, knowing my trainees would carry on my work faithfully. The empty shack looked exactly the same, perhaps more worn, and the noodle business was gone.

Kunsam and Kunil were the first to greet me, followed by their older sister. They had grown so much, especially Dukwah, who was practically a young lady. It filled my heart with peace to see them, yet I was taken aback by their appearance. Their school uniforms were tattered and faded.

"Mother, where were you?" Kunil threw his boyish arms around my hips.

"Mother, I learned a new song today. Would you like me to sing it for you?" Kunsam copied his brother and wrapped his arms around me as well.

I glanced at Dukwah and she stared back at me boldly. "Come closer, let me have a good look at you. I missed you all so much. Have you been obedient?" I smiled.

"How long will you stay before you leave again?" Dukwah's eyes were full of resentment.

"Unfortunately, that is one question I cannot answer. God will call on me when He needs my services again."

"Mother, will you play with us?" Kunsam laced his fingers into mine.

"First I must speak to your aunts. Where are they? Why are they not rolling noodles?"

"The business went badly. People stopped coming even to buy food, though the aunts tried the best they could. Now we barely have enough to feed ourselves." Dukwah stated accusingly. "Come on, boys, I will play with you outside."

I knew I had to make it up to them. As I was thinking of a way, Crippled Sister limped in, leaning on a cane. I was speechless. She stood tall, her legs straight, though one was still several inches shorter.

"Older Sister, your *chiryo* works miracles! After I left you I began to treat myself. At first I was so consumed with pain I thought I was dying. I thought you had broken my bones, because I was black-and-blue all over. Then the bruises began to turn yellowish green, and I was sure I was a leper. For weeks I waited for a toe or an ear to fall off, but nothing rotted. Instead my entwined legs began to loosen. I could not believe what was happening to me, so I began to hit myself. The more I hit, the more the muscles in my legs relaxed and lengthened. Look, my legs are almost even and I have put on good weight. No longer do I depend on the kindness of others to carry me around. See how well I walk. A miracle, I tell you!" The bitterness had left her and there was joy in her face again.

I spent my first week at home washing the children's school uniforms. I was most concerned about Dukwah's appearance. Several washes later the grime still clung to the fabric.

Rummaging through dumpsters, I dug out two large cotton rice sacks. I dyed one black to make a jumper dress for her. The white sack I sewed into a collared blouse. I found some shoes behind a shoemaker's shop. I was fortunate enough to find a pair for the boys as well. They were perfect, almost brand-new, except that they were all made for the left foot.

Then there was nothing more to do. If there had been food to spare, I would have cooked a special meal. If there had been more clothes to wash, I would have washed them. But the thing I most wanted to give them was a home of our own. For a time I felt useless. At least when I was doing *chiryo* I knew I was being useful, but even that did not happen easily. I waited steadfastly for patients who never came, until one showed up gyrating wildly.

"My son is a good boy; only sometimes he likes to dance around and laugh suddenly to himself. I do not know what causes him to act this way," his father said.

The farmer boy danced clumsily as he balanced himself on one bent leg and then on the other. With his bloody chewed fingers he painted a distorted self-portrait on Crippled Sister's only clean wall.

"Bad! Look what you have done to this nice woman's wall," the father scolded.

The boy froze on his left leg, his one arm uplifted and the other in his mouth.

Brushing back his oily bangs, I examined his face closely. It looked pleasant, almost pretty in a girlish way. I reached for his shirt string and he pulled away from me. Could this crazy farm boy comprehend modesty? That was a good sign. He was not completely lost. Then, as if he sensed why I was there, he calmly lay down so I could examine his body. I told him exactly what I was planning to do. He let me open up his shirt and undo the drawstring that held up his burlap trousers. Under the tan skin of my cheeks I felt a flush of shyness. At the leper colony I had treated dozens of men, but never once blushed. Their bodies were so deformed it was inconceivable to imagine them in an intimate sort of way. Not since Husband's death had I seen such a physique. The shoulders were broad and the stomach cut like a finely carved washboard. The opening of the trousers revealed a trail of coarse black hair growing wildly like uncut weeds, hinting at a fully developed man. This hidden fact unnerved me, yet I was curious. All those years I was married to Husband, never once did I fully probe his body with my hands or eyes. The male anatomy was still a bit of a mystery to me. It was one of the forbidden secrets a wife just accepted. As long as his part and my part fit together and conceived babies it was unnecessary to question how it all functioned.

After that first visit, he came regularly. I treated him morning, noon, and night as the Chinese maid had done for me. From time to time I would catch glimpses of his true intelligence behind those glassy eyes. He reminded me of my own lonely childhood—isolated from the rest of the clear-thinking world because of the fire in my belly that deprived me of sleep.

Eventually, *chiryo* stopped the dancing and bloody wall portraits. He began to sleep through the entire night, and in the morning he woke thinking clearly. Ideas and calculations formed in his head far beyond any of ours.

"It seems a waste to bury such brilliance in cow manure." I clucked my tongue.

The old farmer heard me and responded, "Educated, you think my son could be a great man?"

"It would be against God's will if every person did not live up to his full potential."

"I am not a religious man, but I believe what you say is true. If only he could have the chance to go to school and make something of himself, and not become just an ignorant old farmer like his father."

"You can take him to Seoul for the college entrance exam. Great young men are coming out of colleges these days."

"*Ii-ee-goo,* I would take him, but then who would plow the land?" He clasped his hands in despair.

"I will take him," I answered abruptly. My quick response surprised even me.

"*Uh-moh,* you have already been too generous." He bowed his head humbly.

"The boy and I will leave in the morning," I said.

When Crippled Sister discovered what I had promised, she nearly fell over. "You support this retarded boy's education and not your own children's. What kind of mother are you?!"

I wanted to say I was the kind of mother whose daughter's heroic efforts to obtain knowledge taught her the value of education; however, I remained silent as I tied my belongings in a large square cotton kerchief and prepared *ahghee* for our next adventure. This time I pulled Dukwah aside.

"I am going to Seoul. Even if your aunts speak badly of me, be respectful and patient. When I find us a house I will send for you and the boys. Please, Dukwah-yah, I need your support more than ever. You must take my place so I may serve God."

"Take us with you."

"It is better for you to stay. Here you have your studies and a roof over your head."

"Who will look after you and *ahghee?* You need me, Mother."

"I know I do. That is why I am asking you to care for your brothers."

"You will not forget us?"

"No. I will send for you shortly. Be brave."

The farmer boy was waiting for *ahghee* and me on the highway. Together we headed northward, each carrying only a small sack. We were all alone. The sounds of our clumsy footsteps shuffling through gravel echoed into the vast stretch of highway that seemed to have no end. This familiar scene brought back violent memories of our crossing.

After a while on that deserted road, a dim glow of light from the rear caught my attention. Standing in full view in the middle of the road, I waved the approaching truck down. It halted right in front of me, causing its load of chickens to cluck wildly. I hurried over to the driver's side to ask for a ride. He welcomed us aboard.

He rambled on and on about the bad fortune he has had in his miserable life as a widower. He recounted to us tragic war stories, the same stories I had heard so many times before, but always from different lips. By the end of our ride, I was emotionally drained. The unnamed man had shared so much with us and yet we would probably never meet again.

The farmer boy, *ahghee,* and I found ourselves on the outskirts of a shantytown where the boy's uncle lived. It was dinnertime and the alleyways leading to the house were dimly lit with oil lanterns.

The uncle's house was in the basement of a small gift store. I bought the only pencil in the store with my last coin. The woman studied the money suspiciously, then looked me over with those hard slanted eyes of hers. Speaking in an insulting tone, she muttered, "Well, it appears real."

I managed to catch only a few winks of sleep because the farmer boy kept us all up with his nervous pacing. Finally the release siren sounded and we were on our way to Yonsei University. First I took him on a detour up the small hill overlooking the school. There on the hill, closer to God, we knelt down on the grass and prayed. The words always flowed so easily when I prayed for someone else. When I had said all that needed to be said, I showed the boy how to sharpen the pencil.

"Be careful not waste any of it. It is all you have. Write lightly or the point will break."

"Yes, Aunt, I will write with a very light hand."

When we arrived at the university, a sea of expensive automobiles crammed the streets. Anxious students with their parents hovered around the entrance gate. The boy nervously tapped the pencil on his palm. I could tell he felt out of place among all the rich city people.

"Let us turn back and go home," he said timidly.

"Turn back? You unappreciative boy. Your father and I have sacrificed so much to get you to Seoul. This is your chance to change your destiny," I said sternly.

"I do not belong here, Aunt." He dropped his gaze. "I am only the son of a farmer, not a scholar's son."

"True, you are not. Your father is just an ignorant farmer who could not even bring you here in an oxcart. All you have is this pencil and God, but that is more than enough," I said as I combed his knotty hair away from his eyes.

Silently I mumbled another prayer for this frightened boy as he marched into line with all the other students and disappeared into the gray cement building. I waited with the concerned parents outside. Every religious symbol and good-luck charm must have been there that day, warding off bad spirits and calling on the smart ones. All around me parents paced back and forth, or rocked themselves.

At last, the examination was over and the students stumbled out in clusters. I stretched my head over the crowd to find the farmer boy, and there he was, still clutching the pencil, only a stub now.

"See, Aunt, I was very careful not to waste any of it." He beamed proudly.

"You did fine. Now you will have something to write with on the first day of school."

When I said this, he smiled even more broadly. "You think so?" he asked hopefully.

"I am sure of it."

As confident as I sounded, it was not enough to dispel the nervousness of the boy or his uncle. They worried themselves sick waiting for the scores to be posted. On the appointed day we arrived at the university early. A large crowd was already pushed against the bulletin board. A lengthy list of tiny printed names stretched from one end of the long board to the other. At the top of the list we spotted the farmer boy's name. He had scored the highest mark. The boy and his uncle were overjoyed. They joined arms and jigged around like children at play. I was too troubled to join in the celebration. Now I had to find a way to raise the money for his tuition and housing.

I took a stroll, trying to come up with a solution to my dilemma. For three days I strolled around aimlessly, because I sensed we had overstayed our welcome, though the uncle insisted we were not an inconvenience. On the fourth day of my search, I ended up at the Moonsoong Mission, run by American missionaries. These kind people listened to my problem with open minds and compassionate hearts. Generously they offered to take the boy in and arrange for a full scholarship. They, too, believed a great young mind like his should not be wasted.

I rushed back to get the boy before the missionaries changed their minds. When I returned with him a congratulations banner draped from the rafters with his name drawn across it. People clapped and cheered gaily as a round cake, with small candles, was brought out on a platter. The vanilla cake tasted delicious. It was so sweet and so foreign I savored every crumb.

Before all the celebrating ended, I snuck away. I had enough good-byes in recent years to last me for two lifetimes. Besides, I had to find shelter for *ahghee* and myself before the national curfew sounded. I roamed around, looking at the reconstructed city. The last time I was here was when I passed through on the way to Pusan. Husband was wrong; Seoul was more than useless farmland. I could see that even with all the bombed-out structures and the scorched earth it would quickly rebuild itself into a prosperous city. It had already grown in population. City folks had it better than those of us living outside. Life seemed almost normal. I felt intimidated by their style. Right off, they knew I was a refugee from the North by my scratchy burlap dress with the elbows patched, one in brown and the other in gray. I searched for a sympathetic face in the crowd who might take in a mother and her babe, but men and women glanced back sullenly.

Feeling completely unwelcome, I dodged down a dark alley. Only one teenage boy lurked in the distance. He kept looking over his shoulder while increasing his stride. He must have thought I was a bandit with a baby strapped to my back.

I wanted so badly to go back to Yeachun, but I could not return in my present downcast condition, especially when I had asked Dukwah to be brave. I felt absolutely alone. At such low moments I often peered up at the sky to assure myself that someone up there did love me. He judged me not for my patched clothes or Pyongyang accent.

I went to the only place I knew would shelter outcasts. The church looked more like a condemned shed than a house of worship. I would have passed it by if it had not been for the crude wooden cross crookedly nailed above the splintered doorway. Inside, the walls were bare and grimy, and the altar was missing. Someone probably used it to fuel a small fire. Only the pews remained.

There were many like me who had come with their children to rest themselves. I slumped down into the nearest pew, suddenly drained. I kicked off my slippers and rested my head on the back of the row in front of me. Little by little I began to feel better. Just resting, relaxing my eyelids, not praying.

I had hardly dozed off when I woke myself up shouting out Yongwoon's name. "Yongwoon-yah! Yongwoon-yah! Mother is here."

"Are you all right?" a feeble voice asked.

It came from the woman behind me. Her clothes told me she was a woman of affluence, and her bloated face and hands revealed she was not at all well.

"Yes, thank you," I replied, still shaken.

"No one is spared from bad dreams these days," she remarked as she massaged her fingers to alleviate the pressure.

"Your hands must cause you terrible pain," I commented.

"Why, yes," she answered, surprised.

"Let me see your tongue," I asked boldly. Her swollen tongue was covered with a thick coat of white. "There is something that can be done for you. I guarantee it will bring you back to health. I can treat you if you would like."

"Where are you from?"

"Nowhere."

"Where are you going?"

"Nowhere."

"Well, then, if you can do what you claim you must come to my home, for my husband is also very ill."

And so I did. She lived in a house of moderate size with her invalid husband. As with many others, his condition worsened due to the lack of medicine after the war. Before his illness he was a well-respected college music professor. Now his emaciated body curled in a fetal position in the corner of the front room. He was so weak he could barely raise his head. From time to time the servants had to flip him over so he would not suffer from bedsores.

The instant I gazed into his yellow eyes I knew his body was poisoning itself. The blood needed to be cleansed and pumped into every organ and every limb with greater ease.

"There is much work for me to do here. Let us begin at once," I said as I pushed up my sleeves.

I treated the professor and his good wife each day, many times twice a day, alternating between the two. Gradually I began to see some noticeable improvements in the coloring and temperature of the professor's skin. He began by lifting his head, then sitting up on his own. Shortly thereafter he was on his feet and back at the college teaching music.

"Ask anything and I will give it to you if I can," the wife offered graciously.

"Allowing my baby and me to stay here is payment enough."

"Then you must stay on and live with us as long as you wish. Your *chiryo* is good. Many of our people could benefit from your services. You could treat them here free of charge. Do not worry about finances; my husband and I will feed and clothe you and the child."

I stayed with them for a while, working out of their house. The three of us became close friends, though they were much older than I. It happened so easily, so naturally. It was a new experience having people to talk to besides my sisters and Husband. In fact, it was easier because we were unrelated by blood or marriage. There were few expectations or disappointments to fuss about.

Their support and referrals brought forth a steady flow of

patients each day. They came to check out the woman who was either a liar or a miracle worker. I confessed to being neither one; I let the people decide on their own. Some thought I was a mad torturer, but most became convinced followers, spreading the praises of *chiryo*.

Living such an independent existence only added to my hunger for security. I had never wanted a home of my own so badly in my life. A place where my children could feel safe. A place to replant our mangled roots and build upon our shrunken family.

God must have heard my unspoken prayer, for an important man surnamed Kang sought me out. He had an older brother who was ailing from internal bleeding. Without adequate medical attention the blood seeped out from every orifice of his body. I was their last hope.

A chauffeur-driven black sedan came to fetch me. It made me feel important to ride in such a modern automobile. The upholstered seats were of brown leather with white lace cushions and doilies. The driver, who said fewer than three words to me, wore white gloves and a black captain's hat. What a great job he had, I thought, as I watched him turn the wheel left and right. It was definitely better than cleaning outhouses or plowing fields.

I could not believe my eyes when we pulled up to an estate surrounded by a high gate. Inside, the mansion was adorned with rich drapery, crystal chandeliers, and priceless foreign treasures. I was afraid to make a sudden move and break something that I could not afford to replace.

On the floor, an expensive carpet covered the pathway from the door to where I stood. I caught a glimpse of my slippers and the muddy trail I had just left. I wished I had removed them before entering, but the well-dressed servant who let me in said in this house they practiced Western customs. I made a mental note never to adopt this particular custom in my own house. Shoes should not be worn inside living quarters. It would only create more work for me.

For months I treated him, lived with him, cleaned up after him. Gradually there was less blood in his stool. He began to fatten up and even joke on occasion. The doctors attributed his recovery to an incorrect diagnosis, but Mr. Kang's brother and I knew the truth.

To show his gratitude he built me a fine house in Hong-mueng. I was overwhelmed. The house had a tall iron gate and a cement wall surrounding it, a porch to take one's leisure on, and plenty of space. Altogether the house contained seven rooms, excluding the outhouse. The largest room was at the farthest end of the hallway. Above the sliding partition, a hand-carved nameplate as big as a game board hung over it. The letters were so bold that even a person with poor vision standing at the opposite end of the house could read that this office belonged to me.

Life was different now; patients poured in whether I desired them or not. My clientele included company presidents, famous opera singers, magazine editors, school founders, and congressmen. They would arrive as early as five o'clock in the morning in chauffeured cars, on stretchers, on the backs of others.

I worked diligently, but it was never fast enough. My hands were raw and the pounding became torturous. Every nerve and vein pulsated at the slightest touch. I urgently needed assistance. I turned to the only people who I knew would come and help though they disapproved of my work. Unable to clutch a pencil, I dictated a letter to my sisters, imploring them to bring their children and mine to Seoul. When they arrived and saw how worn I was, they did not berate me. They rolled up their sleeves and offered me their extra hands. They worked as hard as I did, even harder; nevertheless, the number of patients kept multiplying instead of diminishing. The small hill that shaded our house was thronged with people. Sometimes pushing and shoving matches arose because desperate people tired of waiting. The fights escalated to the point where I had to devise a fair numbering system. Small pieces of paper numbered from one into the hundreds were distributed on a first-come-first-treated basis.

I accepted any woman who wanted to learn *chiryo*. I began a hands-on internship program. The moment they joined my team, I used their fresh hands. The cement house thundered with *chiryo* from sunrise to curfew. It was music to my ears.

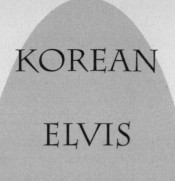

KOREAN

ELVIS

So many strangers in need funneled through my threshold, I hardly noticed my children growing up. I was always too busy to attend their graduations or to remember their birthdays. I took it for granted that Dukwah was forever going to be Mother's little surrogate. But Dukwah had her own dreams. She was sprouting into a woman with her own course in life, apart from mine.

Looking back now with clearer eyes, I see how I failed her. I thought providing food, clothing, and shelter was all that was expected of me. It was not. Dukwah wanted and needed a mother to nag her to study more, eat more, do more chores. However, she did all these things on her own so well, I never bothered. From the day she was born she was always so fearless and self-reliant.

When other mothers were afraid that their children would not get into a top college, I worried very little. I knew Dukwah would rise to the challenge and be accepted into the college of her choice which she did. Korea University was one of the finest and oldest colleges in South Korea. I was so proud.

Those days I seldom saw Dukwah, except when she was fast asleep in bed. Sundays, on our way to church, were the only other times our paths actually merged.

Little did I know there was a young man, in khaki army fatigues, watching Dukwah from afar. Always he waited outside church, half concealed behind a tree, hoping to catch a glimpse of her.

Dukwah had bloomed into a self-confident, poised beauty from all the attention she received from her peers and teachers. They admired her dignity and boyish strength, but there was nothing boyish about her physique. She stood at a tall five feet three inches and had curves from her breasts down to her calves. A perfect thirty-four, twenty-three, thirty-four.

The young soldier first saw her at a college party during her junior year, a party I had no knowledge of. I had heard rumors of such "meetings" where young men and women met without parental supervision. I found it shocking, but I let her be. This was her time to recapture her adolescent years lost to war and then later to piles of schoolbooks.

He had just returned from America on a yearlong radar training program for the military. He stood there cocky in his newly starched white officer's uniform, shoulders back, chin up, and hair styled like his American idol, Elvis. How confident he was as all the young single women admired him shyly from downturned eyes. No beauty was out of his reach that night, or so he thought.

Dukwah and her friend Sukee arrived fashionably late. Sukee was a petite girl, barely five feet tall, with short-cropped hair she curled out, wearing a brand-new pink outfit with a wide skirt. Dukwah, who wore her two-piece green dress with a matching ribbon tied around her ponytail, stood an inch above the tallest girl. As soon as these two lovely pastel creatures entered, a flock of young men swarmed around, wanting an introduction.

The circle of male competitors caught the handsome officer's attention and he went to investigate the commotion. As he casually made his way forward, the two women grew more to his liking.

"My name is Lee, Jaehak." He spoke in his deepest resonant voice, hoping to impress the girls with his manhood.

Dukwah and Sukee saw his pretty face and turned their conversation toward the other suitors, because a man who was too attractive always had many ladies attached to his arm. Now his ego was at stake. He became more determined.

"I have just returned from radar technical training in New Jer-sey, Ah-meh-li-ca," he interjected boastfully. He even spoke a few more English sentences to dazzle them. At last he hooked Dukwah's attention.

"What is it like there?"

"In Ah-meh-li-ca everything is big. There is so much to do and see. You can go into a large theater and view moving colored pictures on the wall anytime you want. My favorite is Er-bis Ples-rey." He grinned proudly as he ran his fingers through his black greased hair the way he had seen his idol do a dozen times in the movies.

"My third cousin traveled there!" a wide-eyed young man bragged, trying to steer her away.

"I have a distant uncle who studies at an university there, too!" another boasted, trying to show off.

Jaehak scoped out the many eager faces that were trying to steal the women away from him. "I will tell you all you want to know, but somewhere else. I shall buy you both a cup of co-pee."

Sukee nodded her head in excitement. Her first almost real date. "How fun," she giggled, hiding her mouth behind her hand.

"Thank you, but I am afraid we cannot accept," Dukwah declined promptly.

"Just for one cup of co-pee," Sukee coaxed. "Our mothers will never know; besides, these are new times. We are modern women."

"One cup, you promise?" Dukwah held out her left pinkie.

"One cup," Sukee echoed, and they locked pinkies.

As they were about to leave, the girls stepped aside the doorway for Jaehak to pass first. Instead, he made a slight gesture toward the door.

"In Ah-meh-li-ca, I learned it is the man who must open the door and wait for the woman to go first."

The girls were flattered; all the Korean boys they had ever met always went first. It felt odd being treated in such a special manner. He held doors open, hung up their coats, and pulled out their chairs. He impressed them further with entertaining stories about America, past the one cup of coffee. For hours they sipped coffee and nibbled on an assortment of cakes. And to end their triple date, Jaehak treated them to a late-night bowl of steaming oysters and *dduk bokum,* rice cakes and beef sautéed, under the stars.

"Order whatever you desire." He was showing off as if he had a fortune in his wallet.

"You have already spent too much," Dukwah protested.

"So I will have to do without my cigarettes for a week, but the company is well worth it."

Dukwah despised cigarettes, though she thought they suited him. He looked like a celebrity the way he let the smoke wisp through his lips.

With their bellies full, they parted. Dukwah thought she would never see the young officer again and left feeling no regrets. A few weeks passed and she had forgotten all about him, until he tried to arrange a meeting with just her alone. He left a note for her at the corner store: "Tomorrow, I will be waiting for you outside your college gate at three o'clock."

The plump weathered woman behind the counter watched with interest as Dukwah read the note. Sensing she might be the focus of snickering gossip, Dukwah nonchalantly tossed the paper into the wastebasket. She thanked the woman politely and walked away. On the outside she appeared calm and poised, but inside she was boiling mad at the foolish soldier's attempt to contact her. The next day at the university, she left class early to avoid bumping into him. When she failed to show up at the requested time and place, he went back the following day and waited for her at the gate. Day after day he stood there; his face became a familiar sight with the guards. Again Jaehak's ego was at stake. This strong-headed woman had cast a spell over him. He had tried to erase her pastel memory in his head by befriending other pretty ladies, but the vision of the staturesque girl crept back, always stronger and more urgent. He had to see her and was determined to win her over.

At church there was talk about a handsome lovesick soldier lurking outside the church, week after week. I paid no heed to the gossip because I thought he was no concern of mine. Fearing I would discover that he was pursuing her, Dukwah could not ignore his annoying presence any longer. She agreed to meet him one final time.

He took her to lunch at the American military commissary in Yongsan. Over their meal of steak and mashed potatoes, he poured out his dreams to her.

"Someday I am going to return to Ah-meh-li-ca. I will have a fine house, car, and family. A little daughter for the first child, I hope, then a son or two. They will be raised there, because—"

Finishing off his thought, she declared, "Because there they will never have to fear war. They can be children and when they become adults they will be God-loving, intelligent, and respectful, so when people see their Oriental faces they will know what a great country Korea is."

He felt a certain awe. Where did this young beautiful woman find such wisdom? She also wondered about this young man who shared her dream. Without realizing it, they had stolen each other's heart. They sat for a long time in silence, their hands so near they almost touched.

For three months they met secretly behind my back. It was difficult for them to get together, for old tradition still held. Young couples, no matter how modern or rebellious they thought they were, must maintain a distance in public. Those days it was considered forward for a man and a woman to clasp hands openly. So the day he dared to take her hand into his, he asked her to marry him. She felt his heart beat through his palm and knew he could feel hers.

She wanted to say "yes," but the final approval must come from me, her mother. And she knew my answer would be an absolute "NO!"

"But he is a good man and educated," Dukwah defended him.

My eyebrows shot up. "His mother is a Buddhist. You cannot marry a man who does not believe in Christ."

"Once we get married I will change him, Mother."

"You cannot change a man for marriage; he must change for his immortal soul."

"Just meet him, please. His name is Lee, Jaehak. He wishes to speak with you."

"No!" I repeated more forcefully. "You ungrateful girl. Have you forgotten about the Reds? I did not risk our lives and the lives of your father and eldest brother to throw it all away for a Buddhist. I will find you someone more suitable, perhaps a doctor. Forget about this soldier. What kind of person picks his own bride? I was married by a matchmaker. It is the only way we can be sure about his background and bloodline. What if his lineage of Lees crosses your father's ancestors? He may be a distant cousin and your children would be born retarded. With a matchmaker such a tragic mistake would be avoided."

"Our two families of Lees are from different villages. There is no risk."

"But the stigma remains. People will think you are marrying a relative."

"Mother, these are different times. Many young people se-lect their own mates."

"What you want to do is unethical. Marriage is a family mat-ter! It is too important to decide on one's own. Do not mea-sure love by the heat in your body, for someday the flesh will age and smother the passion. Listen carefully to your mother, for I am only thinking of your future." My heart was pounding so quickly it throbbed.

Since that moment when Jaehak's name was mentioned, there was no peace in my house. It was my duty as mother and father to steer my children on the right path. But these were indeed radical times. The young did as they pleased. They de-fied their parents' orders. They broke all tradition when Jae-hak showed up at the house alone without an elder, relative, or go-between. He was waiting for me along with my sisters, niece, her husband, and Dukwah when I arrived.

Sensing a trap, I stood at the doorway with one slipper off and one still on, glaring at the soldier sitting next to my daugh-ter. Everyone guiltily diverted their eyes away from mine, wait-ing for me to scold. Instead, I surveyed the whole scene silently. What I saw did not please me, especially this potential son-in-law. He was handsome like Husband, and that scared me the most. From my own personal experience I had learned it was a burden to marry a man who was too beautiful. It had only brought me endless agony and lonely nights.

"Aunt, sit yourself," Crippled Sister's daughter beseeched.

"Why?" I inquired with controlled scorn.

"I wish to ask for your daughter's hand in marriage." Jaehak spoke out of turn.

Now I could not leave. The subject could no longer be avoided. I walked in and Baby Sister slid the door shut behind me. I sat directly in front of the willful pair. He sat upright with his shoulders squared. Dukwah acted timid and even shy, but underneath was an unshakable conviction and a broad streak of stubbornness that drove her to bring us all here today.

Sisters tried to charm me with tea and food, loading my plate with only the best portions. They exhausted themselves with false laughter and chatter to cloak the frigid silence in the room.

"How nice of Dukwah's friend to bring us these foreign cakes all the way from America," Baby Sister said sweetly.

"I have never tasted anything so delicious and . . . rich," Crippled Sister exaggerated as she nearly gagged on the sugar. "Try some, Older Sister." She handed me a round, flat cake with black chocolate buttons melted into it.

I would not speak and they became more flustered, tripping over each other's attempts to win me over.

At last I spoke. "I have given you my answer and still you insist on this marriage."

They all hesitated in fear, anticipating I would raise my voice, but I remained frigidly calm.

"Please listen to him." Baby Sister came to their defense. "We are discussing your daughter's future. She is nearly twenty-two."

"It is true I have not done my duty to find her a husband, and I blame myself. But he is not the man I wish to pick for my daughter."

"Dukwah tells me you desire her to marry a Christian. I will believe in your God if you allow us to marry." Jaehak spoke up without being addressed once again.

"And I will help him, Mother." Dukwah's voice was steady.

What could I do? Young love in bloom made men and women so sure. They were clearly mesmerized by each other.

"There is nothing more I can say to change your minds, I see. Do as you please," I announced dryly.

A
MOTHER'S
LOSS

And so the wedding date was set and it came quickly, for they were married on a bright, cool day in the winter of that same year. The wedding was modeled after a modern Western ceremony. The only thing I insisted on was that it be a Christian wedding with a reverend to marry them. All agreed, even Jaehak's Buddhist mother after some coaxing. On the appointed day the special bouquet I had ordered arrived early and so did friends hauling wagons loaded with delicious foods, the kind only a rich man could afford to offer his guests. I was overwhelmed with their generosity and outpouring of enthusiasm. Nevertheless, I still could not help feeling sad. I knew it was supposed to be a joyous occasion and yet my daughter's getting married and belonging to another family hit me hard. I had purposely busied myself all morning to avoid these feelings, but they kept flooding back. How did this happen? I worried she was going to go through the same torment that I went through as a young wife. Many times I wished I had not married a man I loved so much. If I did not love him and want to possess him for my very own, I would never have expected anything from him, and then there would have been no disappointments. But God worked in mysterious ways. I knew He would not have put Husband in my life if He did not think I could handle it or grow from the experience. Suddenly I longed for my dead husband. The longing was not of the flesh, but for companionship.

When I saw Dukwah in her wedding gown, standing there holding her bouquet, I was struck by the vision of her. She was exquisite, the ideal symbol of Korean feminine beauty. The flowers feathered down the front of her dress, accentuating the sleek line of her hourglass figure. She was an unforgettable sight of purity, beauty, and dignity. I paused to gather myself, searching for the perfect words. I wanted to pass on some wisdom that might help her through the rough years ahead. Then I remembered what my own mother had shared with me moments before I was carried away—secrets to keep peace in the house.

"A woman must always be the strong stone, for she is the foundation of a family. However, your husband must never be threatened by your power and will. Let him believe it is his. Peace and happiness rest upon you and you alone. Guide him, lead him to his full potential, and most important, open his heart toward the light of God, and also your unborn children's."

She stood very still and stiff in her white silk gown, but I sensed she was listening deeply to every word.

"Do not look so gloomy, you are a very lucky girl. You two have chosen each other because of your love. Not everyone is that fortunate. Enjoy your life together. Do not waste one second of it."

The benches were full of guests, all friends and patients of mine. Jaehak walked up the central aisle. Without a doubt he stood out, tall and confident next to his stout friends. As he took his place up front, loud, clear foreign music announced the bride's entrance. She came in on the arm of a male relative. They walked steadily with the music. Her face was half hidden behind a thin white veil. She glanced neither right nor left, but every eye was locked on her.

When the reverend asked Jaehak if he would take Dukwah as his wife, his reply was so loud it echoed off the walls. Stifled laughter rippled from the guests and he looked around wondering if he had said something wrong. And in a few minutes, they were pronounced husband and wife. Together they faced the guests and bowed from the waist. The ceremony was complete. At that very moment she stared up and our eyes met. I saw gratitude in hers. I wondered what she saw in mine. Could she tell my heart was aching?

She hesitated at the first bench, where I sat, for just an instant before her groom led her away, her hand still in the curve of his elbow. Dukwah's face was unchanged, but Jaehak could not conceal his delight. A smile creased his lips; he would have the daughter he wanted.

Nine months later they were expecting a welcome addition. I counted the days when the baby would arrive, for I knew Dukwah would be returning home for the delivery. I had been so lonely for her since my son-in-law took her to Pusan, where he was newly stationed. I wept all the time. I wept more now than when Husband died. Dukwah wrote regularly, though. She was a devoted daughter, always concerned about how much I worked, if I rested enough. Oftentimes I sat for hours, reading these letters over and over again. Her experiences as a young wife were drastically different from mine. She was lucky; she had married a man who was not born the first son. My son-in-law could take his bride wherever they wished to go, even away from the watchful eye of a mother-in-law.

When Dukwah arrived, I noticed that she carried the weight of the babe well. She glowed with motherhood. This birthing of a child would bond her closer to me and forever to generations of women before her. She would be honoring their legacy, the very purpose for which she was brought into this world. She would soon discover there was no greater honor or joy than to create life.

Motherhood had matured her. She was no longer the stubborn girl whose pride often wore at my patience. In the past when I asked her to undress so I could treat her, she would hide her body. Now when I asked to see how her belly hung, she calmly removed her wrap. It was full and the skin taut, but I could not determine whether she carried a male child or a female child. To solve the mystery, I found a pencil with a rubber tip and a needle and thread. I pulled the thread through the needle and poked the needle in the rubber part of the pencil, then suspended the lead tip over Dukwah's wrist. With a steady hand I held it there until the pencil moved one way or another. Back and forth or side to side meant she would have a boy, but it began to slowly circle, round and round. She was carrying a girl child. Surprisingly it did not matter; the old way of thinking had left me. I would openly love her with all my heart and soul, the love I had deprived my own children, because a parent's duty was to discipline the children, and the grandparent's privilege was to spoil them. I could hardly wait!

As soon as Dukwah went into labor, she was whisked off to the hospital. Only the very poor delivered their babes at home nowadays. This modern change I did not agree with. I felt cheated because I was prevented from assisting in my own daughter's delivery. The doctors and nurses treated me like an outsider, shooing me into the waiting area. My anger bubbled as I imagined the pain she was suffering among strangers in white robes. But then all was forgotten when I held my perfectly healthy granddaughter in my arms. Such a little thing she was, all pudgy and pink. She had her father's large round eyes with the double lids and her mother's quiet dignity. I searched the rest of her face to see if her features resembled mine. When I saw none I was relieved, because I was never particularly fond of my dark pouty lips or flattened nose.

I gazed down at this little bundle in my arms and quietly whispered, "Be good to your mother, for there will be no one else in this whole world who will love you more dearly."

She half frowned at me, knowing I spoke the truth, then went to sleep exhausted from breathing her first breath of life. I laid her gently in her mother's arms, and I watched them both sleep for a long time. When Dukwah finally awoke, she looked at me and I looked at her and we both understood what was in each other's heart without uttering a word.

"We must give her a great name," I said.

"Her father has already chosen one."

"Without consulting an elder?" I asked, disturbed that another tradition had been broken.

"If this child was born a son, his name would have been David after King David in the Bible. A girl, she would be called Julie."

"What kind of name is Ju-rie?"

"An American name."

"But you are Korean."

"Someday, Mother, my children will live in America. They will never have to walk through bombs and fire. I want them to grow up slowly and enjoy every day of their childhood."

"Yes, I see." I nodded, respecting the wisdom and courage in her vision though I wanted to be selfish and keep Dukwah and my granddaughter near me. But for their futures, I vowed I would help them find a way to go to America. I turned to tell Dukwah what I had decided when I saw tears swell in her bright eyes.

"What is it?" I slid to her side.

"I regret I can no longer serve you as I have in the past, Mother." She drew a breath.

"I can take care of myself," I said soothingly.

"Now she must be my first concern." Dukwah looked down at the beautiful child she cradled so protectingly.

"As it should be. By caring for this child and giving her all that I have provided you and more, you will be serving me. Rest now, she will need your strength to guide her through life. It is a long and demanding road, believe me." I grinned, remembering the battles I fought with her.

Two years later Dukwah gave birth to a second daughter, Helie, another foreign name. I could tell right off she had a more willful personality than her older sister. She cried all the time, demanding every bit of attention; nevertheless, I loved her just the same.

I enjoyed everything about being a grandmother, and shamelessly poured all my affection into the two of them. My joy, though, was haunted by the possibility of war. I had to get them far away from the 38th parallel, which was a constant reminder of our Cold War situation. I was unwilling to gamble on the political chill. I feared a thaw-down would plunge our beloved country into another war, far worse than the last. My four children and I barely survived. The next time we might not be as fortunate.

Using my *chiryo* connections, I was informed by a devoted patient, whose husband was a congressman, that Canada was accepting Korean immigrants in celebration of the one hundredth anniversary of its independence. It was not America, but close enough. I passed on the exciting news right away to Dukwah and my son-in-law.

"You must act quickly before others find out and apply for their papers," I urged them.

Dukwah went out that very instant to search for the Canadian Embassy, but it was nowhere to be found. The nearest office was located in Hong Kong. So I made many hushed inquiries and discovered that the British Embassy was acting on Canada's behalf. The English gentleman behind the counter handed Dukwah a pile of documents, which she quickly brought back to her husband. We all watched as he filled out their personal history with the aid of a Korean-English dictionary. It took him all day to construct grammatically correct sentences, rounding all the *o*'s and dotting every *i*. First he wrote lightly in pencil, and then, he carefully traced over the words in pen. There was no time to waste, together the family carried their future to the main post office in downtown Seoul. Every day we all waited patiently for a reply. It became the central focus of our daily routine. Waiting and checking, checking and waiting.

As the days turned into excruciatingly long weeks, my son-in-law began to wonder if he did the right thing by giving Julie and Helie their foreign names. Then in early spring of 1968, we received the news. "The Canadian Government invites technically experienced immigrants from Asia." They were approved!

My son-in-law sold everything to buy the four plane tickets. It was decided he would go first to find a place to live and a job requiring his military radar skills, and Dukwah and the girls would move in with me until he sent for them. I was thrilled.

The day he left the air was still a little crisp from the winter before. Dukwah bundled up the girls in sweater jackets and hats she had knitted, elegantly accessorized with mittens and genuine fox-fur scarves, the kind that clipped on when the fox bit onto its own tail. They looked like precious little dolls.

At the airport, the runway was crawling with relatives. They had all come out to see the first man in our family ever to fly in a plane and venture to a new land across the vast ocean.

"When you come to Canada, I will pick you up in a big new car," he bragged to his wide-eyed daughters, each holding a flower for him to take.

"A car! We have never had a car before," Julie cried out in her little voice, jumping with excitement.

Helie was too busy trying to reglue the petals that had fallen off her flower to realize her father was going to a place very, very far away.

"Be good and listen to your mother," he told them before climbing up the steep metal stairs to the plane. How important he looked standing at the top in his new tie and trench coat. "*kimchee-se*," he smiled as Fourth Cousin snapped one last photograph.

Everyone waved good-bye, but I just held on to my grand-children's hands, afraid to let them go. I looked over at Duk-wah and we both had matching tears streaming down our cheeks. I knew exactly how she felt, as if a piece of her was being torn away. Because when a man and a woman became so close, their bodies were fused into one forever. And when they were forced to part, he took a piece of her with him, leaving her walking around with a hole in her heart.

I tried to make her last few months at home the happiest. All of us would gather in the main quarters at the end of the day, as we used to do when their father was alive. Kunil would bring out his scratched-up guitar and strum a melody while Julie and Helie entertained us with their invented dance moves. It was wonderful being surrounded by all my children once again. Well, almost. If Yongwoon were here my happiness would be complete. He would have been proud of his younger brothers and sisters. Kunil and Kunsam were both attending fine universities. And *ahghee*, whom we now called Dukhae, was a young lady in her second year in high school. I cannot claim credit for how well they turned out. Dukwah was more of a mother to them, especially to Dukhae. Seeing Dukhae play with her nieces and taking turns carrying them on her back reminded me of the many times I saw her older sister do the same for her. I knew she would miss Dukwah as much as I would.

Then the dreaded letter arrived from my son-in-law. The envelope was stamped from a place called Montreal, Canada. The letter said he had secured a job and wanted his family to join him immediately. Our final day together was extremely hard on Dukwah and me. We had become so close, almost friends. She pretended to be lost in her packing and I kept busy fussing over my granddaughters. It was summer and I dressed them in identical yellow dresses with huge white lace bib collars. Even their bonnets matched to the last stitch. In case one of them got lost, Dukwah could always point to the other and say in broken English, "Same, same." She was so smart.

Once again every relative showed up at the runway. It felt as though I was going to a funeral more than anything else. I kept having to dab my moist eyes and blow my runny nose so Fourth Cousin could take our pictures. First the three of them stood by themselves; then the entire clan gathered; finally it was just me and Dukwah. We stood stiffly beside each other while Fourth Cousin adjusted the lens. I remembered my son-in-law smiling and saying that funny word "*kimchee-se*," but I was losing too much to even pretend for the sake of the photographs. Click—the moment was over and our images preserved. Turning toward her, I grabbed her hand desperately and she squeezed mine back hard. Through our touch, we communicated a lifetime of apologies and forgiveness. Through our eyes, we confirmed the love that flowed between us.

"I will miss you terribly. You have always been such a faithful daughter," I said, then paused to gather more courage. ". . . You were my strength when I had none. You were my support when I needed someone . . . Every day I thank God for finding me worthy enough to be blessed with a daughter like you."

"Mother, I wish you were coming with us." Dukwah's voice quivered as black tears streaked down her cheeks.

"*Iiii.*" I handed her my damp hankie to wipe her runny makeup. "I will always be with you. Even thousands of miles away, when you rejoice I will share in your happiness. When you cry I will feel your tears down my face like now, because you and I are of the same flesh."

"We will see each other again." Dukwah squeezed my hand harder.

I could not answer her back, the words stuck in my throat. I wanted it to be true as much as she did, but even with the invention of the plane the world was still very large. So we parted with no farewells. That would have been too final, too real.

It was not until I saw my granddaughters' tiny black patent-leather shoes climb those high steps into the metal bird and disappear inside its belly that I felt my heart shatter into a million pieces.

"Older Sister, let us go home," I heard Baby Sister holler above the noise of the engine.

I could not, not yet. Then I saw Dukwah and the little ones poke their heads out of the doorway and wave miniature *Taekuk* flags. I threw my arms into the air and called out, "Dukwah-yah!" But the humming of the engine was too overpowering. Before I had a chance to call out her name again, the iron door slammed shut. They were gone. I stood paralyzed as I watched the plane roll down the runway, picking up speed. I worried it would not get off the ground in time . . . It did. It was frightening and exciting that a child of mine was flying up, up, up, into the clouds.

AMERICA, 1991

These days I cannot sleep very long. I am always the first one awake. I think it is because at the age of eighty my body knows time is precious. But old age hasn't stopped me from living. In fact, I became an American citizen this year on my eightieth birthday. I decided it was about time. I had immigrated here fifteen years ago in 1976. Since the medical profession banned me from practicing *chiryo*. Rather than break my promise to God, I left my beloved Korea to join Dukwah and her family in California.

Every morning I rise with the sun, take my dentures out of the cup in the bathroom and plop them into my mouth, then I get dressed and walk over to the church to say a prayer, thanking God for giving me another day. I love this church. It is in the center of Koreatown in downtown Los Angeles. Dukwah and my son-in-law helped build it. That is why my two sisters and I live in the little yellow house next door. My children keep pressuring me to move in with them in their expensive homes. I tell them I like it right where I am. Here I can walk to the Korean market and buy all kinds of things I enjoy eating. Here I do not have to read or speak English; even my Mexican neighbor on the other side speaks some Korean.

Today, Baby Sister is dishing out a steaming bowl of rice from our new electric rice cooker for the morning meal. Dukwah brought it over yesterday. She is always doing kind things for me. Smelling the food, Crippled Sister limps out of the bathroom, leaning on her cane. She walks better than she ever did. In fact, I have seen her run on occasion when one of her grandchildren gets into mischief.

While this may not be the nicest house in the world, with its cracks, chipping paint, and roaches, it is home to my sisters and me. We are not the same spoiled children living in our rich father's home. We have all swallowed too much sorrow in our lives to be particular. Each one of us has lost a child or a husband or both, but I think Baby Sister has suffered the most. Her only surviving child immigrated to America not long ago and died shortly thereafter. The family decided to keep this tragedy from her until we could fly her here to Los Angeles. Once she arrived, I was the one to tell her her daughter was waiting for her in a grave.

Crippled Sister is the happiest. Her smile is always big, showing off all her original teeth she has managed to keep. She finds humor in the silliest things. That is why the wrinkles all over her face deepen, but she does not mind. She would never think of covering them up with cream or makeup the way old women in America do.

As for me, I would say I am the reserved one. I talk only when I have something to say or have the energy to spend. Others interpret my silent composure as wisdom. Maybe that is why my granddaughter Helie wants to come over today and ask me questions about our family. I am looking forward to seeing her. She has been gone for two years, working in Korea and traveling through China. Just imagining her following my footsteps all over the Orient fills me with pride. Of all my grandchildren, she reminds me the most of myself. She has the same stubborn, spunky streak. There is no place in the world she cannot go. I just wish she would get married, not because I think she needs a husband to take care of her. God only knows, it is the women in our family who support the husbands. I do not want her to miss out on love and the rewards of bearing children.

Oh, it is almost eight o'clock. I have to eat quickly before my first patient arrives. They are coming earlier and earlier every day, it seems.

There is a knock at the door. It is Mr. Park. His coloring looks a little better since last week and the red marks on his neck have almost all faded.

"Have you eaten?"

"Yes," he answers humbly.

"Then let us get started." I motion him to sit down.

Together we bow our heads as I offer a prayer. "Heavenly Father, I ask you to guide my hands to do Your bidding. Amen."

"Amen," he repeats, then pulls off his shirt and lies down on a blanket I had spread out.

I begin with the neck, pinching the skin between my second and middle fingers. My fingers are still strong. I can work for hours at a time, but if I do get tired one of my sisters will take over for me. We three sisters still work well as a team, and we have garnered a reputation for ourselves and *chiryo*. People come to us from far-away places called Florida and Washington, D.C.; some even followed us from Korea. I still charge nothing, though. The fee is whatever patients can afford, because my work is not about the money. It never was.

It is ten minutes before eleven and I hear a car screeching up the driveway. This time I know it is my granddaughter. I recognize the wild music blaring. She comes in and gives me a big hug and kiss while I am in the middle of doing *chiryo* on Mr. Park, then goes over to her other grandmothers and greets them in the same manner. It is very American, but I love her affection.

"Good morning, Grandmother, Middle Grandmother, and Little Grandmother. How are you doing today?" she greets us in Korean. I am pleased at how well she has mastered our language. For the first time I can actually understand her. I stare at her for a while because she has changed. I do not mean her clothes. She still wears jeans that exposes her navel and a baby doll top that is too tight around the breasts. I am referring to her face. Usually she wears a frown whenever she is around her mother or me, because she thinks she has to guard her independence and American identity, as if we could trick them out of her. Not now. There is a confident smile across her lips and warmth in her eyes.

"Can we talk, Grandmother?" she asks.

Before I have a chance to answer, Crippled Sister takes over my work, and Baby Sister rushes out from the kitchen, bringing us a plate of *beandaeduck,* mung bean pancakes. Helie says she is never hungry, but we make her eat anyway. It is not good to be so thin. Having grown up in America, she does not know the meaning of hunger. War taught me to eat everything and anything. I can even make wild weeds taste delicious. Only after we three grandmothers are satisfied that she has eaten enough pancakes, do we let her begin the interviewing.

"Okay, just relax and talk into the microphone," Helie instructs as she hooks a wire to my shirt.

"Let me change into something nicer and comb my hair," I tell her.

"Don't worry about it, Grandmother, I'm only recording your voice."

"Are you sure?"

"Yes. Recording, one, two, three."

"Recording, one, two, three," the machine repeats.

It is amazing what humans can achieve with such a tiny box. It is a pity they cannot achieve world peace as easily.

"Now, Grandmother, I want to ask you where you and Middle Grandmother and Little Grandmother were born."

"That is easy, Pyongyang." Crippled Sister laughs out loud, showing all her teeth.

"What year were you born?"

I had to think for a moment for the exact year. It has been so long.

"The year of the rat, 1912," Baby Sister reminds me.

"Oh yes," I agree.

"Did you have a good childhood?"

"We did. Our father was a kind man. He liked having his daughters around. That is why I think he married me off so late."

"How old were you when you got married?"

"Twenty-two."

"If that's considered 'rotten,' I don't mind spoiling a little." Helie chuckles.

"Do not hold on to your unmarried status as if it is a great prize. A rotten fruit once fallen off the tree is wasted and there are no second chances. Life and the creation of life is the most precious gift given to women. It is not meant to be taken lightly or denied."

Suddenly my head floods with memories of the past that shaped my life. I remember standing in front of my parents as I was being told about my future husband and how he was the first son in a line of first sons. I remember being carried away from my father's home to join another man's. I remember discovering the joy of being a woman and mother. I remember moving to China so our children could grow up free. I remember the Reds and how cruel they treated us for believing in God once we returned. I remember the war and all the suffering. I remember the hardships of raising my children without a father. And of course I have never forgotten about my Yong-woon, who was lost to me. I tell her all this and more, because I cannot stop myself.

By the time I am finished, everyone is exhausted with emotion. All our eyes are red and swollen from too much crying and my throat is dry. Baby Sister has a grocery bag full of freshly made *kimchee* and Korean pears for our granddaughter to take back to her apartment. She hugs and kisses us good-bye as we walk her to her red Japanese-made car. Before she zooms away, she rolls down the window and asks one final question.

"Grandmother, is there anything in your life you would change if you could?"

I know that answer right away. "Yes," I respond, my voice all choked. "If I could change one thing, it would be the fate of my firstborn. That is my one regret."

The lights are all turned off and my sisters are asleep on the floor. I walk into the bathroom, remove my dentures and place them back in the cup, and I stare into the mirror for a while. I see a very old woman. The traces of my youth are all forgotten under a thick patch of silver hair and a mask of cracking wrinkles. Each individual strand and each individual line are born out of tragedy and happiness. The two are never separate. That is why when I remember my life I feel so much, hurt so much, love so much. I am tired, very tired, but I am not ready to die just yet. The uncertainty of my child's fate keeps my heart from stopping.

Even though I rarely speak his name, there is not a day that passes that I do not mourn for what I have lost. I have tried for almost forty years to find him. In 1971, when the two Koreas began a series of talks at Panmunjom, the Demilitarized Zone, my heart was filled with renewed hope. I waited for peace, but power and egos pulled the two sides further and further apart over the years. Then in 1983, I clung to one final hope. The Korean Broadcasting System announced a reunion show. All those who wished to find lost family members could appear on television. So on the designated day Dukwah drove me to the network in her big German car. She was more nervous than I. When we arrived, there was a crowd of people gathered around waiting for the cameraman to take their pictures. Everyone wore signs around their necks with the names of the loved ones they were searching for. Dukwah helped me write mine out in clear bold letters, giving Yongwoon's name, date of birth, and birthplace.

People were so anxious the stage thundered with chatter. The television crew rushed around testing microphones, securing cables, flicking lights. One man, puffing on a cigarette, was directing the whole thing, telling family members to stand out of the way and yelling at his crew to work faster.

"Here we go, everybody!" someone yelled. Bright lights washed over the stage, so powerful I felt myself begin to sweat. "Five, four, three, two . . ." And it was showtime.

The cameraman panned from one face to another. It was getting nearer and nearer to mine. Suddenly I was overwhelmed by it all: the lights, the people, the cameras. For a few perilous moments, I froze and my legs buckled. Dukwah saw how faint I looked and lurched toward me and slid a supportive arm under mine. Then, putting her face close, she said, "You can do it, Mother. Older Brother may be watching."

Those few words inspired me to stand up straight with my

shoulders pushed back. I did not want Yongwoon to see his mother for the first time as a quivering coward. I wanted him to be proud of me. For him, I wore my best Korean dress and let my daughters convinced me to perm and dye my silver hair black.

Before I knew it, my moment of fame was over. The camera came in for a close-up of my face and sign, then moved on to the next person. I was so absorbed in holding my sign still, I hope I did not crack a smile.

"Did I look foolish?" I asked as we left the studio.

"You were great," Dukwah assured me.

For days I felt giggly. When the show finally aired it seemed like every Korean all over the world who could receive the station watched those reunion shows. Letters and phone calls poured in from old friends and neighbors I had lost contact with, but not one offered news about my son. Heartbroken, I gave up. I could not bear another dead end.

It is June 4, 1991. I receive a letter from Pyongyang. He is alive! My Yongwoon is alive! The letter was written by the hand of his twenty-eight-year-old daughter. My God, he had children. All these years he was living behind the lines, and I never knew for sure.

After I had given up, my four children decided to take over my search secretly. They had heard of a Canadian reverend who had reunited many war-torn families as North Korea's unofficial ambassador. Kunsam volunteered to write to the reverend and in turn the reverend offered to carry the letter to North Korea, but with no promises.

Months passed, then news arrived. The Reverend found my Yongwoon, living not in our old house, but in a small depressed province miles away from Pyongyang where I heard living conditions were worse than when we fled. Because after the division, while the rest of the world was making marvelous discoveries and great leaps into the future, North Korea stayed isolated.

Dear Uncle,

How are you? On behalf of the Lee family I write this letter to an uncle whom I have never met in my life, wondering how you are doing. What you look like. Whether you are fine.

My name is Aeran, the oldest daughter from your big brother, Lee, Yongwoon. I understand you have been searching so long for him even in your dreams. Do you remember him clearly?

Time flies as swiftly as stream water. When you and my father were separated forty-one years ago, you both were very young. Now you are in your fifties with lots of gray hair.

I am twenty-eight years old. I was not born at the time when the tragic separation took place. My parents did not know if you had survived or not. They are deeply happy with the news that you are alive and all are well. If you were not in a country far away across the Pacific Ocean, we would run to you with wide-open arms and embrace you tightly. If there were no American barbarian, there would be a chance for blood brothers to meet. Thinking of all the absent years of brotherhood and now your existence fills our hearts with sentimental emotions.

I have great inner feelings about the nature of the war. The country was divided into South and North as a result, but the worst thing to happen to humankind was the forceful split of the family. Though it left our land into two parts divided, the passion to search for our family never divided.

My siblings and I grew up not knowing that we even had a grandmother, uncles, aunts, and cousins. Now we know.

I am sure that you, American uncle, have a big family in California by now. Ours consists of six members: father, mother, two younger brothers, a younger sister, and myself. My father is a trainer in the Revolutionary Construction Unit. My mother is a cook. I work for the Department of Food Quality Control as a quality controller. My younger brother, Hakchung, twenty-six, is a student of Bochunbo Engineering College. My youngest brother, Munchung, twenty-four, is doing his military duty in the North Korean People's Army. My youngest sister, Miran, twenty-one, works as a volunteer for the Visitors' field trip. Thus we are serving and doing our best for the country.

You know all about us, now it is your turn to let us know

all about your life in America. Every minute I count anxiously until your letter arrives. Hope it will be full of exciting news about the family. Please try to visit us in North Korea. I'm sure that it will be a great experience for you to step on the soil of the forbidden fatherland.

We never imagined you were still alive, much less in a big country like America. When the time of rendezvous comes, I would love to embrace you. Though we have never met, I feel very close to you because we share the same piece of flesh. Flesh is a bond of fate. They say blood is thicker than water. I now agree. A family should not be divided under any circumstances, nor the country.

There are endless questions, inquiries, worries, and concerns about the family. Whenever I think of your dear faces in America, I can hardly sleep or work. Ashes fill my heart with such pain knowing you have a difficult and hard life in a foreign country.

I just cannot go on writing.

Please take care. I wish everyone a bright future! I am closing my letter now, with all the love from all of us.

> *Your niece,*
> *Aeran*
> *in North Korea*
> *the nearest and the*
> *farthest*

A mother's worries welled inside me. I was wrong. Knowing he still lives and not being able to touch him is worse than knowing nothing. I agonize more now than before. Is his belly empty? Did he think his mother had abandoned him? Did he suffer much alone?

All I remember of his face is his youthful ready smile and bold eyes like his father's. The rest I cannot retrieve, for my ancient memory is failing me. So much time has been wasted, so much time has passed, and yet I still envision him as being seventeen. Oh my God, would I recognize my own son, now aged and perhaps as gray as me? It is odd to think of him as an old man . . . I am petrified.

Every morning and every night before I go to bed, I pray I will be able to hold my son in my tired arms, just once, then I could leave this earth, for my life would be complete. I pray a lot, because praying is all I can do, and then I wait, hoping, aching, for the political gate that separates my son from me to fling open. And when it does, I will run in laughing and crying and singing out his name. How do I know? I am Korean, and we Koreans have this unshakable faith, for we are a strong-willed people. History proves it to be so. For more than a millennium we have lived as one people and I am certain we will be united again. Unification is possible! I say this as a woman who has survived over eighty years of living; also, I say it as a woman who has given life.

"And now these three remain: faith, hope, and love. But the greatest of these is love." A mother's love. (1 Corinthians 13:13)